HOBBES

BBFAL

BBAL 2000

HOBBES

by
JOHN LAIRD
Regius Professor of Moral Philosophy in the University of Aberdeen
Fellow of the British Academy

So much is unheedy learning a hinderance to the knowledge of the truth, and changeth into elves those that were beginning to be men. (VII, 222.)

NEW YORK / RUSSELL & RUSSELL

0145287

~~103918~~

FIRST PUBLISHED IN 1934
REISSUED, 1968, BY RUSSELL & RUSSELL
A DIVISION OF ATHENEUM PUBLISHERS, INC.
L. C. CATALOG CARD NO: 68-25065
ISBN 0-8462-1238-2
PRINTED IN THE UNITED STATES OF AMERICA

TO THE READER

I HAVE to describe to you, as I apprehend, a philosophy conceived after the grand manner, indefatigably elaborated, and expressed with an art that no other English-born philosopher, always excepting Francis Bacon, ever acquired.

In the substance of his philosophy Hobbes showed himself a psychologist of genius, a notable metaphysician, a political thinker of enduring renown, and a moralist who should be called the father of British ethics in its greatest period, although most of his progeny were anxious to show why and in what ways they could not live down to so disreputable an ancestor. The vast perspective of his philosophy, however, is even better evidence of his stature and of the elevation of his station. He tried to bring all that was new, and all that was old, in genuine science within the scope of the great new instrument called "the philosophy of motion"; and he believed that his eyes were never dazzled.

Cowley, in an ode, compared Hobbes to Columbus, but would have written more aptly had he said: "Thou great *Magellan* of the golden lands of new philosophies." The Columbus of the science of motion (if there was only one) was Galileo, not Hobbes; but Hobbes, in a greater degree than even Descartes, should be called the first philosophical *circumnavigator* of the "new" intellectual globe.

It was Magellan who found his way back, by sea, to the Spice Islands; and Hobbes, similarly, believed he had returned, with fresh confidence and with a circumspection born of knowledge, to the proper understanding of the Socratic maxim: "Know thyself." Cowley, in a sense, was wrong when he said:

> "The Baltic, Euxine and the Caspian,
> And slender-limb'd Mediterranean,
> Seem narrow creeks to thee, and only fit
> For the poor wretched fisher-boats of wit."

For Hobbes saw these seas (all except the Caspian) not simply as narrow creeks but essentially as parts of the unity of the oceans, and as the more intelligible because the oceans themselves had been explored.

Hobbes himself claimed only two great discoveries, the science of optics and the science of civil philosophy. The first, at his own estimate, might be compared to Magellan's discovery of the Philippines ; in other people's opinion it resembled, rather, the two barren rocks that Magellan called " St. Paul's " and " Shark Island." Hobbes's civil philosophy, however, was an achievement of immensely higher order, and since Hobbes, like most men of his time, thought that " leviathan " was the great monster of the seas (although in the Book of Job it may only have been a crocodile), we may perhaps compare this part of his philosophy, not altogether fancifully, to the " Great South Sea " that Magellan was the first to sail and to call the Pacific. Magellan, I suppose, hoped to placate the storms by giving the ocean this soothing name. Hobbes, on the contrary, gave a belligerent title to his great treatise on the ways of peace. Yet, like Magellan, he was determined to push on even if he and his men " had to eat the leather of the rigging."

I know very well that I have been preceded by many eminent expositors, with whom I should not like to match myself, although I believe I have something to say. In England, Croom Robertson's *Hobbes* is far too good for conventional words of praise ; and Mr. Brandt's *Thomas Hobbes' Mechanical Conception of Nature*, the best of all the books hitherto published on its special theme, has been translated into intelligible, if curious, English. On the Continent, Dr. Tönnies, in various works, has collected most valuable evidence with the most scrupulous accuracy. And there have been others besides these.

For myself, I am attempting to enliven an interest in Hobbes that seems less active to-day than it should be among British philosophers. If I succeed in that aim I am not afraid of having wasted my time in writing, or of wasting yours, reader, in perusing. Those who have not read, not some only, but most of Hobbes have missed great enjoyment as well as much profit. The aim of the present series is importunately to prevent such errors. Therefore I present an apology that is no apology. And so farewell.

OLD ABERDEEN,
   September 1933.

BBAL 2000

CONTENTS

ix

0145287

103918

PART III

INFLUENCE

NOTE ON ABBREVIATIONS

WITH the exceptions of the *Elements of Law* (=E.L.) and of the *Behemoth* (=B.), which are quoted as in Tönnies's editions, Hobbes's English Works are quoted as in Molesworth's edition, volume and page being given *simpliciter*. Thus (II, 8) means page 8, Volume II, of " Hobbes's English Works." When the Latin works (Molesworth's ed.) are cited, " L." is prefixed. Thus (L. II, 8) means page 8, Vol. II, of " Hobbes's Latin Works."

A number standing by itself, *e.g.* (n), refers to page n of whatever work has been indicated in the context. When such works have several volumes I have usually printed (at X, n) in order to avoid confusion with the references to Molesworth. Thus (at II, 8) refers to page 8 of Vol. II of some work (other than Molesworth's *Hobbes*) to which the context refers.

Since it seemed to me essential to give a good many references, and to enable the reader to check them, I have had to invent a number of abbreviations for economy of space. The plan I adopted was to explain the contraction to be used on the first occasion some given book was mentioned and thereafter to use the contraction. I used=for the sign of contraction. Thus when I say " Gal.=Galileo's *System of the World*, trans. Salusbury. London, 1661," I mean thereafter to refer to Salusbury's translation as (Gal.).

The sign " q." signifies " as quoted in."

Among the contractions that recur most frequently I may here mention the following for the reader's convenience : A.=Aubrey's *Lives* ; A.G.=*Archiv f. Geschichte d. Philosophie* (principally for Tönnies's *Hobbes-Analekten*, published there) ; Br.=*Frithiof Brandt's Commentary* ; C.M.H.=*Cambridge Modern History* ; Cal.=*Calendar State Papers* ; Car.= Carlyle's *Mediæval Political Theory in the West* ; Cl.=Clarendon's *Survey* ; D.N.B.=*Dictionary of National Biography* ; G.A.=Gierke's *Althusius* ; G.G.=Figgis's *Gerson to Grotius* ; Gen.=Gierke's *Das deutsche Genossenschaftsrecht*, Vol. III ; Gooch=G. P. Gooch's *English Democratic Ideas in the Seventeenth Century* ; H.M.C.=*Historical MSS. Commission* ; P.P. =The *Portland Papers* (in the above) ; R.=Croom Robertson's *Hobbes* ; and St.=Leslie Stephen's *Hobbes*.

PART I
LIFE AND TIMES

I

CHIEFLY BIOGRAPHICAL

(1) LIFE

On Good Friday, the fifth of April 1588, when the menace of the Great Armada lay chilly upon the land, the wife of a certain Thomas Hobbes, vicar of Westport and of Charlton, near Malmesbury in Wiltshire, gave birth prematurely to her second son, the subject of this monograph. Thus Hobbes and Fear were twins, as Hobbes said, long afterwards, in his rhyming autobiography. Nevertheless, his favourable horoscope in Taurus[1] did not lie. A troop of writers, from Bishop Kennet to Miss Rose Macaulay, taking his word for it, have asserted that his nature was womanish, but his intrepid intellect was thoroughly masculine and deserved to be born into the " century of genius."

There is some mystery about Thomas Hobbes, the father. According to Aubrey—who may, indeed, as Wood said (*Athenæ*, I, lx), have " been roving and maggotie-headed," but was a sort of Boswell in his " historiola of our Malmesbury philosopher "—" the old vicar Hobs was a good fellow " who once cried out " Trafells (clubs) is troumps " when he was asleep in church after a Saturday night at cards (A. I, 387). His career at Westport came to an end when he used his fists at the church door upon a person who became the next vicar. Thereafter, having had to fly for the act, he lived in obscurity at Thistleworth

---

[1] Aubrey's *Brief Lives*, ed. Clark (=A.), I, 328. The " life " of Hobbes was the longest.

as a " reader " (A. I, 391).   A doubt, however, must attach
to Aubrey's statement (A. I, 323) that " Thomas, the
father, was one of the ignorant ' Sir Johns ' of Queen
Elizabeth's time ; could only read the prayers of the
church and the homilies ; and disesteemed learning (his
son Edmund told me so) as not knowing the sweetness of
it " ;   for in Foster's *Alumni Oxon* the entry occurs :
" Hobbes, Thomas of county Gloucester, pleb. Brasenose
College, matriculated 29 April, 1587, aged 40, vicar of
Westport and of Charlton, Wilts." One can only speculate
about the aims and attitude of this married undergraduate,
already a vicar and a father.

The mother's maiden name was Middleton, " of a
yeomanly family " at Brokenborough, " appendant to
Charlton vicarage " (A. I, 323).

A generous uncle, Francis Hobbes, glover and alderman,
paid for the boy's education ; and our philosopher had
the luck to be taught by a Mr. Robert Latimer, " a good
Grecian," according to Aubrey (another of his pupils),
" and the first that came into our parts hereabout since
the Reformation " (I, 329).   Well schooled, Thomas
Hobbes proceeded to Magdalen-hall in Oxford at the age
of fourteen, and in due course took his bachelor's degree.
By his own account (L. I, lxxxvi, *sq.*)—which was, however,
an octogenarian's—he had no great opinion, at the time,
of the logic and scholastic physics taught at the University,
and spent his time poring over booksellers' maps.

The Principal of Magdalen-hall recommended him to
William Cavendish, Baron Hardwick (soon to become the
first Earl of Devonshire), as tutor to his son ; and so
Hobbes's lifelong connection with the house of Devonshire
began.   Without the connection there might only have
been a village Hobbes ; with it the Hobbes we know
became possible.   There was no house, he later said
(VIII, iv), in which a man " should less need the
university " or in which it was easier " to study the

liberal arts liberally." And more than the library counted. Foreign travel, leisure to think, constant intercourse with men of letters and of science as well as with statesmen—these things, when Hobbes had shown his worth, gave him his great opportunity. In political affairs he knew from the inside how the more enlightened of the royalist gentry thought. In the new world of science he had the entrée to Welbeck Abbey, where another branch of the Cavendish family lived, *i.e.* William, Earl of Newcastle, and his brother Charles Cavendish, the former of whom had a lively interest and the latter a high proficiency in the new scientific movement.

At first the tall, sallow, handsome, delicate tutor[1] with the hazel eyes that shone like "a bright live-coal" (A. I, 349) was a page to his young lord (who was much of an age with himself and had recently been married to a Scottish bride of twelve) and had many unpleasant tasks. He had even to stand about in wet, unshapely shoes trying to borrow the money that his pupil was ashamed to solicit in person (A. I, 347). Hobbes took many colds but he did not take offence, and he contrived to retain some acquaintance with the classics by reading pocket editions of Cæsar and other ancient authors while he waited in draughty antechambers. He went abroad with his pupil in 1610 (the year of the assassination of Henri IV by Ravaillac, a lay-Jesuit), visiting France and Italy, acquiring a "passable" acquaintance with the languages of those countries (L. I, xiii), and discovering that the logic and philosophy of Magdalen-hall were of no account in learned Europe (*ibid.*).

Returning to England, Hobbes continued his studies in the classics, and diligently acquired his effective Latin and his admirable English style. The long apprenticeship continued until 1628-9, when he published his translation of *Thucydides*; but at that date he must have been

[1] In later life his health and complexion improved.

conscious of his mastery of English prose, since he asked
Ayton the poet, and also Ben Jonson, to be his
" Aristarchus " regarding the style of the dedication of
his book. In later life he regretted that he had read so
many romances and plays about this time, but Aubrey
said truly that the frivolity was fortunate since it increased
his remarkable " copie of words " (A. I, 361).

It is natural to think of this translation of *Thucydides*
as a sort of philosophical reconnaissance comparable (as
W. Nichols thought[1]) to Machiavelli's *Discourses on Livy*.
Thus Tenison, a later critic, opined that the speech of
Euphemus, the Athenian ambassador, in Book VI, was
the substance of Hobbes's " sandy politics,"[2] and Hobbes
himself, forty years later, said that he had wanted to
convince his fellow-citizens of the folly of the Athenian
democracy (L. I, xiv). The book itself, however, provides
rather better evidence. Hobbes wrote, he said, as the
instructor of " noblemen and such as may come to have
the management of great and weighty actions " (VIII, v).
A historian's business was to show where honour and
dishonour might be found, although " in the present age "
these were " grossly mistaken " (VIII, vi). Thucydides
hated democracy and the ambition of demagogues (VIII,
xvi). He even, in reality, " approved of regal government " (VIII, xvii), and was falsely accounted an atheist
because he could not assent to the " ridiculous religion "
of the common people. Again (1st ed., p. 103) : " In
Athens no man so poor but was a statesman. So St. Luke,
Acts 17, 21. All the Athenians spend their time in nothing
but hearing and telling of news. The true character of
politicians without employment."

The first Earl of Devonshire died in 1626, the second in
1628, leaving his estates embarrassed, and Hobbes, a little
ruefully, undertook to accompany the son of Sir Gervase

---

[1] *The Religion of a Prince* (1704).
[2] *The Creed of Mr. Hobbes examined*, p. 162.

Clinton to Paris, Orleans,[1] and perhaps (VII, 451) to
Venice. About this time he also made his first acquaintance with geometry. "Being in a gentleman's library
in . . .," said Aubrey (at I, 332), "Euclid's *Elements* lay
open, and 'twas the 47 El. libri I. He read the proposition.
'By G—,' said he, 'this is impossible.' So he reads the
demonstration of it, which referred him back to such a
proposition; which proposition he read. That referred
him back to another, which he also read. *Et sic deinceps*,
that at last he was demonstratively convinced of that
truth. This made him in love with geometry. . . . I have
heard Mr. Hobbes say that he was wont to draw lines on
his thigh and on the sheets, abed, and also multiply and
divide." In later life, again, he was careful to explain
that in 1630 he had told Newcastle and Charles Cavendish
that he believed light and sound to be only phantasms,[2]
and so that he had not been anticipated by Descartes
(VII, 468). He was a student of physics, therefore, as
well as a wooer of geometry, in his dangerous forties.

Hobbes had returned to the service of the Devonshires[3]
by November 1630 (H.M.C. VII, 399), and, as he said
(L. I, lxxxix), spent seven sedulous years in teaching the
next Earl Latin, rhetoric, and other such subjects. But his
own studies continued apace.

A third and prolonged visit to the Continent with his
new pupil found him obsessed (L. I, xiv) with the problem
of motion, its relation to the new physics and especially
to our senses. On this he meditated, afloat, on horseback,
on the road; and during his stay in Paris he began to
formulate his system of philosophy under the very best
auspices, for he became the friend of Marin Mersenne, a
monk of the Franciscan order of the Minimi, whose cell

---

[1] *Hist. MSS. Comm.* (=H.M.C.), VIIth Report, 1914, p. 396.
[2] *Arch. f. Gesch. der Philosophie* (=A.G.), XIX, 154.
[3] On the title-page of a reprint of the *Thucydides* in 1634 Hobbes
described himself as "*Secretary* to the late Earl of Devonshire."

was a very "whirlpool of all the studies,"[1] where all the newest ideas swam. According to Wood, Hobbes, at this time, communicated his results to Mersenne "once or twice a week" (*Athenæ*, iii, 1207). Furthermore, Hobbes visited the great Galileo about the year 1636,[2] and when he returned to England in 1637 believed himself ready to put his philosophical system into proper order in three great divisions : Of Body ; Of Man ; Of Citizenship.

If, as Mr. Brandt[3] provisionally supposes (Br. 55), the *Short Tract*, first published by Dr. Tönnies,[4] might have been written as early as 1630, it is plain that Hobbes, in that year, had anticipated much of his later system, although he retained certain scholastic views that he later repudiated. Such conjectures apart, however—and 1630 seems very early—there is sufficient evidence that Hobbes, a few years later, was regarded as a philosopher of standing. Thus Kenelm Digby, the eminent pirate-diplomat and chemist-philosopher, writing to Hobbes in 1637 went so far as to say : " You that know more than all men living . . . I summon you of your promise, which is that as soon as you have done any part of your Logic, you will let me see it."[5]

Again, in the *Portland Papers*,[6] several letters plainly indicate Hobbes's scientific interests, aspirations, and reputation. In 1633 (p. 124) he tried to purchase a copy of Galileo's *Dialogues* for Newcastle, but could not " get it for money." He was keenly interested in Mr. Warner's experiments with multiplying and burning glasses (126). He studied optics busily, and discussed some of Galileo's views on that subject (129).

---

[1] De Coste, *Vie de Mersenne*, p. 59.
[2] Probably at Arcetri, despite L. I, xxviii.
[3] *Thomas Hobbes' Mechanical Conception of Nature* (=Br.), Eng. trans. Copenhagen, 1928.
[4] See *Elements of Law* (=E.L.), ed. Tönnies. Cambridge, 1928.
[5] Rawlinson MSS., 1104 Bodl.
[6] H.M.C. XIII, App. Pt. II, Vol. II (=P.P.).

On the personal side he said : " Though my Lady and my Lord do both accept so well of my service as I could almost engage my self to serve them as a domestique all my life, yet the extreme pleasure I take in study overcomes in me all other appetites " (129). Again, speaking of a certain Mr. Payne in 1635, he wrote : " I would he could give good reason for the faculties and passions of the soul, such as may be expressed in plain English, *if* he can ; he is the first—that I ever heard of—could speak sense in that subject. If he cannot I hope to be the first." This remark, taken along with the discussion of the passions in the *Short Tract*, casts doubt upon the picturesque rumour (A.G. III, 232) that Galileo, at their interview, had been the first to suggest to Hobbes that ethics might be treated in a geometrical way.

Hobbes's first philosophical book, however—the *Elements of Law*, which was circulated in manuscript in 1640—scarcely mentioned " Body," but discussed man and his citizenship. In a sense it was a tract for the times, although its absolutism professed to be based upon perennial principles of psychology, ethics, and politics. Indeed, it must be presumed to have grown out of discussion at Chatsworth or at Welbeck, where cultured patricians like Falkland and " all the excellent of that peaceable time " (A. I, 151) kept aloof both from Puritans and " Arminians," distrusted the growing opulence of the cities, and yet, despite their culture and their honest delight in " reason," were compelled by their traditions and their station to unite with a party they could not wholly approve, and to oppose a party they did not understand. An indication of their intellectual temper is to be found in Clarendon's account of the character of Newcastle, and in Con's[1] account to Cardinal Barberini of that nobleman. " He loved monarchy," said Clarendon, " as it was the foun-

[1] The Pope's agent to Henrietta Maria. Clarendon's and Con's statements are quoted together in Gardiner's *History*, VIII, 244.

dation of his own greatness ; and the Church as it was constituted for the splendour and security of the Crown ; and religion as it cherished and maintained that order and obedience that was necessary to both. . . . He detested whatsoever was like to disturb the public peace." " In matters of religion," said Con, " the Earl is too indifferent. He hates the Puritans ; he laughs at the Protestants, and has little confidence in the Catholics."

In these times the high points of political theory were regarded rather as the spearheads of active forces than as cloud-capped peaks to be reached only if a man had wings. Henry Parker's *Observations*,[1] for instance, was the most effective political pamphlet of 1642, and was quite as abstract as Hobbes's manuscript. Therefore Hobbes, in his own words, " doubting how they [the Long Parliament] would use him, went over into France, the first of all that fled, and there continued eleven years, to his damage some thousands of pounds deep " (IV, 414)—which seems a lot of money. This action is commonly regarded as an instance of prodigious poltroonery ; and perhaps it was. Certainly Aubrey's account of it was historically misleading. " Bishop Manwaring of St. David's," said Aubrey, " preached this doctrine [absolute monarchy], for which he was committed prisoner to the Tower. Then, thought Mr. Hobbes, 'tis time for me to shift for myself."[2] For Manwaring was imprisoned in 1628, and in 1640 the House *desisted*, on the King's appeal, from an attempt to censure him ; and Hobbes can hardly have thought that he had the same reasons for apprehension as Strafford, Laud or Finch

It is to be remembered, however, that Hobbes was fifty, determined to elaborate a very comprehensive philosophy, sure of his welcome from Mersenne

---

[1] Parker became secretary to Essex, the head of the Parliamentary army.

[2] Clark's *Wood's Life and Times*, II, 472 n.

and other learned friends, and firmly convinced (A. II, 169) that men " contracted a moss on them for want of ingeniose conversation." If moss (in the Tower), not blood, was what he had to fear—for there was no war in 1640, and, if there had been, an elderly scholar could not have been expected to become a cornet of horse—why should he not decide that Paris—where his philosophy had made such progress only three years before, and where Richelieu, the great patron of the sciences, was still alive —was a better place than England under its fierce new Parliament ? It is possible, even, that Hobbes's patron, who was a pupil no longer, trembled for his estates (which in fact were sequestrated in 1642, although a composition was allowed in 1645).

In Paris, Hobbes, with Mersenne's backing, was accepted as a leader in philosophy, and was especially anxious to vindicate his independence *vis-à-vis* to Descartes (*e.g.* A.G. XIX, 153 *sqq.*): For a time, however, his political theory competed with his metaphysical, and his world-famous treatise, the *De Cive*, appeared in a small edition in 1642. This completed, he returned to natural philosophy. According to his own statement (L. I, xci) he spent four of these years upon the further elaboration of the book that was to be the *De Corpore*. In 1646 his friend Sorbière wrote that he was avidly expecting the publication of Hobbes's *Elements of all Philosophy* (A.G. III, 193) ; and Hobbes himself said, in a letter of 1647 (A.G. III, 207), that, but for illness, he would have completed the first part of his philosophy, the discussion ' Of Body."

By 1646 he had completed at least one draft of an optical treatise, and earlier had contributed to Mersenne's *Ballistica* (published 1644), one of the contributions being an important *précis* of his doctrine of sensation. Again, as Mr. Brandt has shown (Br. 170), portions of the later *De Corpore* existed in draft in 1664, since Mersenne in the

Ballistica referred to Chapter 28 of the *De Motu, Loco et Tempore* of " the very subtle Hobbes," and the topics of Mersenne's reference were those of Chapter 28 of the later *De Corpore.*

We need not infer, however, that the draft was very complete. When Hobbes wrote his *Leviathan* (A. I, 334 *sq.*) his ·" manner of writing . . . was thus. He walked much and contemplated ; and he had at the head of his staff a pen and ink-horn, carried always a note-book in his pocket, and as soon as a thought darted, he presently entered it into his book, or otherwise he might perhaps have lost it. He had drawn the design of the book into chapters, etc., so he knew whereabout it would come in." If this were his usual method of composition, the relative completeness of Chapter 28 does not give much evidence regarding the progress of the work as a whole ; and we know that some of Hobbes's friends were sceptical on the point. Thus in December 1644 Charles Cavendish wrote from Hamburg to Pell the mathematician : " Mr. Hobbes puts me in hope of his philosophy, which he writes he is now putting in order ; but I fear that will take a long time ";[1] and, in 1645, " he proceeds every day somewhat, but he has a great deal to do."[2]   Since, however, Hobbes had resolved (A.G. III, 69) to make his physics and metaphysics, like his *De Cive,* completely unassailable, it may have been " somewhat of polishing " that occupied him every day.

There was much that was pleasant during this busy period. Hobbes did not take his intellectual separation from Descartes to heart. He thought himself the better man, and was reassured upon the point by obsequious friends like Sorbière, who told him (A.G. III, 68) that he and Gassendi, not Descartes, were the phœnixes of the age. Hobbes and Gassendi, as Aubrey said simply (A. I, 366),

[1] J. O. Halliwell's *Collection of Letters,* p. 87.
[2] q. Br. 180, from Vaughan's *The Protectorate.*

"loved each other entirely"; and Gassendi, writing to Sorbière in 1646, said that no one was more profound in political theory than Hobbes, and that, in general philosophy, his penetration and impartiality were peerless.[1] Mersenne was as friendly as he was appreciative, and Hobbes could refresh himself with the company of the unbelligerent English, among whom a young man, who became the celebrated Sir William Petty, read Vesalius's *Anatomy* with him and drew the diagrams for his optical treatises (A. II, 140).

Yet the deep cloud over England cast its gloom over Paris, and the trickle of despairing refugees became a steady stream. The Earl of Devonshire was not a combatant, but his younger brother Charles had been the first of the English nobility to fall in action. He "would fain have delivered himself," Cromwell wrote in an early dispatch (1643), but "my Captain-lieutenant slew him with a thrust under his short ribs," and the event did more to show that the Parliament-men were implacable than any that had preceded it. Newcastle, Charles's mediocre generalissimo, left the service and his country after his defeat at Marston Moor, and with his brother, who was physically incapacitated for soldiering, came via Hamburg to Paris, where he married his "mad duchess," the future authoress, *en secondes noces*, and attempted, with her assistance, to expel the memory of his campaigns with scientific and theological discussion. It was in their house that Hobbes debated free-will with the Arminian, John Bramhall, refugee Bishop of Derry. The misery of the exiles, however, cannot have yielded readily to these intellectual consolations, and Hobbes himself seems to have been threatened with poverty, since he thought seriously of accepting the offer of an admirer, Du Verdus, to join his household, permanently, in Languedoc.

In the same year the Prince of Wales fled, by way of

[1] *Œuvres*, Florentine ed., VI, p. 223.

Jersey, to his mother at St. Germains, and Hobbes's fortunes took a turn for the better, since he was appointed the Prince's instructor in mathematics, partly, it may be presumed, through the influence of Newcastle, who had once been the Prince's " governor." At the time, however, Hobbes had a high reputation in mathematics. Indeed, by one of the ironies of history, he had been one of a very learned jury of twelve (which included Roberval, Professor of Mathematics at Paris) to decide upon a case of circle-squaring, Pell *v.* Longomontanus (L. I, xxxi). If Charles Stuart, in the years between Naseby and Worcester, must have been rather a preoccupied pupil, he may well have owed much of his lively interest in science to Newcastle and to Hobbes.

Hobbes's position, however, was very uncomfortable. Ormonde and the Queen looked askance at the anti-Arminian, anti-papal author of the *De Cive* ; and the Scots, from whom most was to be hoped, were shocked that the Court should include a " professed atheist."[1] Hobbes had to promise to teach mathematics *only*, and not politics (A.G. III, 194); and when Sorbière, in 1647, with all the indiscretion of a literary hanger-on, described Hobbes as " preceptor to the Prince of Wales," in the second edition of the *De Cive*, which he was then seeing through the Elzevir Press, Hobbes wrote him as sharp a letter as a grateful man could. He was only a super-numerary, he said (A.G. III, 199). He was *not* of the Royal household. Charles should not be tainted with the odium attaching to Hobbist politics ; and Hobbes himself could not hope to return to England if he really did belong to the exiled Court.

Nevertheless, Hobbes elected to write his *Leviathan*, his masterpiece in political theory and one of the great books of the world ; and the time of its publication has aroused comment. After the Restoration, Wallis, Hobbes's enemy,

---

[1] Baillie to Henderson, q. Masson's *Life of Milton*, III, 430.

said that the *Leviathan* was " written in defence of Oliver's
title, or whoever, by whatsoever means, can get to be
upmost " (IV, 413); and Wallis may have been primed
by Clarendon, who said that the book was " a sly address
to Cromwell,"[1] and narrated how, having remonstrated
with Hobbes in Paris when some sheets of the *Leviathan*
were printing, Hobbes told him " after a discourse between
jest and earnest . . . *the truth is I have a mind to go home* "
(Cl. 8). Hobbes had no difficulty in showing that his own
" little story " compared very favourably with Wallis's—
for Wallis had been a " decipherer " of the royalist correspondence captured at Naseby—and he pointed out quite
truly that Oliver was not Lord Protector in 1651 (IV, 415).
But it seems plain that he *had* a mind to go home.

Indeed, when Hobbes said (1656) that the *Leviathan* had
" framed the minds of 1000 gentlemen to a conscientious
obedience " to the new regime (VII, 336), he was boasting
of a result that could not have pleased the exiled Court ;
and in his post-Restoration reply to Wallis he defended
the action of those royalists who submitted to the only
protection they could find (IV, 420 *sq.*). It is hardly
surprising, therefore, that although he presented a manuscript copy of the *Leviathan*, " engrossed in vellum in a
marvellous fair hand "[2] (Cl. 8) to the young Prince, who
had just returned from his useless expedition to Scotland
and to Worcester, he was forbidden the Court shortly
afterwards, even if " Wat Montagu and other Papists (to
the great shame of the true Protestants) were the chief
cause that that great atheist was sent away."[3]

It does not follow, however, that the *Leviathan* was
written with the purpose of facilitating Hobbes's return.
In the *De Cive* (II, 107) Hobbes had maintained that after

---

[1] *Brief View and Survey* of Hobbes's Errors (=Cl.), 2nd imp. Oxford,
1676, p. 317.
[2] British Museum. Egerton, 1910.
[3] *Nicholas Papers* (=N.P.), p. 285. Camden Society, 1886.

a conquest a subject was bound to *support* the new government, and although he attempted to demonstrate the truth of *absolutism*, he never held that the supreme power was demonstrably monarchical. It was the assumption that the royalist cause was lost, not any novel point of high theory, that made Clarendon so bitter; and although we may reasonably assume that a philosopher of sixty, whose cosmopolitanism may well have been surfeited, occasionally remembered discretion, there is little in the *Leviathan* that looks like a bid, astute or otherwise, for a return to England. Hobbes wrote the book because his ideas were in the saddle. In certain incidentals, however (*e.g.* III, 704), he does seem to have advised the royalists in England; and the *Leviathan* (III, 696) contains the very significant statement, quite inconsistent with Hobbes's usual ultra-Erastianism, that once the " knots " of " præterpolitical " power had been untied, first of papacy, second of episcopacy, and third of presbytery, a return to the " independency of the primitive Christians " was " perhaps the best."[1]

According to Hobbes (IV, 415) it was distrust of the French clergy, not the coldness of the exiled Court, that made him fly back to England; and Clarendon (Cl. 8) in part confirmed this statement by saying that " the Justice had endeavoured to apprehend " our philosopher. The insults to the papacy in the *Leviathan*, we must suppose, had made the Church forget its Gallicanism for the moment; and the Fronde may have made the French Government particularly wary of a theorist who might be supposed to countenance successful rebellion. In any case, Hobbes returned to England, never to leave it again, in wintry weather and in some danger from freebooters and pirates.[2] The royalists heard (N.P. 286) that he was " much caressed " in London, and certainly it was stated

---

[1] Omitted in the Latin edition.
[2] Cf. Evelyn's *Diary*, 13th Jan. 1651.

in a government sheet of 8th–15th January 1651–2—the *Mercurius Politicus*, conducted by Marchamont Nedham— that " Mr. Hobbes declines in credit with his friends there [in Paris] of the Royal stamp," and was called an atheist only because his views " did not square with the clergy interest." On the other hand, the later rumour[1] that Cromwell offered Hobbes a secretaryship was accompanied by no evidence.

The article in the *Mercurius Politicus* was occasioned by the publication, shortly before the *Leviathan*, of the *Elements of Law* in two successive books under different titles. In a sense, therefore, the very book that had driven Hobbes into semi-voluntary exile helped his semi-voluntary return. It was rumoured, too, that Seth Ward, a very astute person, who soon became one of Hobbes's tormentors, had superintended the publication (*Athenæ*, iii, 1210), and had declared (*ibid.*, iii, 1215) that he " had rather be the author of one of Mr. Hobbs his books than be King of England," by which Ward did not mean that he would rather be dead. In short, many who afterwards said something very different were then inclined to suppose that Hobbist principles might bring peace to a distracted country. Hobbes, however, as he had said in the penultimate sentence of his *Leviathan*, " hoped to return to his interrupted speculation of bodies natural," and he did so return, first in London, and later (1653) in Derbyshire, at his patron's.

He had leisure for these speculations, but not entire quiet. The *Leviathan's* lashing of the waters roused a tempest that would never subside during Hobbes's lifetime, and Seth Ward's *Vindiciæ Academiarum* (1654) was one of the portents of the coming storm, although most of it dealt with the views of Webster (a friar) and of Dell (an enthusiast). Hobbes, said Ward, besides being highly magisterial (6) had stolen his optical theories from Warner (7),

---

[1] John Dowel, *The Leviathan Heretical*, 1683, p. 137.

and had as little knowledge of the present state of
English universities as one of the seven sleepers (59).
There was no Popish fairyland in Oxford, whatever the
Leviathan might have said ; but " hobgoblins were spiteful
and mischievous in their friskings " (54).

In the same year a very unscrupulous Hobbist, John
Davys of Kidwelly (A. I, 359), who had procured a manuscript copy, not intended for publication, of Hobbes's
theses against Bramhall in their Paris discussion about
free-will, published the same along with a highly provocative preface, in which the " black coats " were compared
to " ignorant tinkers " who made more holes than they
found in the consciences they tried to solder (IV, 235).
The book, like everything else that Hobbes wrote, was
widely read. " So to bed," Pepys wrote (Wheatley's ed.,
II, 140), " . . . and lay long reading Hobbes his Liberty
and Necessity, and a little but very shrewd piece ; and
so to sleep." The shrewd piece, however, and the circumstances of its publication, led Bramhall to make a lengthy
retort (1665), traversing each of Hobbes's arguments ;
and Hobbes replied in a substantial volume, printing the
Bishop's replies *in extenso* and giving long and highly
delectable " animadversions " upon each reply. His
patience was exhausted. " Vindex " (Seth Ward) had
been barking like a little dog to please his masters (V, 455).
Now came Bramhall. And Hobbes (V, 455) thought it
" necessary at last " to " make an example " of this bishop.
Yet the " little dogs " (which, of course, were pedigree
Episcopalians) were to bark till Hobbes was buried (and
over his grave, too). Some of them grew into very big
dogs ; and when *De Corpore* was published at last, in 1655,
the snarling tribe, not altogether to their surprise, had
something to bite.

" Vindex " produced his *Exercitatio epistolica* in about
a year, and Wallis was still more prompt with his *Elenchus*
of Hobbian geometry, and especially of Hobbes's extensive

circle-squaring in the *De Corpore*. The pair, who worked as a team, were Savilian professors at Oxford, imported from Cambridge, and they had reason to claim that they had a much better knowledge of modern mathematics than anyone (except Hobbes himself) ever supposed that Hobbes had. Ward, Professor of Astronomy, who later became a bishop at an age that " went to the very hearts " (A. II, 287) of some of the older ecclesiastics, was the less active controversialist of the two ; but Wallis, an unpleasant and unscrupulous but extremely able person, was the greatest mathematician in England, and continued the paper warfare almost as long as Hobbes did.

Hobbes saw from the first that he was very hard pressed. In January 1656 he wrote to Sorbière (A.G. III, 209) that he had all the ecclesiastics of England against him. (But what was really so very trying, as Wallis said,[1] was that a mere " minister " should outdo him at mathematics.) In the next year Hobbes wrote that the kingdom of truth was not of this world (A.G. III, 213), and six years later, a little more cheerfully, that posterity would side with him (*ibid.*, 214). He also declared (*ibid.*, 217) that although he could not convince Huygens and others, he would eventually convince all who were not too dense to see that a stone multiplied by the number ten did not become ten square stones.

Something of the manner of the controversy may be indicated here. On the score of moral character Hobbes was much the more effective because his case was the better. Wallis had no such deadly thrust as " there, doctor, you deciphered ill." While each had some reason to impugn the other's classical scholarship, Hobbes, when he chose to be suave, was unapproachable, as in his remark (about mathematical proportion), " There is within you some special cause of intenebration which you should do well to look to " (VII, 240) ; and Wallis's taunts concerning Hobbes's plebeian standing and rustic speech—we learn

[1] *Hobbiani Puncti Dispunctio*, p. 9.

from Aubrey (at I, 354) that Hobbes always retained " a little touch of our [West-country] pronunciation," and of course the word *hob*, among other things, meant a rustic— was very neatly countered by Hobbes's " It was perhaps an imagination that you were talking to your inferior, which I will not grant you, nor will the heralds " (VII, 388). In the main, however, the disputants were too angry for very polished gibing. " Very witty " (VII, 389) was all that the spluttering Hobbes could find to say when Wallis twitted him with the fact that, not being a university doctor, he had to wear a hat, not a cap ; and each of the adversaries opined that the other had defæcated his arguments.

At the Restoration, Hobbes's natural anxieties were quickly relieved. In Aubrey's words (I, 340), " it hap- pened, about two or three days after his Majesty's happy return, that, as he was passing in his coach through the Strand, Mr. Hobbes was standing at Little Salisbury House gate (where his lord then lived). The King espied him, put off his hat very kindly to him, and asked him how he did." Ever after, Charles was Hobbes's very good friend, delighting in his wit, pensioning him in a hundred pounds a year[1] (a pension that seems generally to have

---

[1] According to Aubrey (I, 346), Hobbes " died worth near £1000, which (considering his charity) was more than I expected." If so, the residuary legatee, James Wheldon, received considerably more than Hobbes anticipated ; and, apart from £100 contributed by Devonshire, Hobbes specified the sum of £290 only, although he directed his executor to maintain a child, " the daughter of Thomas Alaby " for some years. (If Hobbes had a natural daughter, it looks as if this child was a descendant.) During his lifetime Hobbes had made over to his elder brother the " mowing ground," worth £16 or £18 per annum, bequeathed him by Francis Hobbes (A. I, 324. Tönnies, *Leben und Lehre*, 67), and (Tönnies, *ibid.*) had paid off a mortgage of £200 incurred by a spendthrift nephew (cf. A. I, 385).

Hobbes received £5 for the dedication of *De Mirabilibus Pecci* from the Devonshires, and £40 (from the same) for the dedication of *De Corpore* (Tönnies, *ibid.*). In his later life, the Devonshires (*ibid.*) paid him £50 per annum. It is unlikely that this was supplementary to the original bequest of his first pupil (A.G. XVII, 293), viz. £80 per annum. Charles's irregularly paid pension was £100 per annum. While travelling with Mr. Clinton (*Hist. MSS. Comm.*, VII, 396) Hobbes acknowledged

been paid, although (VII, 472) unpunctually and perhaps not always in full) and studying the old man's interests as well as his own when, for example, he forbade the publication of Hobbes's *Behemoth* (B. viii),[1] a provocative history of the Long Parliament.

Some evidence from Sorbière is relevant here. That gossipy camp-follower of the sciences visited England in 1653, and narrated his experiences in a small volume.[2] He was received by Charles, who knew of his connection with Hobbes, and he recorded the interview thus (p. 97) : " His Majesty showed me Hobbes's portrait, done by Cooper, which hung among his scientific curiosities, and asked me if I knew the man and what I thought of him. I answered suitably, and we agreed that if he had been a little less dogmatic he would have been indispensable to the Royal Society. For there are few who scan things more closely than he. . . . He had alarmed the clergy of his country, I don't know how, as well as the Oxford mathematicians and their followers. So his Majesty compared him very aptly to the bear that the dogs had to bait for their exercise."

Except for one incident Hobbes was not even threatened with molestation. The exception was the action of the House of Commons[3] in 1666 when, to prevent any future Great Fires or Great Plagues, it ordered an examination of the profane and atheistical works of Thomas Hobbes and of Thomas White.[4] Nothing, however, came of the

---

the sum of £65 as " part of our half-year's allowance," and in a letter to Newcastle (P.P. II, 125) thanked Newcastle for a gift, but said that friendship without " silver spurs " was quite enough. Hobbes had about £500 when he fled to France (Tönnies, *ibid.*) and (St. 37) received, about 1646, a half of the £200 left him by Sidney Godolphin. Harvey left him £10 (A. I, 299) ; and, according to Aubrey, Selden did so also (at I, 369), but Tönnies found no mention of the circumstance in Selden's will (*op. cit.*, p. 283).

[1] Tönnies's edition (=B.). [2] *Voyage en Angleterre*, 1664.
[3] *Calendar State Papers* (=Cal.), 20th October 1666.
[4] Thomas White (or Albus, or Albius, or Blackloe), the papist author of forty-eight books, the book in question being *Of Purgatory*. According

matter, and Hobbes (Cal., 9th June 1667) was able to thank Arlington " for his favourable treatment." He also wrote a short treatise to prove that he could not be a heretic on any showing.

Further, Hobbes was relatively affluent ; and the King's favour, combined with the affection of his patrons, gave sufficient shelter to a sharp-penned controversialist who had all episcopacy against him.   According to Sorbière, the Earl loved and revered Hobbes, and Bishop Kennet, although contriving to instil a doubt, admitted that " the Earl, for his whole life, entertained Mr. Hobbes in his family as his old tutor rather than as his friend or confidant ; he let him live under his roof in ease and plenty, and his own way, without making use of him in any public, or so much as domestic affairs.   He would often express an abhorrence of some of his principles in policy and religion, and both he and his lady would frequently put off the mention of his name and say ' he was an humorist and that nobody could account for him.' "[1]

As Warburton said a century afterwards :   " The philosopher of Malmesbury was the terror of the last age as Tindall and Collins are of this.   The press sweated with controversy ;   and every young churchman militant would try his arms in thundering on Hobbes's steel cap."[2] Hobbes was glad to be (under the bishops) the unofficial examiner of ecclesiastical merit, but not so pleased to have any further printing of the *Leviathan* prohibited by the " licensers " (who were, for the most part, the bishops' chaplains, or members of the Royal Society or of the University of Oxford).   In 1668 (Pepys's *Diary*, 3rd September) the price of the book had risen to thirty shillings, and in 1670 (Cal., 28th September) the Master of the

---

to Wood (*Athenæ*, Art. " Glanvil "), White was a crony of Hobbes, and the two " would wrangle, squabble and scold about philosophical matters like young sophisters, though either of them was eighty years of age."
[1] *Memoirs of the Family of Cavendish*, p. 14, 1708.
[2] *Divine Legation*, II, Pref.

Stationers' Company, with an escort, seized the sheets of the *Leviathan* which were then a-printing. Hobbes had to publish in Amsterdam, writing a Latin translation of the book, slightly altered in details, for the benefit of learned Europe, with some remarks in the last pages (L. III, 509 *sq.*) upon lessons to be learned from the surrender of the democrats to Oliver's autocracy, and accompanied by a theological Appendix in place of the original " Review and Conclusion." " Some things in it," said Tillotson, writing to Worthington in April 1669 (Worthington's *Diary*), " seem to be knavishly intended, but the greatest part is very foolish."

Such baiting the bear could endure. It was less pleasant, however, to hear in 1669 that the disreputable Daniel Scargil, when deprived of his fellowship, had edified Cambridge by attributing his vicious ways to Hobbian principles, especially as the aged philosopher had always prided himself upon his justice and generosity (*e.g.* L. I, xxi), and was admitted by Clarendon (Cl. 3) and nearly all other detractors to be " a man of probity," living a life " free from scandal."

More vexatious still was the attitude of the scientists and of the newly formed Royal Society. According to its own contemporary historian,[1] the Society was " a mixed assembly " ; and Devonshire, Aubrey, Pepys, and Evelyn were Fellows. Hobbes's exclusion from it, therefore, was an insult. He was regarded by some competent judges (including Petty, a prominent member of the Society, who ranked him[2] as one of the eight truly great men of post-classical Europe) as the greatest living English thinker. He was still in active correspondence with the Parisian scientific circles in which he had occupied a place of honour for so long ; and he enjoyed royal favour. Hobbes presented many memoranda and demonstrations

---

[1] Sprat, Bishop of Rochester, *History of the Royal Society*, p. 91, 1667.
[2] *The Petty-Southwell Correspondence*, p. 158, 1928.

from " your most humble servant who hath spent much time upon the same subject " (VII, 431) ; but he never became a Fellow.

Every one understood the reason. The Society, which Charles made Royal, had begun at Oxford (Sprat, 53), in Dr. Wilkins's rooms, during the Protectorate ; and Wallis and Ward were Hobbes's enemies. They had no intention of inviting Hobbes into their " free way of reasoning " (*ibid.*), which was also properly devout (p. 4) ; and Wren, the Honourable and pious Robert Boyle, and others were of the same mind. They claimed that they were founding laboratories and not schools (p. 68), and therefore that (although they could deal effectively with Hobbes's mathematical papers), they were opposed, in principle, to his non-experimental ideals. Charles himself could not jest them out of this attitude, when, as Pepys said (Feb. 1, 1663/4) : " Gresham College he mightily laughed at, for spending time only in weighing of air and doing nothing else since they sat."

Hobbes advised the Society to alter its ways. " Not every one that brings from beyond seas a new gin, or other jaunty device," said he, " is therefore a philosopher. For if you reckon that way, not only apothecaries and gardeners, but many other sorts of workmen, will put in for, and get, the prize. Then when I see the gentlemen of Gresham College apply themselves to the doctrine of motion (as Mr. Hobbes has done, and will be ready to help them in it if they please, and so long as they use him civilly), I will look to know some causes of natural events from them, and their register, and not before ; for nature does nothing but by motion " (IV, 437). He also entered into a vigorous controversy with Boyle about vacuum and the nature of air, not seriously to the disadvantage of that great experimentalist.

In short, despite his many friends, Hobbes became a lonely belligerent, called by his enemies " peevish " and

" morose," and comforting himself because his Continental renown (as he thought) stood secure. " His reputation beyond the seas fades not yet " (IV, 435). " His picture also is in great esteem in France, insomuch that the virtuosi thereof have come in pilgrimage to the house of the said Sorbière to see it " (Wood's *Life, Athenæ*, I, cxxxvi). (And, indeed, he was the handsomest of all British philosophers, although (A. I, 348) he disdained to have " the reputation of his wisdom taken from the cut of his beard " and so was " shaved close except a little tip.") " Outlandish gentlemen also, when they came to London, did make it one of their prime businesses to visit him " (*Ath. ibid.*), including Cosmo de Medici, Prince of Tuscany, who went away with a portrait and kept it (*ibid.*) among the " cimilia or rarities " in his closet.[1]

Two accounts of Hobbes in the early Restoration period may be quoted here, the first from Hooke, a friend of Boyle's, the second, more sympathetic, from Pell the mathematician.

" I should sooner," Hooke wrote to Boyle in 1663,[2] " have given you an account of an interview I had of

---

[1] The portrait in the National Portrait Gallery is by J. Michael Wright, and shows at least one of the eyes as " quick " (A. I, 347) as well as the " ample forehead," although the " ruddy complexion " had become a little subdued. Aubrey referred more than once to the portrait by Caspars (A. I, 354, cf. 372) that he himself had presented to the Royal Society (which body at present possesses two) ; and also referred (at I, 354 *sq.*) to Cooper's portrait in the King's possession (which Loggan might engrave). There were, he said (at I, 368) two copies. In addition, there was a portrait at Sir Charles Scarborough's (A. I, 355) and one of Hobbes in extreme age by " a good painter " at the Earl of Devonshire's (*ibid.*) (cf. Wood's *Athenæ*, iii, 1208, of the portrait at Chatsworth " with a glass in his hand "). Horace Walpole (Masson, *Life of Milton*, VI, 648) mentioned an engraving by Faithorne (1664) in a collection of engravings of distinguished royalists ; and there was the Duke of Tuscany's portrait or engraving. In Granger's *Biographical History* (3rd ed., 1779, Vol. IV, p. 92) mention is made of a small oval in the *Homer*, and it is stated that Faithorne's engraving appeared in the octavo edition of Hobbes's *Latin Works*, that Clark and Hollar copied from Faithorne, that Faithorne probably worked from Cooper's portrait, and that there was a portrait by Dobson at " the Grange in Hampshire."

[2] q. Masson's *Life of Milton*, VI, 289.

Mr. Hobbes, which was at Mr. Reeve's, he coming along with my lord Devonshire to be assistant in the choosing of a glass. I was, I confess, a little surprised at first to see an old man so view me and survey me in every way, without saying any thing to me ; but I quickly shaked off my surprisal when I heard my lord call him Mr. Hobbes, supposing he had been informed to whom I belonged. I soon found, by staying that little while he was there, that the character I had formerly received of him was very significant. I found him to lard and seal every asseveration with a round oath, to undervalue all other men's opinions and judgments, to defend to the utmost what he asserted, though never so absurd, to have a high conceit of his own abilities and performances, though never so absurd and pitiful, &c. He would not be persuaded but that a common spectacle-glass was as good as an eye-glass for a thirty-six foot glass as the best in the world, and pretended to see better than all the rest by holding his spectacle in his hand, which shook as fast one way as his head did the other ; which, I confess, made me bite my tongue."

Pell's narrative (1662) was more sedate (Halliwell, 96 *sq.*) :

" This morning Mr. Thomas Hobbes met me in the Strand, and led me back to Salisbury-house, where he brought me into his chambers and there showed me his construction of that problem, which he said he had solved, namely the doubling of a cube. He then told me that Viscount Brouncker was writing against him. ' But,' said he, ' I have written a confirmation and illustration of my demonstration and to-morrow I intend to send it to the press, that with the next opportunity I may send printed copies to transmarine mathematicians, craving their censure of it.' I answered that I was then busy, and could not persuade myself to pronounce of any such question before I had very thoroughly considered it at leisure in my own chamber. Whereupon he gave me these two papers, bidding me take as much time as I pleased. 'Well,' said I, 'if your work seems true to me I shall not be afraid to tell the *world* so, but if I find it false, you will be content that I shall tell *you* so ; but privately, seeing you have only thus privately desired my opinion of it.' ' Yes,' said he, ' I shall be content, and thank you too. But, I pray you, do not dispute against my construction, but show me the fault of my demonstration, if you find any.' "

Hobbes continued to defend his politics, his theology, and, more particularly, his mathematics and natural philosophy, until his ninetieth year, the palsied fingers moving clumsily to the bidding of a mind that was still " vegete," nimble, and powerful. Among these later writings, the *Behemoth*, an historical dialogue relating the sinister but instructive story of the Long Parliament, would have brought lasting fame to a lesser man ; and the indefatigable old gentleman, pouring forth in his age what he had so long restrained in his youth, produced, as an octogenarian, complete metrical translations of the *Iliad* and of the *Odyssey*, prefaced by a most judicious essay on the " virtues of an heroic poem," which ended with the delightful remark : " Why, then, did I write it ? Because I had nothing else to do. Why publish it ? Because I thought it might take off my adversaries from showing their folly upon my more serious writings, and set them upon my verses to show their wisdom. But why without annotations ? Because I had no hope to do it better than it had been already done by Mr. Ogilby " (X, x). Even Hobbes's enemies admired his spirit, for one of them parodied Cowley's ode in Hobbes's honour thus :[1]

[1] *The True Effigies of the Monster of Malmesbury* (1680).

0145287

Tom's grown another man, and now himself betakes
To poetry and sonnets makes
Of gods and goddesses and such like things:
He's now the echo of what Homer sings.
If versifying be a sign of youth
The man of politics is youthful still:
He does not here pretend to show the truth
On which pretence how much ink did he spill:
O that he had spent all the time
In hard translations and in rhyme
Which he spent in opposing truths by which to Heaven
we climb.

At ninety, however, he was writing his *Decameron Physiologicum*, a dialogue which concluded with the statement: " So God forgive us both as we do one another. But forget not to take with you the demonstration of a straight line equal to an arc of a circle " (VII, 177).

At eighty-four he wrote a spirited autobiography in Latin couplets, having previously supplied Anthony à Wood with a prose autobiography which occasioned one of his later vexations. The unloved Dr. John Fell, Dean of Christ Church, who financed Wood's venture in large part and supervised the Latinity of the *Lives* in their academic dress, arrogated a good many powers to himself in consequence, and besides excising several passages in Hobbes's *Vita*, altered other parts of the narrative, calling the *Leviathan* " monstrosissimum," saying that Hobbes's " sober " judgment was only " sharp," and hinting that his *De Cive* was meant to stir up trouble (Wood's *Life* in *Ath.* I, cxxxvi; A. I, 343 *sqq.*; L. I, xliii *sqq.*). Mr. Hobbes " took it ill," complained to the King, and was allowed to print an epistle about it to which Fell made a " scurrilous answer " (Wood, *Athenæ*, iii, 1213).

Hobbes's general health improved from middle life onwards, but he had several illnesses, some serious. In 1646 he was at the point of death, but turned the con-

103918

versation when Mersenne approached the delicate question of the possible offices of the Church, and, a little later, took the Anglican sacrament from Cosin, afterwards Bishop of Durham. , In 1651 Guy Patin,[1] the celebrated Paris physician, found him unwilling to be bled, and thought he was contemplating suicide ; but, as we saw, there were other reasons for his melancholy at that time. According to Aubrey (at I, 350) he was " very sick and like to die . . . about 1668."

Minor infirmities began to accumulate. He had shaking palsy in his hands after 1650, to the ruin of his hand-writing. He complained to Sorbière (A.G. III, 218) that he had had pain in his side and unsteadiness in his gait from the age of sixty onwards ; but according to Aubrey (I, 349) he " went indifferently erect, or rather, considering his great age, very erect." And he tried to assist his natural longevity by a self-invented treatment on philo-sophical principles. His theory was (A. I, 357) that " old men were drowned inwardly by their own moisture." The obvious remedy was profuse perspiration. Therefore he was rubbed after his daily walk in the morning—his habit (A. I, 351) was to pen his morning thought in the afternoon—and well rubbed after tennis which (although not very often) he played " at about 75 " (*ibid.*). He also wore very warm clothing.

The passage of air through the lungs was another part of his regimen. Therefore, when the doors were made fast so that nobody heard him (A. I, 352) he sang aloud for his health's sake. After sixty he was studiously temperate in his diet, drinking no wine, and eating fish rather than flesh ; but he had been temperate all his life, not drinking wine every day, being " in excess," by his own computa-tion, only one hundred times in his whole life, and then making his stomach relieve the disorder in his head (A. I, 350). While Bishop Kennet spoke of " 10 or 12

[1] *Letters*, ii, 593 *sq.*, 1846.

pipes of tobacco a day" (*Memoirs*, etc., p. 14) Aubrey
mentioned but one (I, 351). Hobbes was "not a woman
hater" (A. I, 350), but "even in his youth" was prudent
in that matter, and we have only Bishop Kennet's
word for it (*Athenæ*, iii, 1218) that he had a natural
daughter.

His age, then, was busy with exercise, meditation, and
writing, but perhaps not so very much with reading.
Clarendon (Cl., Ded.) complained, like some others, that
Hobbes "consulted too few authors, and made use of too
few books." The latter complaint, however, was accompanied by the untenable accusation that Hobbes should
have discussed more frequently with his intellectual equals,
and the former was probably an echo of Hobbes's boast
(A. I, 349) that "if he had read as much as other men
he should have known no more than other men" (cf. V,
311 and 441). He had, however, little interest in scholarship for its own sake, except, perhaps, in the classics ;
for he belonged, as he thought, to the new order, and held
that the learning of such men as Suarez or Bramhall (he
might have added Gassendi) smothered their wit. His
own learning was used for sharp dialectical thrusts, which,
as in his reference to Luther and Calvin on free-will,
(V, 64 *sq.*) had little relation to the general position of the
authors quoted, and may have been helped (cf. VI, 6) by
his knowledge of the use of an index.

James Wheldon, "servant to the Earl of Devonshire"
and Hobbes's executor, gave Aubrey a full account of the
philosopher's last illness, saying in substance that he died
on 4th December 1679 "rather for want of the fuel of life
than by the power of his disease" (A. I, 383), although
there had been a strangury for nearly two months, and
although, for a week before his death, "his whole right side
was taken with the dead palsy," so that he could not
speak. According to a very probable anecdote he had
once been pleased with the suggestion that the inscription

on his tomb should be " Here is the true philosopher's stone " ; and another anecdote relates that he said : " on his death-bed " that " he was 91 years finding a hole to go out of this world, and at length found it."[1] Southwell, however, wrote to Ormonde in Ireland that Hobbes had died " in all the forms of a very good Christian."[2] He was buried at Hault Hucknall, beside the park of Hardwick Hall, and it was written on his tombstone that he was a just man renowned for his learning at home and abroad.

(2) WRITINGS

The scope and variety of Hobbes's industry are best seen in the list of his published works. (His unpublished manuscripts would increase the bulk, but scarcely the substance, of British letters.) For the reader's convenience of reference, it seems best to offer a classified catalogue with annotations. If the catalogue is dry, I beg the reader's pardon. I cannot make it succulent, but I can make it instructive.

As we have seen, Hobbes repeatedly returned to the same themes. For example, he gave three major accounts of his political theory in a period of about a dozen years. The reader should also recall that his first political treatise was " plucked from him " (II, xx) by the contemporary crisis when he was " studying philosophy for his mind sake " (II, xix), and had planned, and to some extent written, a comprehensive system in the three sections : Body ; Man ; Citizenship. The treatment of Body was to include " first philosophy," the general principles of matter and motion, and all that was not peculiar to any species of moving beings. The treatment of Man was to deal with man's *special* faculties and affections. Civil Government had to do with the duties of subjects (II, xx).

---

[1] Clark, *Wood's Life and Times*, ii, 471 *sq.*
[2] Ormonde Papers, H.M.C., N.S. IV., 13th December 1679.

(A) *The Major Philosophical Works*

(*a*) Political ; or the third section of the philosophy.

(1) " Elements of Law, Natural and Politic," the title of the manuscript circulated in 1640, reprinted by Tönnies and accessible in its second impression, Cambridge, 1928.

The manuscript, although divided into two parts, was planned as a unity. In 1650 it was published in two companion volumes, the first being entitled *Human Nature*, the second *De Corpore Politico : or the Elements of Law, Moral and Political.* A " friend " saw it through the press, and it was signed " F. B.," *i.e.* Francis Bowman, bookseller at Oxford (E.L. viii). Obviously the first volume was not intended as a complete exposition of the second section of Hobbes's philosophy. Reprinted in 1652. Several early translations.

(2) " *De Cive* " (in Latin, L. II).

A small edition was printed " privately " in Paris in 1642, bearing the initials " T. H." on the dedicatory letter (Robertson's *Philosophical Remains*, p. 304). The title then was *Elementorum Philosophiæ Sectio Tertia : De Cive,* and the book received attention at once in the highest scientific quarters, as a letter of Grotius shows (April 1643 ; No. 648, additional, in *Epistolæ*, Amsterdam, 1687). In the larger edition (Amsterdam, Elzevir Press, 1647, supervised by Sorbière) some important notes, a dedication, and the justly celebrated " Preface to the Reader " were added. In 1651 Hobbes published an English translation entitled *Philosophical Rudiments concerning Government and Society* (II).

(3) " Leviathan : Or the Matter, Forme & Power of a Commonwealth, Ecclesiasticall and Civill." London, 1651.

Job's " leviathan " was " a king over all the children of pride " (xli, 34) ; and so was Hobbes's " artificial man," the sovereign. The idea that the sovereign was a " mortal God " was, of course, not new, and may be found, *e.g.* in

Bacon's essay on kingship. It did not necessarily imply *divine* right.

The Latin edition (L. III) was published at Amsterdam in 1668. Its new appendix contained three short dialogues (On the Nicene Creed ; On Heresy ; Reply to Objections).

Mr. Lubienski, in his recent book *Die Grundlagen des ethisch-politischen Systems von Hobbes* (München, 1932), has shown, in some detail, that the minor differences between the English and the Latin texts deserve attention, and suggests (*e.g.* p. 261) that Hobbes may have written (a draft or a great part of ?) the *Leviathan* in Latin *before* he wrote the English book, and used this material in the Amsterdam edition. Hobbes's own statement was (IV, 317) that he had " converted " the *Leviathan* into Latin " with the omission of some such passages as strangers are not concerned in," because he had been " solicited from beyond sea " to do so and feared that " some other man might do it not to his liking." Since, as we have seen, so much of his time between 1642 and 1649 was devoted to the later *De Corpore* (*e.g.* A.G. III, 208), it seems unnecessary to suppose really superhuman energy on his part. Hobbes clearly regarded the Latin edition as the definitive one, at any rate in so far as it corrected the English (IV, 317). Its Latin form was designed for the learned. But *the* book is the English book (III). A Dutch translation appeared in 1667.

(*b*) Body : or the first section of the philosophy.

" *De Corpore* " (in Latin), 1655 (L. I).

This important work, whose publication had been so long delayed, was succeeded in 1656 by a translation, superintended by Hobbes although not wholly satisfactory, entitled *Elements of Philosophy, the first Section, concerning Body* (I). The translation substantially modified the mathematical argument, especially (Chapters XVIII and XX) regarding circle-squaring, and contained other modifications elicited by criticism.

(c) Human Nature : or the second section of the philosophy.

" *De Homine* " (in Latin), 1658 (L. II).

This was the official second section of the system, although the psychological introductions to the *Elements of Law* and to the *Leviathan* remain by far Hobbes's most important contributions. He wrote the book, he said (L. II, Ded.), " to keep his promise " ; and, although he did not keep the promise very well, he (i) gave an account of optics (partly psychological and partly physiological), and (ii) gave a very condensed psychological introduction to politics.

(B) *Minor Philosophical Pieces*

(a) On Politics, Ethics, and Religion.

(1) The translation of *Thucydides*, published in 1629, perhaps written earlier. Reprinted 1634 and 1648 (with a different publisher). "Second edition," 1676 (VIII and IX).

(2) " Of Liberty and Necessity " (IV).

A short statement of Hobbes's position in his debate with Bramhall, drawn up in 1646 at Newcastle's request. Hobbes (V, 434) did not mean to publish, " but I barred not myself from showing it privately to my friends." Davys, in a pirated edition, published the piece in 1654, except for its " postscript " ; and Bramhall (*Works*, ed. 1842, IV, 251 *sq.*) held that Hobbes should at least have prevented Davys's "lewd epistle," Hobbes being in London at the time. Republished with comments by Bishop Laney, 1677.

(3) " The Questions concerning Liberty, Necessity and Chance," 1656 (V).

The incensed Bramhall printed, as he said (*Works*, IV, 19), " all that had passed between us upon this subject without any addition or the least variation from the original." Hobbes, protesting that he could not recall any uncivil word or charges of atheism in their debate,

printed Bramhall's book *plus* his own new animadversions.
In 1658 Bramhall published his *Castigations of Mr. Hobbes
his last Animadversions* ; but Hobbes did not reply.

(4) Five posthumous publications here enumerated
according to the probable date of composition :

(4) (i) *"Historia Ecclesiastica carmine elegiaco concinnata."*
Probably begun about 1659, but written, for the most
part, some years later (cf. L. I, xx) ; published 1688 with
a preface by T. Rymer of Gray's Inn (L.V). The verses—
there are 2242 lines—were a dialogue between Primus and
Secundus, and were a sort of sequel to the *Leviathan*, the
history being compiled (A. I, 338) from Cluverius's *Historia
Universalis.* An anonymous and lengthy translation into
English verse was published in 1722.

(4) (ii) " A Dialogue between a Philosopher and a
Student of the Common Laws of England " (VI).
Written about 1666 (Robertson's *Hobbes* (=R.), p. 199).
Aubrey (at I, 341) took credit for having " drawn Hobbes
on " to write it, his blandishments having begun in 1664.
When published (1681) in its present incomplete form it
was said by the publisher to have been " finished many
years " (VI, 422). It seems to have been circulated in
manuscript, and so was known to Sir Matthew Hale
(Burnet's *Life*, 193).

(4) (iii) " An Answer to a Book published by Dr.
Bramhall, late Bishop of Derry, called the ' Catching of
the Leviathan ' " (IV).
Written about 1668. Bramhall's book was an appendix
to his *Castigations*, and tried to plant three " harping
irons " in the monster's side regarding its anti-Christianity,
subversive proposals, and inconsistency. Hobbes's reply
contains a full defence of his theological position. As he
said (IV, 282) : " If you want leisure or care of the questions between us, I pray you condemn me not upon report."

(4) (iv) " An Historical Narration concerning Heresy
and the Punishment thereof " (IV).

Written about 1668. In the Cal. State Papers (30th June 1668) there is a letter from Hobbes to Williamson stating that certain sentences should be excised if a licence could not be obtained otherwise. The licence was presumably withheld, but the peccant sentences appear verbatim in the posthumously published text (IV, 406). The " narrative " should be compared with the contemporary appendix to the Latin edition of the *Leviathan*.

(4) (v) " Behemoth or the Long Parliament " (VI).

Completed about 1668 and best studied in Tönnies's edition (London, 1889), printed from a manuscript in St. John's College, Oxford. Crooke, the publisher of the posthumous edition (1682), complained that there had been several spurious editions of the *History of the Civil Wars*—a much more intelligible title for these dialogues.

The name " Behemoth " seems to have run in Hobbes's mind at least as early as 1656, when he suggested to Bramhall (V, 27) that " Behemoth against Leviathan " would be a " fit title " for those who undertook to refute the *Leviathan* ; but this fitness, properly speaking, should only have been the superiority of a land-monster to a sea-monster, or perhaps of a hippopotamus to a crocodile. One would naturally think that the Long Parliament was supposed to be a detestable monster, Hobbes's artificial man a benign giant ; but in Job xl. 19, Behemoth was said to be " the chief of the ways of God."

Obstructionists may have prevented the publication of sundry minor pieces, *e.g.* Hobbes's views of the Scargil incident in a letter to Sir John Birkenhead (A. I, 360 *sqq.*).

(*b*) Scientific papers before 1655.

(1) " A Short Tract on First Principles."

Tönnies's title for a manuscript printed by him (E.L. 152–67). Probably written between 1630 and 1636, and important evidence of Hobbes's philosophical development.

(2) Objections to Descartes' *Meditations*, 1641, and

Correspondence with Descartes, beginning in the preceding year (L. V, 251 *sqq.*).

(3) " *Tractatus Opticus* " (L. V, 215-48).

Published as the seventh book of Mersenne's *Optique* in 1644. Mr. Brandt has shown (Br. 97) that the greater part of this tract is identical with a letter written by Hobbes to Descartes in 1641, and formerly supposed to be lost. He also (Br. 205 *sq.*) explains the fate of certain corrections (A.G. XIX, 174) that Hobbes made for a projected second edition of Mersenne's publication in 1648.

(4) The *"Præfatio"* (concerning sensation) to Mersenne's *Ballistica*, 1644 (L. V), and part of Prop. XXIV of that work (at pp. 74–82). [Not in Molesworth. See Br. 168.]

(5) A manuscript entitled " A Minute or First Draught of the Optiques."

The date was 1646. Fragments have been published by Molesworth (VII, 467 *sqq.*) and by Köhler (A.G. XVI, 71 *sq.*).

(6) A Latin optical treatise in manuscript.

Most probably written before 1649, since in that year (I, xii) Hobbes said he had the optical part of *De Homine* ready and laid aside. Portions have been published by Tönnies (E.L. 168 *sqq.*). I shall refer to this work as *Tractatus Opticus II*.

(c) Later controversial pieces on Mathematics and Physics.

(1) 1656. " Six Lessons," etc. (VII).

The " lessons " were given to the two Savilian professors in reply (*a*) to Wallis's *Elenchus* (1655) and (*b*) to Seth Ward's *Exercitatio Epistolica* (1656), and were an appendix to the English translation of the *De Corpore*. The last lesson was on manners.

(2) 1657. Στίγμαι, etc., " or Marks of the Absurd Geometry, Rural Language, Scottish Church Politics and Barbarisms of John Wallis," etc. (VII).

Rather more than half was about geometry, but Henry Stubbe, a tempestuous person, much hated by Glanvil, whom Wallis contemptuously called Hobbes's "journeyman," made a lengthy defence (VII, 401–28) of Hobbes's Greek, impugned on account of an alleged confusion between στίγμη and στίγμα, and attacked Wallis's Latinity, *e.g.* the phrase "adducis malleum." The book was Hobbes's reply to Wallis's *Due Correction for Mr. Hobbes ; or School Discipline for not saying his Lessons right* (1656), and was succeeded by Wallis's *Hobbiani Puncti Dispunctio* (1657).

(3) 1660. "*Examinatio et Emendatio Mathematicæ Hodiernæ.*"

Six Latin dialogues between A and B, or, as Wallis later said (H.H. 15), between "Thomas and Hobs," so that "when Hobs hath occasion to assume what he cannot prove, Thomas, by a *Manifestum est* saves him the trouble of attempting a demonstration" (p. 103). Molesworth's text (L. IV, 1–232) prints from the edition of 1668, omitting forty-six propositions on the circle from the sixth dialogue.

(4) 1661. "*Dialogus Physicus de Natura Aeris*" (L. IV).

A Latin dialogue criticising Boyle and the methods of the Royal Society. The book also contained a duplication of the cube, which was a republication of what Hobbes, in the same year, had previously published in Paris, and, in the interim, had been refuted by Wallis.

Wallis's reply had the Terentian title, *Hobbius Heautontimoroumenos* (=H.H.), Boyle's was his *Examen of the greatest Part of Mr. Hobb's Dialogus Physicus*, etc. ; both in 1662. Boyle also published a *Dissertation on Vacuum against Mr. Hobbes* in 1674, and criticised Hobbes in two works published in 1682, *New Experiments Physico-Mechanical*, etc., and *A Defence touching the Spring and Weight of the Air.*

(5) 1662. "*Problemata Physica*" (L. IV).

Latin dialogues dedicated to the King. Translated into

English under the title *Seven Philosophical Problems* and published posthumously (1682) (VII).

(6) 1666. *"De Principiis et Ratiocinatione Geometrarum."*

A Latin argument still against Wallis, who replied in the *Philosophical Transactions* of the same year. The sub-title affirmed that professors of geometry showed as much uncertainty and falsity in that subject as writers on ethics or physics (L. IV, 385).

(7) 1669. *"Quadratura Circuli, Cubatio Sphæræ, Duplicatio Cubi"* (in Latin, L. IV).

With a dedication to Cosmo, Prince of Etruria. Wallis replied in a pamphlet, Hobbes reprinted with an answer to Wallis, and Wallis wrote another pamphlet, all in the same year.

(8) 1671. *"Rosetum Geometricum"* (in Latin, L. V).

The sub-title stated that the book dealt with problems hitherto attempted in vain. The book also contained a " short censure " of Wallis's doctrine of motion. The " fragrant posy " was for the geometrical reader to smell ; Wallis might eat it. This idea of a " posy " may have been suggested by Bramhall (IV, 374). The book and No. 11 were translated and published as Books II and III of a work entitled *Mellificium Mensionis or the Marrow of Measuring* (1681), by Venterus Mandey, and were there stated to be " translations from a Latin author " (to the Reader).

(9) 1671. Three Papers to the Royal Society (VII, 429–32).

Against Wallis. Wallis replied, and Hobbes counter-replied with " Considerations " (VII, 435-48).

(10) 1672. *" Lux Mathematica"* (in Latin, L. V).

According to the sub-title the light arose from the collision between Hobbes and Wallis, and had been increased by many effulgent rays, the author being " R. R." (*i.e.* Roseti Repertor). It was dedicated to the Royal Society, and Wallis replied in the *Transactions*.

(11) 1674. *"Principia et Problemata aliquot Geometrica"* (in Latin, L. V).

As the title proceeded to say, these problems had formerly been despaired of, but were now briefly explained and demonstrated by " T. H."

(12) 1678. *"Decameron Physiologicum"* (VII).

Ten dialogues in English on natural philosophy, with an Appendix concerning the proportion of a straight line to half the arc of a quadrant.

(*d*) Pieces principally of biographical interest.

(1) 1662. " Considerations upon the Reputation, Loyalty, Manners and Religion of Thomas Hobbes " (IV).

An effective reply in the third person to Wallis's charges of disloyalty, etc., in his *Hobbius Heautontimoroumenos*.

(2) The " *Vita* " (L. I).

A Latin autobiography, published posthumously by " R. B." (Richard Blackbourne) in 1681 along with a supplement (*auctarium*) containing a good deal of information. The *Vita* contains a reference to Hobbes's ninety-first year (L. I, xx).

(3) " *Vita Carmine Expressa.*" Written 1672 (L. I).

A Latin autobiography in elegiac couplets (382 lines) posthumously published, but written in 1672. According to Aubrey (I, 363), Blackbourne altered the final couplet, which had read :

> Octoginta annos complevi, jam quatuorque
> Et prope stans dictat Mors mihi, Ne metue.

(*e*) Literary pieces.

(1) Printed 1636, written before 1628, *De Mirabilibus Pecci* (L. V).

The wonders of the Peak in Derbyshire extolled in Latin hexameters. The book showed some local patriotism as well as enthusiasm for Chatsworth. The edition of 1677 contained an English version by a " person of quality," and the popularity of the verses is shown by the printing of editions in 1675 (Blaeu, Amsterdam; and also by Crook, at sixpence). See Arber: *Term Catalogues*. To a taunt of Wallis's regarding the quality of the verses, Hobbes replied (VII, 389) that although in his own opinion " ill," yet they were " not so obscene as that they ought to be blamed by Dr. Wallis." The local name for the Peak (in Latin, *podex diaboli*) *is* rather obscene.

(2) 1650–1. " The Answer of Mr. Hobbes to Sir Wm. Davenant's Preface before *Gondibert*" (IV).

Davenant, who had succeeded Ben Jonson as Poet Laureate in 1637 and was reappointed at the Restoration, published his *Gondibert* in 1651. The poem was written, for the most part, at Paris, where Hobbes considered it " in parcels " during its composition, and Hobbes's essay, or letter, on Davenant's preface, was frequently published in later editions of the poem (Masson's *Milton*, VI, 274 *sqq.*). In my ignorance of these things, I shall rashly affirm that Hobbes was a very good literary critic. Among the remarks in this essay most germane to his philosophy, I may mention the following : (1) that although certain heathen poets " had the name of prophets," the best of them were free from the " indiscretions " of seventeenth-century divines ; (2) that since fancy was really memory, her " voyage was not very great, herself being all she seeks."

(3) 1669. Letter to the Rt. Hon. Mr. Edward Howard.

A short and mediocre effort of the same kind, printed along with Howard's poem, *The British Princes* (IV).

(4) 1673–5. Translations of Homer (X).

These began (1673 or 1674) with a small volume in twelves, *The Travels of Ulysses*, a translation of the " Odysses," Books X–XII, published at one shilling. In 1675 the entire "Odysses" was published at 3s. 6d. " with a large preface," and, in the same year, the " Iliads " in twelves at 4s. 6d. In the next year there was an edition of both together at six shillings. (See Arber, *op. cit.*)

Arber mentions further editions in 1685 and 1686. Hobbes's *Homer* was therefore read, whether or not it deserved to be. Pope (in the Preface to his own *Homer*) thought it " too mean for criticism," and Sir Henry Craik (as quoted in Catlin's *Hobbes*, p. 11) said there were only two lines of true poetry in it. It is well that Sir Henry was quite certain about the two.

(5) Posthumously published in 1681. " The Whole Art of Rhetoric," " The Art of Rhetoric," " The Art of Sophistry " (VI).

The first of these is a pithy summary of Aristotle's *Rhetoric*, very faithful to the original in substance, although only about half the length. It was a relic (R. 29 n.) of Hobbes's activities as a tutor. According to Wood (*Athenæ*, III, 1212) Ramus was drawn upon in the others.

I can find no evidence of the existence of two books mentioned by Wood, viz. (1) an alleged Letter III, 1213, to Newcastle in answer to Bishop Laney (about free-will), and (2) an alleged *Apology for Himself and his Writings*, asserting Hobbes's due and habitual submission to ecclesiastical power. Regarding the latter, Wood, III, 1215, supplied neither place nor date of publication. The former he described as published, " London, 1676 in tw.," which describes *Laney's* book. The latter is also mentioned by Bishop Kennet (*Memoirs of the Family of Cavendish*, p. 15).

Certain letters were published by Molesworth (VII, 449 *sqq.*, and L. V, 277 *sqq.*). Some others, with appropriate references, are mentioned in the text of the present work.

II

THE CLIMATE OF HOBBIAN OPINIONS

(1) RELATIONS TO BACON AND TO DESCARTES

HOBBES believed himself to be in the van of all the new ideas. In political theory, he thought he was the very first to demonstrate the truth. In matters of general philosophy he dunged and watered what Galileo and Harvey had sown. The chief of all problems for a commentator, therefore, is whether these beliefs were true ; that is to say, whether Hobbes, a mediæval born, had changed his heart or only his garments.

I hope to deal with this question in the sequel, but for the moment will linger over a minor but inescapable problem. What were Hobbes's relations to his two great contemporaries—Bacon and Descartes—the first of them so much his senior, the second his junior by eight years ?

(a) Bacon

It is natural to compare Hobbes with Bacon, partly because of their eminence, partly because Hobbes's boast that although neglected at home he was revered abroad seems reminiscent of Bacon's attitude as described in Rawley's *Life*, principally because Hobbes, in his earlier days, had known Bacon pretty well. His lordship, we learn from Aubrey (I, 83 and 331) used to meditate in the coppice to the west of his princely park at Gorhambury, and dictate his notions as they came to him, either to " his servant Mr. Bushell " or to " some other of his

gentlemen," among them Hobbes, " whilest he was there " ;
and Aubrey had been informed, very likely by Hobbes
himself, that Bacon found Hobbes the most intelligent of
these attendant amanuenses, "because he understood
what he wrote." It was Hobbes who told Aubrey (I, 75)
the well-known story of the manner of Bacon's death,
i.e. that he died of pneumonia after impulsively alighting
from his coach in winter in order to buy a fowl from a
poor woman, and experiment *instanter* upon the pre-
servative virtues of snow.

These meetings at Gorhambury occurred, almost certainly, during the years of Bacon's retirement (1621-5),
when the *Novum Organum* (1620) was very new, and
the former Chancellor composed the *De Augmentis*, the
History of Henry the Seventh, and chronicled the thousand
experiments of the *Sylva Sylvarum*. According to Aubrey,
Hobbes helped to translate three of Bacon's *Essays* into
Latin, one of them being " Of the Greatness of Cities "
(*i.e.* Aubrey's slightly inaccurate recollection of the title
of Essay XXIX). At that time Hobbes had not turned
to philosophy in earnest ; but he may have dreamed of
some such enterprise. It has to be confessed, however, that
Hobbes's explicit references to Bacon were only two, each
very brief. They both had to do with the " circular
motion " of water, one of them (VII, 112) citing the *Sylva
Sylvarum* (1st Cent. 9), the other (L. IV, 316 *sq.*) indicating
more generally an argument to be found in the *De Fluxu et
Refluxu Maris*. If Hobbes had thought that Bacon was
such another as Galileo or Harvey, I think he would have
said so. On the other hand, many of Bacon's phrases
and metaphors stuck in Hobbes's memory, and on the
literary side at least there is interest, if not good evidence,
in Sorbière's dubious opinion that Hobbes was " a survival
from Bacon, under whom he wrote in his youth ; and from
everything I have heard him say and have noticed about
his style, I can see that he has retained a great deal. He

˙has learned, by study, Bacon's way of turning things, and he slips easily into allegory, but he has, by nature, much of Bacon's pleasant wit, and even of his graceful mien " (*Voyage*, etc., p. 97).

If it is asked whether Hobbes, besides being influenced by Bacon, was a close student, or, in the extreme case, a disciple of that author, the answer, I think, should be a clear, but not a truculent, negative. I shall try to support this opinion, by considering, in their order, experimentalism, induction, metaphysics, mathematics, physics, and politics.

(1) The experimentalism of the Royal Society really was, as it professed to be (Sprat's *History*, 18 and 36), Baconian in spirit. Glanvil said (*Scepsis Scientifica*, 1661) that Solomon's House, in the *New Atlantis*, was a " prophetic Scheme of the Royal Society." In Hobbes's view, Solomon's House would have been a magniloquent and expensive futility ; and he thought the Royal Society (unless it changed its ways) no better, although rather cheaper. Hobbes had, indeed, some interest in experiments, particularly in optical experiments, but he firmly believed, and stoutly asserted, that Galileo, not Bacon, had discovered the key to the secrets of nature ; and it was the deductive, not the experimental, side of Galileo that he wished to follow. Bacon would have called Hobbes a dogmatist, a "spider"(*Nov. Org.* I, 95) spinning the "higher generalities," not a " bee " that transformed experiments into the honey of " the middle propositions." If Hobbes had played with these metaphors, he would have said that he spun silk, not gossamer, and that the " middle propositions " were neither honest fact nor fruitful theory.

(2) Bacon's reliance upon induction might be supposed to separate him very effectively from Hobbes, whose solitary reference to induction, so far as I know, was a statement (L. IV, 179) to the effect that *mathematical* induction was invalid. Yet although Bacon believed that

induction " first gave the breast to philosophy " (E.S.[1] I,
501), he had nothing but scorn for " induction by simple
enumeration," holding that it concluded from simple
presence without thinking of possible absentees, " as if
Samuel should have rested upon those sons of Issay which
were brought before him, and failed of David which was
in the field " (E.S. III, 387). What Bacon hoped to obtain
by inductive comparison was an alphabet of essences of
Forms (*ibid.* 536) ; and he declared in the *Novum Organum*
(II, 20) that a " Form " was a *definition*. If so, and with
the further explanation (N.O. I, 69) that demonstrations
were the very marrow of science and philosophy, it would
not be impossible for Baconians and Hobbists to join
hands. Indeed, in a part of his thought, Bacon affirmed
that " educated experience " was only a " degree or rudi-
ment " of the (rational) " anticipation of nature " (E.S.
III, 389).

(3) Bacon's account of the relation of " first philosophy "
to metaphysics and to the more general ideas in physics in
The Advancement of Learning was somewhat entangled,
but Hobbes's account in the *De Corpore* showed parallel
difficulties. Indeed, I take the view that Hobbes remembered Bacon's work when he drew up his table of the
sciences in the *Leviathan* (III, 72 *sq.*), and when he divided
the sciences in the *De Corpore*.[2] In support of this view
I would mention the following points in the *Advancement*
with which Hobbes, in *De Corpore*, agreed : the virtual
extrusion of final and of formal causes (E.S. III, 357) ;
the statement (*ibid.* 353) that " physic should handle that
which supposeth in nature only a being and moving " ;
the statement (*ibid.* 359) that " quantity indefinite belongeth to *philosophia prima*."

(4) Despite certain laudatory statements about mathe-

---

[1] E.S. = the edition of Ellis and Spedding.
[2] Hallam (*Lit. of Europe*, III, 295, ed. 1839) thought Hobbes much
inferior to Bacon in this particular.

matics (*e.g. ibid.* 397), Bacon, on the whole, was definitely non-mathematical in his scientific ideals. Mathematics, he thought, came in at the end in the application of science (N.O. I, 96), and had only "some shadow" (E.S. III, 404) of the true roots of the sciences. In short, while Galileo asserted (*Il Saggiatore,* V, vi) that the universe was written in mathematical characters where the characters were geometrical figures, Bacon held that it was written in a non-mathematical alphabet where the letters were a largish number of physical Forms. Hobbes agreed entirely with Galileo, and must have thought that if Bacon, as the title-page of the *Novum Organum* depicted, had sailed through the Pillars of Hercules, he had not the equipment to become a circumnavigator.

This point ran very deep. Bacon was willing to admit that, whatever the senses might suggest, a precise inquiry showed that all motion was local (E.S. III, 626) and (N.O. I, 50 *sq.*) that all alteration was local motion of minute parts. He was convinced, however, that the geometry and mechanics of motion could not *explain* anything. Movement, he held, was intelligible only in terms of some ultimate and quasi-psychological *appetite* of things, and this appetite, allegorically described as the naked Cupid (E.S. VI, 655), was the reality that was translated into the natural notion of an atom. Without it, to expand his metaphor, we should be dealing with Pluto, not with Cupid ; that is to say, with the shadows of genuine activity. For, although it was not true that every thing had *sense*, every thing had a "perception" that might be "more subtle than the sense" and had also a "kind of election" (*Syl.* Syl. IX, at the beginning). On these assumptions, Galileo's methods, if sound, would not tell us what we wanted to know.

There may a trace of "Cupid" in Hobbes's account of "impetus" and of "conatus," but, in the main, Hobbes's view was that "Cupid" was a superstition who should not be supposed to be lurking moodily behind rulers and compasses and inclined planes.

(5) Hobbes, I think, owed very little to Bacon's views on ethics and politics. Bacon, it is true, complained that the ancients should have " stayed a little longer upon the inquiry concerning the roots of good and evil and the strings of those roots " (E.S. III, 420) ; but his own stay was brief and barren of consequences. In politics he was no dialectician. " Preserve the right of thy place," he said (Essay XI), " but stir not questions of jurisdiction ; and rather assume thy right in silence than voice it with claims and challenges." Again, Bacon was very much of a Machiavellian, especially in the essay Hobbes helped to translate. And Hobbes, as I shall submit, was not a Machiavellian.

(b) Descartes

Told in general terms, the story of the very strained relations between Hobbes and Descartes is that of two men working independently for a great revolution in the sciences, the younger man deciding too hastily, although perhaps *prima facie* upon evidence, that the senior had pillaged from his arsenal. This, for Hobbes, was a great misfortune. He had to vindicate his independence as well as to express his ideas, and part of the reason why his theories were (and remained) disregarded was that the Cartesian philosophy of nature came to be considered, even in England, as *the* new movement.

When Hobbes fled to Paris in 1646, Mersenne had published two works on Galileo's physics (in 1634 and 1639), and was eager to effect an intellectual introduction (Descartes being then in Holland) between two distinguished philosophers, each of whom had a natural philosophy of his own. Descartes' physics, it is true, were to some extent in hiding, since he had declined to publish *Le Monde* (written about 1634) on hearing of Galileo's condemnation. On the other hand, his *Dioptrique* (published in 1637, the year of the *Discours*) was evidence of his views in the calmer atmosphere of optics. Again, just when Hobbes arrived in Paris, Mersenne had in his possession the manuscript of Descartes' *Meditations*, and was inviting the " objections " of learned men in order to publish them, along with Descartes' replies, in the first edition of the book. The book was published in 1641, Hobbes's set of objections being the third.

Hobbes's objections were obviously those of a man who had made up his mind about metaphysics[1] in a sense very definitely opposed to Descartes ; and Descartes must have felt that his published comment was briefer than was civil, since he excused himself to Mersenne (A.T.[2] III, 360), by saying that a fuller reply would be rating Hobbes too high. There was, however, a different reason for his asperity. Along with the objections, Hobbes had forwarded another paper which reached Descartes in two instalments, the first of which, being now lost, has to be guessed at from their correspondence about it (*ibid.* 287 *sqq.* and 300 *sqq.*), the second of which (Br. 92–9) was largely identical with Hobbes's *Tractatus Opticus*. This other paper seems to have been impolitic on the face of it, since Constantin Huygens, in forwarding the first instalment, wrote prudently that it seemed to be directed against the *Dioptrique*, and that Huygens would not put his nose to it until he had heard Descartes' opinion.[3]

Descartes leapt to the conclusion that " the Englishman " was a mere plagiary, who, however, was not a dangerous rival, since he argued a good case so very badly (*ibid.* 283). On receipt of the second instalment he wrote to Mersenne (*ibid.* 320) that if Hobbes had the disposition Descartes suspected he had, they had better

---

[1] Metaphysics, not physics.
[2] A.T.=the edition of Adam and Tannery.
[3] *Correspondence of Descartes and C. Huygens*, ed. Roth, p. 148.

have nothing to do with one another ; and he added, with great bitterness, " I also beg you to tell him as little as possible about my unpublished opinions, for, unless I am very much mistaken, he is trying to acquire a reputation at my expense and in shabby ways."

Since Hobbes, before the publication of the *Dioptrique*, had been regarded as a high authority, and Mr. Warner's equal, on optical questions (see *Portland Papers*, 128 *sqq.*), the charge of plagiarism had a certain improbability, and plagiaries do not usually send their stolen goods to be inspected by the former owner. Indeed, Hobbes behaved with dignity. The tone of his first reply (A.T. III, 302), including its statement that he wrote to satisfy Mersenne only, was (I think) proper to the occasion, and his later letters about this time showed commendable restraint. In particular he had to say, as he did say to Mersenne (*ibid*. 342), that it was not he who had begun the altercations about priority.

Here Descartes' specific charges were : (1) that if Hobbes's " spiritus internus " were really, as Descartes denied, the same as Descartes' " materia subtilis," Hobbes might very easily have borrowed the notion and changed the name (*ibid*. 322) ; and (2) that there was nothing in Hobbes's account of colour that Descartes had not already published.

The first of these conceptions referred to the universal medium of mechanical shock, and Hobbes asked Mersenne to remember that Hobbes, in the presence of another witness, had stated his later views in Mersenne's house seven years before (*ibid*. 342). Regarding the second, he said (*ibid*.) that he had told Newcastle and Charles Cavendish, as early as 1630, that he believed colours, sounds, etc., to be personal and private phantasms (cf. VII, 468). This doctrine of the subjectivity of the secondary qualities, much more sweeping than the opinion of Democritus, that sweet, fragrant, and the like were in some sense less " natural " than atoms and the void,[1] had the important consequence of banishing the secondary qualities altogether from the domain of physics proper. Since, however, Galileo had expressed the full new theory, with the utmost clearness and at adequate length, in his *Il Saggiatore* (1623), it is hard to see why either Hobbes or Descartes took so much credit for it.

When he heard about what Hobbes had said, Descartes replied that it was puerile to suppose that Hobbes's opinions in 1630 had ever reached his ears—a puerility Hobbes had not suggested—and that if Hobbes were nervous about his philosophical property he had better publish it (*ibid.* 354). Thereafter Descartes showed a calculated boredom concerning Hobbes's opinions (*ibid.* 633 and 639), and may have purposely destroyed both parts of Hobbes's offending epistle. When the *De Cive* appeared, however, he said (A.T. IV, 67) that Hobbes had a much better head for ethics than for physics or metaphysics, but that his account of man's depravity was a pernicious doctrine, and that his defence of monarchy was capable of being argued upon solider and more virtuous grounds. The book ought to be banned because of its strictures on the Church of Rome, unless Hobbes enjoyed some private and particular favour.

In 1644 Charles Cavendish, writing from Hamburg (Halliwell Letters), hoped that Hobbes and Descartes might come to esteem one another, since (he thought) Hobbes must like the *Principia* (which had just appeared) although he might dislike its metaphysics. In December, however, he admitted that Hobbes " utterly misliked " the book and was " joined in a great friendship with Gassendi." It is likely enough, however, as Mr. Brandt argues (Br. 190), that the *Principia*, by giving Hobbes " plenty to think

---

[1] According to Democritus the spatio-temporal qualities were "true-born," the secondary qualities "base-born" (Sextus Empiricus *adv. Math.* vii, 139). Aristotle had held (*Met.* 1061 a 32) that mathe-maticians *neglected* the secondary qualities.

about," delayed his own *De Corpore* and diverted him to his various attempts to make his optical theories tidy.

In the next year (q. Br. 180) Cavendish wrote that Hobbes had declined to meet Descartes in Paris, and although it is possible that Descartes, Gassendi, and Hobbes dined together at Newcastle's table in 1647 (A.T. XII, 468), I am not satisfied that the evidence shows that they dined there *together*. If there were a reconciliation, it must have been sudden ; for in 1646 Hobbes wrote to Sorbière (A.G. III, 68) that he knew for certain that Descartes would try, if he could, to hinder the publication of the new edition of the *De Cive* in Amsterdam.

Descartes died in Sweden on 11th February 1650, and Hobbes, according to Aubrey (I, 367, cf. I, 222) spoke of him, in later years, without bitterness. " Des Cartes and he were acquainted and mutually respected one another. He [*i.e.* Hobbes] would say that had he kept himself to Geometry he had been the best geometer in the world, but that his head did not lie for philosophy . . . but he could not pardon him for writing in defence of trans-substantiation, which he knew was absolutely against his opinion." In his later writings Hobbes referred very little to Descartes, although he was naturally incensed when Vindex accused him of plagiarism. " Let any man read Des Cartes," said Hobbes (VII, 340), " he shall find that he attributeth no motion at all to the object of sense, but an inclination to action, which inclination no man can imagine what it meaneth." On this point, at least, one of the original subjects of their controversy, Hobbes, like the rest of the world, knew that he had scored. In another passage (L. IV, 250), where " materia subtilis " came in, Hobbes said that Descartes' hypothesis was scarcely sane.

(2) HOBBES ON HIS OWN TIMES

I have to concede that this brief indication of the nature of Hobbes's relation to two great contemporaries with whom he was *not* in close accord is a *very* scurvy indication of the atmosphere of the early seventeenth century in metaphysics and in science, but I propose, now, to turn to the climate of Hobbes's political opinions. My reason is simply convenience. It is difficult to describe Hobbes's philosophy of body without indicating its relation to Aristotelianism and to the new ideas of Galileo as the exposition proceeds. To avoid repetition, therefore, I shall include most of what I have to say about the climate of Hobbian opinions concerning physics and metaphysics in the main discussion of Hobbes's philosophy to be given in Part II. of this book. In the present place, however, it seems expedient to attempt : firstly, a brief account of Hobbes's view of the political situation in England, as set forth in his *Behemoth* ; secondly, a rapid survey of the political notions that Hobbes had been trained in when he set about to construct his new and demonstrative science of politics ; thirdly, Hobbes's special relation to certain particular political theorists.

Hobbes's *Behemoth* was an attempt to show, by an historical narration of the deeds of the Long Parliament drawn out of Mr. Heath's chronicle (B.[1] iv), that mistaken views in political philosophy, when generally accepted, brought disaster to the commonwealth.

The " seed " of the rebellion, Hobbes said (*ibid.*), was " certain opinions in divinity and politics," viz. those of the Presbyterians, the Papists, the Independents, together with the educators of members of Parliament, the City of London, and all impecunious adventurers.

While the Presbyterians were the immediate mischief-

---

[1] B. = Tönnies's edition of the *Behemoth*, to which all the references in this section are made.

makers, their seditious notions, Hobbes affirmed, had come, a little damaged, from Rome. The Roman Church, although its authority had in fact been derived from the Emperor (*e.g.* 21), laid claim, most uncivilly, to " as absolute a sovereignty as is possible to be " (8) ; for it claimed an effective (if, according to certain of its doctors, an indirect) superiority in the business of kings. Maintaining that spiritual things overrode temporal, and had much more enduring rewards, it deposed and excommunicated legitimate sovereigns, absolved subjects from their allegiance, and, by regulating marriage, regulated the succession itself (12). (All Hobbes's readers, of course, thinking of Elizabeth's title to the throne, or of the reputed attitude of Spain and the Spanish Jesuits to the British succession, were convinced that these questions were much more than merely academic.)

Presbyterianism, Hobbes averred, was a special development of this Church-bred sedition. In terms of the reformers' appeal to the Scriptures, " every man, nay, every boy and wench that could read English " (21) set themselves up as judges, and the private conscience of " these petty men " (172) made the Romish claim to " govern in all points of religion and manners " (47). The ready-tongued, histrionic Presbyterian " ministers," helped by a politic silence concerning the vices of the trading community (25), arrogated the *power* that most men desired (*e.g.* 193) ; and they were backed by such of the gentry as were ambitious (23) and also " democratical " (28). In one of his sharpest sentences Hobbes said (133) : " They were Presbyterians *id est* cruel." The substance of his complaint was that too many of them were Scots *id est* indigent.

The Independents, in Hobbes's view, were " a brood of Presbyterian hatching " (136). Therefore, whether they were Brownists, Anabaptists, Fifth-monarchy men, or Quakers (*ibid.*), they did not need separate discussion.

And Hobbes was a little reticent about the party of prelacy. He said, however, that the Anglican bishops had invariably held that their authority, within their own dioceses, came directly from God without the Pope's intermediation. Therefore they had not been discontented with the Reformation (*e.g.* 56). Again, he said that Laud's " punctilios " about " the service book and its rubrics " (73) were as unstatesmanlike as his Arminianism (61 *sq.*). Free-will was a subtlety very ill adapted to popular discussion— although King James had sent " a divine or two " (61) to debate the point at the Synod of Dort.

Again, Hobbes held that the classical education of some of the Parliament men was thoroughly objectionable. (He may have been thinking of Oliver's Latinity as well as (163) of the peculiar elegance of Milton's Latin.) Aristotle and Cicero (43), Plato (56), Cato (158), Seneca, " or other enemies of monarchy " (158), were committed to " democratical principles." The universities were therefore to blame.[1] A university (148) had always been " an excellent servant to the clergy," and the clergy had always been " an excellent means to divide a kingdom into factions " (*ibid.*).

The early universities (*e.g.* Paris and Oxford) had been founded by the papacy for the better arguing of its

[1] Hobbes's views on this matter were unintentionally justified by many of his opponents. Thus, Bramhall in his *Serpent Salve* (*Works*, III, 478) described the attack on the universities—" the two eyes of the kingdom "—as part of an attack on the clergy (1643). Much later, John Edwards (*A Brief Vindication*, etc.), 1697, writing against Hobbes and Locke, remarked : " See how naturally a man passes from arraigning and vilifying the Universities to affront and abuse religion " (Ep. dedicatory). The abortive attempt to " purge " the universities in the time of the Barebones Parliament professed to justify itself on moral grounds, but had a political object, too ; and this may have been the aim of many who announced that their object was to weaken professorial scholasticism, and give the new philosophy its freedom. In Clark's *Wood's Life and Times*, ii, 294, information may be found regarding attempts to annul the universities from 1653 onwards " to the end that drones might not be nursed up," and the list of books and pamphlets mentioned there (Webster, Dell, Stubbe, Sprigge, Poole, Boreman) indicates the nature of the controversy.

seditious claims (17), and, in particular, to strengthen the clergy (90) by making the subtleties of divinity supersede the simplicities of religion. This device was as old as the Druids and the Assyrians (90 *sqq.*) ; but it was very effective. In Hobbes's view, what was necessary to salvation could be understood of all (55) ; and, in any case, religion was not an art but a *law* to be settled (in England) by the sovereign. The popish device of adopting the worst parts of Aristotle's philosophy (such as Separated Essences (42) and Undetermined Action), of concealing ignorance with classical terms " wryed a little at the point " (43), of repeating the incomprehensible nonsense of Peter Lombard and Scotus, " two of the most egregious blockheads in the world " (41), or, again, of Suarez (17), was rife among the Protestants. Even Gresham College (96) had to have the bishops' licence for publishing its (possibly valuable) contributions to the new mathematics and natural science.

It may perhaps be thought that this attack on the universities, combined with the calm suggestion that the works of an " obscure " author of international reputation (*i.e.* T. H. himself) should become university text-books, was a striking example of what might be called the Tutor's Fallacy. Certainly, Hobbes's cure for these discontents was *knowledge*, and his diagnosis of the country's sickness was simply *ignorance*. Hobbes's point, however, was that the *leaders* should be taught that sovereignty was absolute and indivisible. The common people always followed their immediate leaders, whether clergy or " potent gentlemen." The science of politics—for it was an exact science (70)—was *deep* (159) ; but if it were taught in the universities the clever would learn it, the less clever would repeat it, and all would be well. What had happened in England was that the sectaries had taught fallaciously, and that the gentry had been confused. The royalist gentlemen had accepted the absurdity of mixed government (33). They may have had too little *spite* to win the war (110), but they partly sympathised with the theories of their opponents. The *whole nation* had been ignorant (114). The lawyers had "infected most of the gentry" with their untenable ideas about the Common Law. The Lords were ignorant. The King's counsellors were ignorant (114). The City was ignorant (142). Under such circumstances nothing but chance could make men law-abiding.

(3) ETHICS AND POLITICS

What England needed, then, and what all the world needed, was the true science of politics. Nothing but *knowledge* could deliver the peoples, and the knowledge must exist before the right people could use it, or the ignorant be persuaded to act as they should. Hobbes believed that he had discovered this all-important science.

Yet he did not invent new weapons. Instead, he rearranged and to a small extent refashioned the old. In matters of metaphysics, it is permissible to suggest that while Hobbes's voice had all the modernity of the new mechanics, his hands—that is to say, his technique—were scholastic, and even Aristotelian. In ethical and political theory, however, voice and hands were both mediæval, although he may have done more than any other Englishman of his time to break the older order of political theory, and, as he claimed, to innovate profoundly.

The truth is that his fundamental notions on these matters were those of the Civil and of the Canon Law, the latter notions being secularised, it is true, but not made much more secular than those of Gratian or of any other great Canonist. Right (*ius*), law (*lex*), obligation (*obligatio*), the eternal "laws of nature," and their relation to positive law and to coercion, these, as with Fortescue two centuries before, were the leading ethical conceptions both for Hobbes and for his predecessors. Their very legalism shows their origin in Roman jurisprudence adapted to the ecclesiastical hierarchy. Even the Erastianism of Hobbes's ultimate theory (which went far beyond Erastus) was matched, if not excelled by Marsilio of Padua ; and Hobbes's substitution of a " public " for a " private " conscience was only the secularisation of the *public ecclesiastical conscience* accepted in some form by all except Brownists and Anabaptists, and, in England, already half secularised by the fact that the secular monarch was the head of the church and the defender of its faith, whatever that faith might be.

Somewhat similar remarks might be made concerning Hobbes's political theory. He claimed, indeed, to be the first founder of a new science of politics, demonstrable like geometry, and capable of enduring so long as men preserved their reason. The foundations of this science were based upon the introspective observation of ineluctable human motives. Here Hobbes may have innovated, not indeed in the motives he admitted, but in the form which his theory necessarily assumed when he refused to admit any others. In the main, however, Hobbes innovated, not by introducing new conceptions, but (as he thought) by logical rigour and ruthlessness.

There is no abrupt transition, indeed there is no transition, from Hobbes's pages to those of Bellarmine, Barclay, Buchanan, Suarez, Du Plessis Mornay (if he was the author of the *Vindiciæ contra Tyrannos*), or to the Declaration of the States General of Holland in 1581, declaring that Philip had forfeited his sovereignty. Every one of these authors would have admitted that Hobbes had played his hand without revoking. None of them would have thought that he was inviting them to play a new game. And the game that they all played had also been played by Hildebrand, Aquinas, Gerson, Occam, and Calvin—old-fashioned players, no doubt, but players who always knew how many trumps were out. Hobbes believed that he could beat them at their own game, than which he neither desired nor admitted any other.

Was government derived, proximately at least, from the people ? Did the " people " form a *universitas* or corporate body before the appointment of a ruler or rulers, and, if so, in what sense ? Was their assent an antecedaneous paction,"[1] a contract tacit or express ? If so, was the donation of power revocable, and on what conditions ? Was it in perpetuity, and was it bilateral ? Was the ruler above or exempt from law ? Did he remain, in some carefully defined sense, *under* the entire body and only *above* the subjects taken severally ? Did he " bear the person of the people," and, if so, by what kind of representation ? How could subjection be " natural " if all private men were " naturally " free and equal ? How was instituted government related to government by conquest or to a patriarchate ? Were barons and magistrates lesser kings, or did they derive their authority mediately from the supreme ruler ? When was there a *communitas perfecta* or politically self-governing body, and what conditions determined the size of its territory and the limits of its jurisdiction ? How far was such a community an affair of *maiestas* or *public* purposes, and how far could it or should it intermeddle with men's private lives, fortunes, women, and other property ?

Such were the questions debated by the " publicists " or political theorists, who derived their conceptions from the *imperium* of the elected Roman Emperors and from the constitution of the Church with its elected Pope. And the debate, in all essentials, was international. Buchanan[2] tried to justify the Scottish people in the eyes of Europe. King James argued against Bellarmine when he defended the terms of the Oath of Allegiance. Samuel Rutherford's

---

[1] Bramhall's phrase (*Works*, III, 366).
[2] In his famous dialogue, *De jure regni apud Scotos* (1579). I shall quote from the edition of 1727 (Edinburgh).

Lex Rex, which superseded Buchanan's book among the
Presbyterians in 1643, abounded with references to Althusius, Arnisæus, and other continental authors. Bramhall's
Serpent Salve, its royalist counterpart, inveighed, about
the same time, against the two branches of the anti-
monarchical family, viz. the Jesuits, Bellarmine, Simancha,
and Mariana, on the one hand, and the Protestants Beza,
Buchanan, and the author of the *Vindiciæ* on the other.
(Bramhall (*Works*, III, 301) traced the first branch to
Pope Zachary, and the second to the Pharisees.) No doubt
all the disputants betrayed their own nationality. Bramhall, as well as Hobbes, repudiated the theory of the
Common Law of England with special reference to Bracton,
Fleta, and Coke, but the Teutonic and feudal principle
of custom affected the legal theory of all the northern
countries, and the contrast between Hobbes and Bracton
was no greater than that between Du Plessis Mornay and
Bodin.

Hobbes himself carefully distinguished between law (*lex*)
and right (*ius*), but this distinction did not affect his
differentiation between the law or laws of Nature and the
positive or civil law, which may now be examined.

The general contrast was very old. According to Paulus,[1]
a lawyer who wrote a little later than Gaius, natural
justice was " that which is always equitable and good,"
civil justice that which was useful to all, or to the majority
in a political community. And the distinction perdured.
The law eternal, Hooker[2] said, was " laid up in the bosom
of God. . . . That part of it which ordereth natural agents
we usually call Nature's law . . . the law of reason, that
which bindeth creatures reasonable in this world, and
with which by reason they most plainly perceive themselves bound " ; and Hooker (*ibid.*), following Aquinas,
defined positive " human " or civil law as " that which

---

[1] See Carlyle, *Mediæval Political Theory in the West* (=Car.), I, 38.
[2] *Ecclesiastical Polity* (=E.P.), as in *Works*, ed. 1836, I, 255.

out of the law either of reason or of God, men probably gathering to be expedient, they make it a law." In short, civil law was a device enacted for men's convenience in some particular community. Natural law was conceived in the way in which simple-minded persons (perhaps profoundly) understand their moral duty, that is to say, as a binding principle of righteousness to which every civil law should ultimately conform.

The general conception of natural justice or equity was of great antiquity. Hooker (E.P. I, 251) cited Homer, Trismegistus, Anaxagoras, Plato, and the Stoics ; and it came to Roman jurisprudence through the Stoics with some help from Cicero. It was apt, indeed, to be confused with the law of nations (*ius gentium*) ; for nations, in their general and international practices, might be thrown back upon common principles of equity. It seems to be clear, however, that Ulpian and Justinian (whatever may have been true of Gaius) fully appreciated the distinction between international practice with regard, say, to war or slavery, and the more fundamental question whether war and slavery themselves could be countenanced by eternal justice. In other words, they distinguished between immutable reason and the best that could reasonably be expected in an imperfect world (Car. I, 42 *sqq.*).

The Fathers, the canonists, and Hooker maintained that the eternal law was *God's*, but this theological aura did not greatly affect their general theory, since both the Scriptures and the Holy Spirit, acting through the Church, laid down many laws that were in their essence positive, although sacred (cf. Hobbes, III, 271). A distinction had therefore to be drawn within the *ius divinum* between God's eternal righteousness and his more special or ceremonial injunctions. Even Suarez[1] reluctantly admitted that, by general theological admission, there was an eternal law *in* God, although he would not concede to the jurists and to the

---

[1] *De Legibus ac Deo Legislatore* (=L.L.), II, i (ed. 1619).

philosophers that laws according to *mere* Nature could be
equalled with laws of divine grace; and he held, like
Bellarmine,[1] that such natural justice as was necessary
for the peace and well-being of human communities, even
allowing it (L.L. I, ii) to be conformable to equity and
reason, was temporal and fleshly, not spiritual.

In its secular dress, the law of Nature was one of Hobbes's
fundamental ideas; for it is mere misconception to say
with Figgis[2] that Hobbes " denied all meaning " to it.
According to Hobbes, the laws of Nature were general
theorems declaring the essential ways of peace. They
obliged if they did not coerce, and the denial of their
obligation was an attempt to transform the thing that is
into the thing that is not. Hobbes even called them
" eternal," partly, no doubt, because, being matter of
reason, they had the timelessness of logical implications,
partly to show that there need be no magic or religiosity
about the idea. So long as there were men on earth, they
were foolish if they did not seek peace; and he who sought
peace had to use the rational ways to peace. True, the
ways of peace would bring peace, in an imperfect world,
only if they were enforced; and so Hobbes also agreed
with the principle of Roman law that *ius*, to be effective,
required *iussio* and *imperium*, that is to say, command as
well as precept. In this, however, he was no innovator.
" The corruption of our nature being presupposed," said
Hooker, voicing the general opinion, " we may not deny
but that the Law of Nature doth now require of necessity
some kind of regiment " (E.P. I, 304). Since " the greatest
part of men are such as prefer their own private good
before all things " (*ibid*. 305), coercion must be. " Laws
do not only teach what is good, they have in them a
certain constraining force " (306) derived from " that
power which doth give them the strength of laws " (307).

---

[1] *De Summo Pontifice* (ed. 1620), I, 7 and v, 6.
[2] *From Gerson to Grotius* (=G.G.), p. 7.

The idea of natural justice was full of meaning, but its application to men " full of mischief " needed more than its idea.

Hobbes, like Bodin, believed he could prove that coercive civil authority must of necessity be vested in the central government, which he regarded as the *soul* of the body politic, not, as many held, merely its executive organ. Consequently (II, xxiii) he found his theory " most bitterly excepted against. That I had made the civil powers too large ; but this by ecclesiastical persons. That I had utterly taken away liberty of conscience ; but this by sectaries. That I had set princes above the civil laws ; but this by lawyers."

Each of these statements (both of them made in 1647) is of considerable interest. Hobbes never agreed with Andrewes or Laud, but from the first rejected their Arminianism, if that term be understood to mean, not simply the rejection of Calvinistic determinism, but the love of churchly tradition that moved Jakob Hermanns (Arminius) as well as the English " Arminians." To use a convenient term in its proper historical sense, Hobbes had never been an Anglo-Catholic, and his readers understood very well that his attacks on the papacy were also attacks upon a certain form of prelacy. Again, Hobbes frankly rejected the substance of the claim to the divine right of kings as that doctrine was understood in his day. A king, according to King James—whom we may call a royal professor, since it is disputed whether he was a royal pedant or a royal scholar—was ordained for the people " and not they for him,"[1] and although there *were* elected monarchs, the kings of Scotland derived their title from the conquest of that country by one Fergus, a legitimate Irish sovereign (*ibid*. p. 62). Hobbes was altogether of the opposite opinion. Like Gerson, Cusa, and other leaders of the conciliar movement against the

[1] *The Trew Law*, etc., in *Political Works*, ed. McIlwain, p. 55.

papacy ; like Buchanan and Du Plessis Mornay ; like the Spanish Jesuits—Hobbes was called a Don-friend, as well as a " debauchee "[1]—he stoutly asserted that sovereignty in all instituted governments came from the people. Instead of concluding, however, like some of the royalists,[2] that this doctrine made the sovereign the people's mere servant, if not their dog, he inferred the unlimited autocracy of the sovereign in spiritual and temporal affairs.

Hobbes's attitude towards the sectaries was uniformly wary and hostile. In Geneva, it is true, there had been no anxiety to un-king legitimate rulers ; but Knox cared very little for Calvin's objections to his proceedings, and was indifferent to the fact that Luther, Melanchthon, and Bucer might also be quoted against him.[3] And every political pamphleteer had heard of Buchanan's views. " A king," said that author (*De Jure*, etc., § 77) " is not intended for restraining the law, but the law for restraining the king." " When the king is called before the tribunal of the people, an inferior is summoned to appear before a superior" (§ 78). " The people from whom he derived his power should have the liberty of prescribing its bounds " (§ 27).

Similarly, Rutherford wrote that " human laws were not so obscure as tyranny was legible " (*Lex Rex*, p. 213), that the covenant between king and people " giveth a coactive power to each " (p. 100)—for it was absurd (p. 106) for the " court-bellies " to demand a " written authentic covenant betwixt the first king and his people " —and produced thirteen arguments to prove that " the estates in Scotland are to help their brethren the protestants in England against the cavaliers " (pp. 378 *sqq.*). In short, (Hobbes held) the sectaries were seditiously independent, and, what was worse, sanctimoniously so. They repudiated

---

[1] Camb. Mod. Hist. (=C.M.H.), VI, 791.
[2] Symmons, *A Loyal Subject's Belief*, p. 3, 1643.
[3] See Gooch, *English Democratic Ideas* (=Gooch), pp. 38 *sq.*

what Maitland in Buchanan's dialogue called " the doctrine of the imperial lawyers," viz. that the *whole* power of the people was transferred to the Emperor, whose pleasure, therefore, " stood as law " (§ 49), and their theory of a conditional contract necessarily led to anarchy, however reluctant Huguenots, most Englishmen, and some Scotsmen might originally have been to proceed to such extremes.

Hobbes, for his part, agreed with the *imperial* lawyers, but not with many even of the royalist lawyers in England. He would have agreed, indeed, with the account of the prerogative given in Cowell's *The Interpreter* (a sort of law dictionary), that the king was above the laws by his absolute power (Art. King), and (Art. Prerogative) that " for these regalities which are of the higher nature . . . there is not one that belonged to the most absolute prince in the world, which doth not also belong to our king."[1] Yet if we compare Hobbes's views with the arguments of the royalist counsel and judges at the Hampden trial, we perceive that a similarity in sentiment and in conclusions should be offset by a profound difference in premises. Even the most explicit of the Tudor statutes (24 Hen. VIII, ch. 12) was not really Hobbian, because it was too historical and too little secular. It ran : " By divers old authentic histories and chronicles it is manifestly declared that the realm of England is an empire, governed by one supreme head and king, having the dignity and royal estate of the same, unto whom a body politic compact of all sorts and degrees of people . . . being bounden and owen [to bear] next to God a natural and humble obedience, he being instituted and furnished by the goodness and sufference of Almighty God with plenary, whole and entire power," etc.

Hobbes's principal quarrel, however, was with the lawyers who followed Coke, quoted Bracton, and supported

[1] Quoted from the second edition, 1637.

the Parliament. Since Bracton (*De Legibus Angliæ*) spoke
with a very divided voice, Hobbes was prepared (*e.g.* VI,
31) to quote him with glee, but he utterly resisted the
semi-Teutonic, anti-imperialist theory of the English
Common Lawyers that custom was an independent source
of law, and strenuously opposed such Bractonian sentiments as that law was a bit between the royal teeth
(q. Car. III, 36), or that, reverence apart, the tenant's
homage under the feudal system implied strict reciprocity
between the rights and duties of overlord and subject
(*ibid*. III, 27). According to Hobbes, all law was derived
from the sovereign, who might or might not *permit* certain
customary usages ; and Hobbes would not have been at all
perturbed had it been shown him that feudal and other
practice was against his theory. He may have known that
well enough (see B. 77 *sq.*) ; and it was not really his affair
if the Crusaders, the Franks, and the Saxons had mis-
understood the nature of law, or if Sir Edward Coke had
tried to erect much lucrative mischief upon a confused
foundation.

In different ways, then, Hobbes held that Arminians,
sectaries, and Common Lawyers were all mistaken ; and
he set about to turn the arguments of the Jesuits and
the Protestant publicists against their conclusions. Du
Plessis Mornay had said : " If man become a wolf to man,
who hinders that man (according to the proverb) may not be
instead of God to the needy."[1] His contrast was between
the tyrant and the benign and legitimate monarch. *Per
contra*, Hobbes, who was no tyrannophobe, declared instead
that political citizens were as a God to one another, while
non-political men were to one another as arrant wolves
(II, ii).

According to Hobbes, a proper understanding of the

---

[1] *Vindiciæ*, Laski's ed., p. 228. For the first part of the proverb see
Hooker (E.P. I, 313). It was obviously an adaptation of Aristotle's
aphorism that the solitary man is either a brute or a God (*Pols*. I, iii).

institution of government settled the question, and this problem, for all these thinkers, was analytical rather than historical (since " tacit pacts " could always be countered by " tacit reservations "), although it had to be tested by historical practice.

On the one hand, it had been suggested by the Stoics and others that an age of innocence—a nuggety rather than a golden age—had preceded the ages of political regiment, but that civil laws became necessary when mischievous persons had to be restrained. This view was easily assimilated to the story of the Fall, and of the subsequent deplorable behaviour of Cain.

On the other hand, it had been maintained, at least as early as Polybius (History Book VI), that the origins of government had to be sought in man's attempt to escape from a solitary and almost brutish condition ; and, more generally, that ordinary prudence showed the wisdom of taking shelter within walled towns. According to Mariana civic life was a device to avoid "imbecilities and indigence."[1] According to the *Vindiciæ* (p. 150) without the laws " nor kings nor subjects can cohabit in security, but must be forced to live brutishly in caves and deserts like wild beasts." There was no occasion for such writers to accept the dominant Aristotelian view that man was *by nature* a political animal.

Hobbes denied the Aristotelian thesis, and put in its stead one that was ultra-Polybian. Hence he has been censured on the ground that, to use Mr. Graham Wallas's happy phrase, "man is at least semi-gregarious." The main point that Hobbes disputed, however, was the theory that man was a *political* animal by nature, that is to say, the theory that an orderly coercive political government could simply *grow* instead of being *made* by deliberate rational contrivance, and more particularly that an *instituted* government could develop in this " natural " way. The

[1] *De Rege*, I, i, q. Gierke's *Althusius* (=G.A.), 3rd ed., 1913, 98 n.

historical examples that he and most of his contemporaries had in mind were the election of Saul by the Hebrews, of an Emperor by the Romans, of a Pope by the ecclesia.

This principal contention was so obviously true that even the Aristotelians admitted a great deal of it. Political government, they had to say, was " quasi-natural," that is to say there was *something* " natural " about it. Suarez, quoting Aquinas, said (L.L. III, 1) that since each private man sought his private good, " there must necessarily be in a perfect community a public power whose office is to intend and procure the *common* good," adding that this public power was man's in the ordinary course of nature and not a peculiar dispensation of deity. *Dominion*, Suarez went on to say (*ibid*.), was not " natural," although it was " congruent with man's rationality " to be governed politically. Similarly, Hooker maintained (E.P. I, 304) that " all public regiment, of what kind whatsoever, seemeth evidently to have risen from deliberate advice, consultation and composition between men judging it convenient and behoveful ; there being no impossibility in nature considered by itself but that men might have lived without any public regiment."

Indeed, it was asserted in several quarters that the *parity* of human beings rendered every kind of political subjection unnatural in itself and defensible only on the inevitable " supposition " that strife and penury had to be met with some subtlety. King James and his fellow-theorists, of course, disputed this theory of parity. Kings might look like other men, but God had seen to it that they were really very different. Less obviously, it might be argued that the Holy Spirit, using human means, made a Pope quite different from a mere man. In the main, however, Aristotle's theory of " natural slavery " was rejected, and the Stoic and legal tradition that men originally were " free and equal " dominated the arguments of the publicists. Even Hildebrand said that " all were

equal by nature " (Car. I, 114). Atto of Vercelli, in the
tenth century, pointed out that no one could make himself
a king, but had to be chosen (*ibid.* III, 117). According to
Cusa (q. G.G. 204) this parity implied that subjection was
due to concordance and consent.   " The king," said Du
Plessis Mornay, " rules not as a God over men, nor as men
over beasts ; but is a man composed of the same matter
and of the same nature with the rest " (p. 195).

The last author put a very usual opinion very neatly
when he said that kings should remember " that it is *from*
God but *by* the people and *for* the people's sake that they
do reign " (p. 120). On the other hand, when he said
(p. 122, cf. p. 125), " No man can be a king by himself,
nor reign without people, whereas, on the contrary, the
people may subsist of themselves *and were, long before they
had any kings*," he drew an inference which, although not
uncommon, was highly disputable.   No one had any
difficulty in believing that some sort of pre-political condition had preceded instituted government, but how could
there be a *people*—that is to say, a united *body* of men—
without rulers ? A " people " was a " universitas " ; being
a body, it must have a head, or else be a monster ; and
what kind of head could it have except its government ?

Supposing, however, that there *was* a people or " universitas " and not a mere multitude of private persons
(*singuli*), the essential question concerned the transfer of
coercive power from the would-be subjects to their would-
be rulers. Ulpian, in the *Digest*, while admitting that
inveterate custom, by tacit consent, might be regarded
as legal (i, 3, 32), concluded that the prince's will had the
force of law because the people had conferred all its power
and command upon him (i, 4, 1), and this was the general
opinion of all legally minded authoritarians, papal or
civilian. Very naturally, however, especially among
publicists who were half-consciously influenced by the
traditions of Teutonic or feudal countries, this doctrine of

the transfer of power could be interpreted in very different ways ; and the most fundamental difference was between a complete *translation* of power and a mere *concession* of it for specific purposes.

The " translation " theory held that those who became subjects conferred irrevocable and plenary power upon their elected rulers. The " concession " theory, on the other hand, while also speaking of a " pact of subjection,"[1] maintained that the voluntary assent to subjection and obedience was, or must be presumed to be, conditional and revocable. According to Manegold of Lautenbach, in the Hildebrandine age (*Ad Gebehardum*, xliii) kingship was the name for an *office*. According to Buchanan (§ 27), " the king should exercise over the people those rights only which he had received from their hands." According to Cusa and to Zabarella (q. G.G. 51), both kings and popes were to be treated as public enemies if they were unfaithful to the trust that had been committed to them. Even Hooker, who was not a " monarchomach " (Barclay's name for Buchanan and the Jesuits), held (E.P. III, Pt. I, 437 *sq.*) that the " articles of compact " must show " how far the sovereign's power extends over the people," and had to be inferred " from subsequent laws or silent allowance," since the first beginnings of a government were " either clean worn out of knowledge or else known unto very few."

The use of the term, social " pact " or " contract " is not of great importance. Gierke (Gen.[2] 569 n.) pointed out that Manegold of Lautenbach had spoken of the " pact " by which government was instituted. Figgis added that Augustine had used the phrase " generale pactum societatis " (G.G. 204). Carlyle noted (Car. I, 17) that Cicero had said (De Rep. III, 13) : " quasi pactio fit inter populum et potentes." Whatever the history of

---

[1] See quotations from Marsilio, Occam, and Cusa, in G.A. 79 n.

[2] Gen. = *Das deutsche Genossenschaftsrecht*, Bd. III.

the phrase, however, the substantial consideration remains that the " social contract " doctrine applied both to the " translation " and to the " concession " theories, and that, according to both, an *unequal* obligation was instituted by consent of persons naturally equal.

On the other hand, the " concession " theory was much liker an ordinary contract.   The coronation oath of the Kings of Aragon, frequently mentioned in these disputes, ran : " We who are as much worth as you, and have more power than you, choose you King upon these and these conditions."[1]   This, very nearly, was a legal covenant.   It would have been a definitive legal bargain if there had been a machinery for keeping the King to his word ; and in the feudal system there *was* a traditional machinery for overriding the monarch (Car. III, 21 *sqq.* and 71).   According to the " translation " theory, on the other hand, although the donation of rule was made for a definite purpose, the givers surrendered all control for all future time, and ceased to be even potentially contracting parties.   In virtue of the gift, the ruler, or ruling body, became the *only* " public person."   There was no " universitas populi " except in so far as it was constituted by the government ; and consequently there was no one within the government's territory with whom the government could contract.   (This, of course, was an essential part of Hobbes's theory.)

Two subordinate, but important, ideas should also be noted.

The usual imperialist statement had been that voluntary subjection meant the donation of power to the elected government, but these traditional expressions were subject, in mediæval times, to a significant explanation that brought the theory appreciably nearer to Hobbes's form of it. The point was that what was donated was not mere

[1] A free translation in the *Vindiciæ*, p. 179.   For the Spanish form see Figgis (G.G. 197).

power—although " plenitude of power," as for Hildebrand, was a very important part of it—but, in essence, the sort of command or authority that a man has over his own actions. Thus, according to Suarez (L.L. III, iii), a man was " the lord of his own actions," and therefore had something to give. According to Occam (q. G.A. 214), the ruler bore the functions of the entire community. In short, the technical Hobbian view that the ruler in his official capacity was a representative or public person who bore the *persona* of the subjects was quite frequent in the literature. John of Salisbury had said it (*Polycraticus*, IV, 2). Bellarmine had said it (*op. cit.*, I, 6). Baldus had said it (q. G.A. 137). Suarez had said it (L.L. I, viii). Marsilio had pointed out that, by means of the representative principle, laws were self-imposed by each subject (q. Gen. 630 n.) ; Salomonius, that the prince represented the people and carried their persona by the authority of the entire people (G.A. 216) ; Cusa (*ibid.*, cf. 212), that government resided "in uno compendio repræsentivo." Similarly, Hooker wrote (E.P. I, 307) : " What we do by others, no reason but that it should *stand as our deed*, no less effectively to bind us than if ourselves had done it in person."

In the second place, it should be remembered that the mediæval publicists had not missed the point that when they said " all," they meant, for practical purposes, " the majority." Thus Marsilio, in a famous phrase, said that the " effective agent " in these matters was the " anima universitatis " or *soul* of the people " or of its stronger part " (q. G.A. 95) ; and Occam, Rosellus, and others (Gen. 571), as well as Augustinus Triumphus (Gen. 582 n.), spoke to the same effect.

I should add that of the two opposing catchwords between translationists and concessionists (*i.e.* of " the prince is above the laws " against " what touches everyone should be dealt with by all or by their representatives "), the latter (from the Decretals) had been used in the summons of a Parliament of Edward I, a fact often noted by the Parliament men.

(4) RELATIONS TO BODIN AND OTHERS

Hobbes's account of absolute sovereignty bore marked resemblances to Bodin's, and our historians[1] often tell us that Bodin had dug to the root of the theory, and that it only remained for Hobbes to clear away a little earth. On this view it was not to Hobbes's credit that he was habitually silent about Bodin, restricting himself (IV, 206) to an expression of agreement regarding the corruption of sovereignty in a so-called " mixed government."

Such an inference, I think, would be unfair. Hobbes was a philosopher, and Bodin was a jurist. Only philosophy, Hobbes believed, could reach the roots ; jurists could at the best expose the tree. Again, Hobbes's theory differed from Bodin's on many important points, especially on the rationale of property ; and Hobbes must be presumed to have believed that a philosopher's method, regarding these points of difference, was immensely superior to a jurist's prejudices.

Since Bodin's *Six Bookes of a Commonweale*, translated into English in 1606, appear to have been a standard university text-book in England, it is clear that any extensive larceny on Hobbes's part ran a very good chance of being detected. We may therefore assume that Hobbes was prudent enough to be honest, even if we doubted his honesty on other grounds (which do not, in fact, exist) ; and I shall content myself with classifying some of Bodin's principal opinions in a way that will make comparison with Hobbes easy, when we come to the corresponding part of Hobbes's theory.

(1) *The Law of Nature.*—The " first law of natural

---

[1] *e.g.* Holdsworth, *A History of English Law*, IV, 195.

command," said Bodin (14),[1] was to " give unto reason the
sovereignty of command " in every " commonwealth, cor-
poration, college, society, and family " ; and princes (104)
were " more straitly bound than their subjects " to " the
Law ᴏᴜ God and Nature." In a rather hesitating way,
however (312 *sqq.*), Bodin suggested that magistrates
might dispute the justice of royal commands and (*ibid.*)
that an inequitable prince was no prince. In some places
(*e.g.* 183) he accepted the possibility of aristocratic or
democratic sovereignty, but usually (unlike Hobbes) held
that sovereignty must be not only absolute · but also
monarchical. " If the prince be subtle and wicked he
will plant a tyranny ; if he be cruel, he will make a
butchery of the commonweal ; or a brothel-house if he
be licentious ; or both together ; if he be covetous, he
will pull both hair and skin from his subjects ; if he be
prodigal he will suck their blood and marrow to glut some
dozens of horse-leeches that are about his person. . . .
These be the dangers of a monarchy . . . but the chief
point of a commonweal, which is the right of sovereignty,
cannot be nor subsist (to speak properly) but in a
monarchy ; for none can be sovereign in a commonweal
but one alone " (714 *sq.*).

(2) *Social Psychology.*—Unlike Hobbes, Bodin usually
held (*e.g.* 379) that " love and amity " were the principal
bonds of all associations and of " the very commonweal
itself," although (47) " force and violence " made men
submit to some captain or other ruler. In a " royal "
monarchy, he said, the king " placed in sovereignty
yieldeth himself as obedient unto the Laws of Nature as
he desireth his subjects to be toward himself, leaving unto
every man his natural liberty and the propriety of his
own goods " (204).

(3) *The Donation of Sovereignty.*—Like Hobbes, Bodin
held that temporary or conditional powers might be

---

[1] The references are to the English translation of 1606.

granted to persons who were really officers, but that such powers were not sovereignty. " Unto majesty or sovereignty belongeth an absolute power not subject to any law. For the people or the lords of a commonweal may purely and simply give the sovereign and perpetual power to any one, to dispose of the goods and lives, and of all the state, at his pleasure ; and so afterward to leave it to whom he list ; like as the proprietary or owner may purely and simply give his own goods, without any other cause to be expressed than of his own mere bounty ; which is indeed the true donation, which no more receiveth condition being once accomplished " (88 *sq.*). " The vassal giveth his oath unto his lord, but receiveth none from him again, although they be mutually bound the one of them unto the other " (99).

(4) *The Nature of Sovereignty.*—Bodin believed that he was the first to define and explain the true nature of sovereignty. " What majesty or sovereignty is," he said (84), " neither lawyer nor political philosopher hath yet defined ; although it be the principal and most necessary point for the understanding of the nature of a commonweal." He himself defined it (*ibid.*) as " the most high, absolute, and perpetual power over the citizens and subjects in a commonweal . . . the greatest power to command. For majesty (as Festus saith) is so called of mightiness." Without it (9) the commonweal dissolved as a ship without a keel became " an evil-favoured hoop of wood." It was " most sacred and holy " (101), absolute (*e.g.* 153), indivisible, and without a peer (155), the division of it being (194) mere " confusion of the state." England, Scotland, Turkey, Muscovy, Tartary, Persia, Ethiopia, and India were said (222) to be examples of this confusion, " the inviolate nature of unity being such as that it can abide no partition (741). The fundamental " mark " of sovereignty (162) was " to have power to give laws unto all and to every one of the subjects and to receive none

from them." But Bodin enumerated other "marks," including the privilege of the French kings " to seal with yellow wax " (181).

(5) *Personal Property and Taxes.*—Despite these claims, Bodin, with an inconsistency with which Hobbes could not be charged, opposed private rights of property (lawyer-wise) to the sovereign power. Ownership of a pair of shoes, it would seem, violated the alleged inviolate unity. In the alternative, *maiestas*, in Bodin's actual use of the term, had a *limited*, if exalted, sphere. Necessity, indeed, might justify the sovereign in imposing taxes without Parliament (97) ; but (201) " every subject hath the true propriety of his own things, and may thereof dispose at his pleasure, although the prince, for pomp and show, challenge unto himself the sovereignty thereof." Otherwise (204) there would be no difference " betwixt a lawful prince and a thief."

(6) *Minor Matters.*—There was much agreement between Hobbes and Bodin on less fundamental questions. Thus Bodin (25, cf. 162) denied that custom could abrogate any law, affirmed natural parity against Aristotle's natural slavery (33), and complained (154) that Aristotle and Polybius " wrote with great brevity and obscurity about sovereignty." He believed that the French kings " were never in any thing beholden unto the popes " (146), and that, in infidel regions, " when we may not publicly use the true religion . . . it is better to come unto the public service " (539 *sq.*). For his own part he " put no difference between a good man and a good citizen " (4) ; and, to take another point, declared that " all divines and the wiser sort of philosophers " had been determinists (436).

Among English writers, I think Hobbes probably owed most to Hooker, and I shall try to support this opinion by incidental allusions. The mere circumstance, however, that Charles I thought that the Lady Elizabeth and his other children should ponder Hooker's book more closely

than any other except the Bible, is evidence that Hooker's
" Arminianism " was quite un-Hobbian, and also that
Hobbes would have risked misunderstanding if (as he did
not) he had referred to Hooker either as an ally or as an
opponent.

It is always possible, of course, that some very learned
person may discover some obscure source from which
Hobbes had borrowed pretty freely. I cannot believe,
however, with a distinguished writer in the *Cambridge
Modern History* (VI, 965), that E. Forset's *A Comparative
Discourse of the Bodies Natural and Politique* (1606) was
" the source of much of Hobbes."

This little book explored the analogies between a human
and a political body in an amiable and slightly apologetic
fashion—for Forset admitted (to the Reader) that the
" state's body " was not " entirely marchable " to a man's
—and it maintained that the King was the " soul " of the
political body. Forset's reason for the latter assertion,
however, was directly opposed to Hobbes's, for instead
of holding, like Hobbes, that the sovereign received his
authority (irrevocably) from the people, Forset argued that
the King was the animating principle of what, without
him, would have nothing to give, since it would be but " a
lump of moulded earth " (6). The book, in the main,
was a rather feeble defence of Divine Right, as may be
seen (regarding divinity) from the author's horror at the
Gunpowder Plot for " the blowing up, shivering into pieces
and whirling about of those honourable, anointed, and
sacred bodies " (52 *sq.*), and (regarding its feebleness) by
the admission that the Laws (being the quintessence of
" reason ") might be the *soul* of the King (4).

I can see no internal evidence that Hobbes had read the
book, and am confident that if he did read it, it could not
have impressed him. The comparison of a human to a
political body, whether the *corpus mysticum* of the Church or
a city of men, was at least as old as Plato, and was part of

the staple diet of mediæval publicists. Indeed, Occam found it necessary to say that although a *man* would be a monster if he had two heads, a *corpus mysticum* might have several (q. Gen. 547 n.). It was also a commonplace that either the laws or the ruler was the *soul* of the body politic. As we have seen, Marsilio of Padua said so. Althusius also said so (G.G. 181) ; and Charles's Attorney-General, Sir John Bankes, said so at the Hampden trial, although he made even higher claims. "Let us obey the King's command by writ and not dispute," said Bankes. "He is the first mover among these orbs of ours. . . . He is the soul of this body whose proper act is to command."

Quite a different question arises when, instead of this alleged influence of persons like Forset, we examine the supposed influence of a great and universally known writer such as Machiavelli (about whom Hobbes was silent also). Hobbes must have been familiar with Machiavelli's principal views ; but I cannot think he was appreciably influenced by them. I shall try to examine this problem, firstly with reference to *The Prince*, secondly with reference to the *Discourses on Livy*.

(1) Machiavelli, like Hobbes, may be said to have taken a "low" view of human nature. He said, for example, that fear was stronger than love, and hatred stronger than both (*The Prince*, p. 76)[1], but he was not, like Hobbes, a pure psychological egoist, or indeed interested in such questions of "pure" theory. Again, Machiavelli's theory was much *wickeder* than Hobbes's. According to Hobbes, an obedient citizen might not *overtly* oppose his private (or denominational) conscience to his lawful sovereign, at any rate in a Christian commonwealth ; but Hobbes never denied that the sovereign had moral duties of the ordinary, respectable kind, both towards his subjects and towards other sovereigns, although these could not be enforced in any court. Machiavelli, while not denying (*e.g.* 81) that

[1] Edition 1929 of the translation by Dacres.

there were moral duties in Utopia, simply assumed the perfidy of all princes, especially towards one another. Any prince, he said, who practised peace and faith (instead of merely preaching them) would lose both his principality and his reputation (*ibid.*).

Both Hobbes and Machiavelli may be said to have taken " utilitarian " views, but Hobbes's utilitarianism, understood in the light of his interpretation of the Laws of Nature, dealt with the eternal ways of peace, and *such* utilitarianism was a part, although not the whole, of all traditional ethics, Stoic, civilian, canonical, and scholastic. Thus Cicero (q. Car. I, 4) said that a citizen was " utilitatis communione sociatus " ; Zabarella (q. G.G. 206) said that the Pope had to serve what was ordained " ad perpetuam utilitatem " ; Isidore (*apud* Suarez, L.L. I, vi) explained that the ideal was " pro communi omnium utilitate."

Indeed, Hobbes counselled the ways of peace, Machiavelli assumed the existence of the ways of war. The prince, he said (83, cf. 65), " shall always stand sure at home if he have good arms ; and all things shall always stand sure at home when those abroad are firm." He was working, in short, for the redemption of Italy from barbarians and oppressors (122). Hobbes was thinking of an England rent internally after the defeat of the Great Armada had made it externally secure. Certainly Hobbes said that, *in war*, force and fraud were the two cardinal virtues ; but if that statement is Machiavellian, where are the anti-Machiavellians ?

Machiavelli had no interest in abstract theory. He was and professed to be a student of history, and his illustrations were either topical or drawn from the classics, the very last place to which Hobbes would have willingly gone. Hobbes, slighting history and its methods, was concerned to apply a pure abstract science of politics. " Men," said Machiavelli (5), " do willingly change their lord believing to better their condition." Is it likely that he would have been impressed by arguments based on the stultification of the original contract ? According to Machiavelli, a prudent prince should leave the wives and property of his subjects alone. Is it likely that he would have responded, without a Florentine smile, to an abstract analysis of property ? In Machiavelli's view (43) the great men desired only to oppress, the little men only not to be oppressed. Is it likely that he would have given so much as a thought to the argument that, since sovereignty was implied in the original pact, " oppression " could have no meaning ?

(2) In the *Discourses* Machiavelli accepted the Polybian view of the origin of society (at I, 2), but held, unlike Hobbes, that while a single legislator (*e.g.* Lycurgus) was most useful at first (I, 9), at a later stage the best government was *mixed*. He even held what Hobbes would have called the seditious doctrine (I, 57), that a " people " was more honest and more constant than a prince. Like the classical writers whom Hobbes detested, Machiavelli was a tyranno-phobe (see *e.g.* II, 2, and its praise of Xenophon's *De Tyrannide*). And Machiavelli (I, 4) took sedition as a matter of course. He also maintained, in a way at least partly un-Hobbian (at I, 58), that " the prince who can do what he pleases is a madman, and the people that can do as it pleases is never wise."

I do not think, then, that the lessons (largely " seditious," according to Hobbes) that Machiavelli learned from the classical writers, whom he adored, were lessons that Hobbes, for the most part, could have approved. On the other hand, it may very well be true that Hobbes assimilated Machiavelli's great assumption regarding the ultimate reason for the unity of history, viz. that " anyone compar-ing the present with the past will soon perceive that in all cities and in all nations there prevail the same desires and passions as always have prevailed " (I, 39). Again, although Hobbes might easily have invented his epigram about the cardinal virtues in war, he might also have found it in Machiavelli. "Although in all other affairs," said Machiavelli (at III, 40), "it be hateful to use fraud, in the operations of war it is praiseworthy and glorious, so that he who gets the better of his enemy by fraud is as much extolled as he who prevails by force."

Hobbes also agreed with Machiavelli, that religion was useful only when it was regarded as a sort of national asset (I, 11 and 12). But many others had said the same.

PART II
PHILOSOPHY

III

MATERIALISM

(1) THE NATURE OF PHILOSOPHY

" I would very fain commend philosophy to you," said
Hobbes to his readers (I, xiv), " that is to say, the study
of wisdom, for want of which we have all suffered much
damage lately." Elsewhere (II, iii) he described wisdom
as " the perfect knowledge of the truth in all matters
whatsoever," an affair of " a well-balanced reason " and
not merely of " a sudden acuteness."

In short, Hobbes distinguished between *mere* " knowledge " and that *perfect* knowledge which was philosophy
or science. Sense and memory, he said, gave " knowledge "
to " all living creatures " " immediately by nature " (I, 3).
" Experience," which was " nothing but memory," and
prudence, which was expectation begotten of memory,
naturally extended the " knowledge " of sense ; and so
did the records of " history " (I, 10 *sq.*). Philosophy,
however, was the product of " true ratiocination " (I, 3),
and it had to be *cultivated* methodically. Otherwise man's
natural reason would be like the straggling vines and odd
stalks of corn that grew in a wilderness (I, 1). Indeed,
philosophy (III, 665) needed the security of a commonwealth.

This methodical philosophy (I, xiii) had but one source,
" the natural reason of man, busily flying up and down
among the creatures, and bringing back a true report of
their order, causes, and effects." It was employed about
natural things and tutored by our senses. Yet Hobbes, in

85

a very stubborn part of him, was also a naïve rationalist. " Philosophy," he said (*ibid.*), " the child of the world and your own mind is within yourself. . . . Imitate the Creation ; if you will be a philosopher in good earnest, let your reason move upon the deep of your own cogitations and experience. . . . The order of the Creation was—light, distinction of day and night, the firmament, the luminaries, sensible creatures, man ; and after the Creation the commandment. Therefore the order of contemplation will be reason, definition, space, the stars, sensible quality, man; and, after man is grown up, subjection to command."

Nevertheless, and principally, Hobbes was a rationalistic *materialist.* The " creatures " among which *natural* reason flew up and down were *bodies,* and their " causes " were physical motions. " The subject of philosophy, or the matter it treats of, is every body of which we can conceive any generation, and which we may, by any consideration thereof, compare with other bodies " (I, 10). Theology was excluded because God was ingenerable and indivisible, and there could be no philosophy of angels or other incorporeal beings, " there being in them no place neither for composition nor for division, nor any capacity of more and less, that is to say, no place for ratiocination " (*ibid.*). Our natural reason, Hobbes said, was confined to the quantity of moving bodies, and if any perplexed person desired some other philosophical ideal he must " seek it from other principles " (I, 12).

In his formal definition of philosophy in the *Leviathan* (III, 664) Hobbes said, as in other places (*e.g.* I, 8 *sqq.*), that knowledge was *power,* including the power of settled government, as well as, say, the instruments of navigation that effectively distinguished good Europeans from North American savages. This Baconian view was Hobbes's considered opinion (*e.g.* I, 7), although he went as far as most intellectual men (III, 44 ; IV, 51 and 453) in admitting the strength of curiosity, and the delight of curiosity satisfied. He also pointed out (in this as in other places) that there were two employments of philosophical reason, viz. the progress from causes to their effects and the regress from effects to their causes.[1]

Superficially it might seem that this double employment must simply describe the same path traversed in different directions ; but Hobbes did not think so. The regressive movement that he habitually contemplated (*e.g.* I, 388) proceeded from certain quite determinate effects, like the tides, to a supposition which, in conformity with the general laws of motion, *might* account for them (for he did not deny that, in such cases, several different hypotheses might be admissible). The progressive movement, on the contrary, had, to Hobbes's mind, a different and indeed a magisterial function. Human reason, he believed, could unite itself, by intuition, with the first principles of the generation of natural things, and from its own resources (here assumed to be identical in principle with Nature's) could evolve, with inevitable necessity, not, indeed, determinate natural facts like the tides, but the general abstract structure of the mechanical universe.

Hobbes's clearest account of this fundamental process was given in his chapter on philosophical method (I, 65 *sqq.*), the relevant part of which may be summarised as follows :

The first beginnings of knowledge were the phantasms of sense and imagination, but these were manifested as a crude factual datum, a mere ὅτι in Aristotelian language ;[2] and, as philosophers, men had to seek their causes or their διότι. Again, the " nature " of such data had to be resolved into their physical constituents.

In philosophy (I, 68) men might attempt to solve some *limited* problem (*e.g.* the cause of light or heat), or they might search " indefinitely ; that is, to know as much as

[1] Cf. Bacon, E.S. III, 351 : " The inquisition of causes and the production of effects."
[2] See, *e.g. Met.* A, 981 a 29.

they can without propounding to themselves any limited
question." In the latter case " it is necessary that they
know the causes of universal things,[1] or of such accidents
as are common to all bodies, that is, to all matter, before
they can know the causes of singular things, that is, of
the accidents by which one thing is distinguished from
another." Again (I, 69), " the causes of universal things
(of those, at least, that have any cause) are manifest of
themselves, or (as they say commonly) known to nature ;
so that they need no method at all ; for they have all but
one universal cause, which is motion. For the variety of
all figures arises out of the variety of those motions by
which they are made ; and motion cannot be understood
to have any other cause besides motion."

Such " causes of universal things " could be expressed in
" universal definitions " (I, 87) which were logically fertile
and also philoprogenitive. Definitions were *principles*, and
a principle (VII, 199) was " the beginning of something."
Such principles, " because they are principles, cannot be
demonstrated, and seeing they are known by nature . . .
they need no demonstration, though they need explication.
The whole method of demonstration is synthetical, con-
sisting of that order of speech which begins from primary
or most universal propositions, which are manifest of
themselves, and proceeds by a perpetual composition of
propositions into syllogisms " (I, 80 *sq.*).

Accordingly, Hobbes persuaded himself that the synthetic methods of the Greek geometers were the nerve, and
the very life, of philosophy ; and we may now consider,
firstly, the manner in which he subdivided philosophy in
terms of these explanations (I, 87), and, secondly, the
extent to which his philosophy was an innovation in its
mere conception.

From the definitions of space and motion, Hobbes
said (I, 70 *sq.*, cf. L. IV, 28 *sq.*), geometry and the

[1] Cf. Aristotle, *Met.* A, 981 b 29.

laws of *uniform* motion could be deduced. Next came the laws of action and reaction ; and this was followed by the science of *alteration* without visible translation. Naturally, the causes of *sensible* changes had to be sought in this third division of the subject ; and it led, in the fourth place, to the explanation, in detail, of the sensations and appetites of men, from which, in the last place, civil philosophy could be deduced. Of these five groups, the first three, remaining abstract, could all be deduced from the primary definitions " manifest to nature." In the fourth, the deduction, " in special " was more complicated and a good deal less direct. In the fifth (I, 73 *sq.*) philosophy might legitimately advance from a half-way house. Ultimately civil philosophy, like everything else, was a consequence of matter and motion. Political philosophers, however, might legitimately build their theories upon the passions and appetites of men.

On the score of innovation, Hobbes claimed that he was the first founder of any intelligible science of *Optics* and of *Natural Justice* (VII, 471), and otherwise (I, vii) disclaimed " any offensive novelty," having made it his business to develop the new knowledge of motion. In this domain, he said (I, vii *sq.*), the ancients, although they had accomplished much, had also missed much. Even Copernicus had dealt with too limited a problem. It had been left to Galileo, in Hobbes's own time, to be " the first that opened to us the gate of natural philosophy *universal*," although Kepler, Gassendi, and Mersenne had " extraordinarily advanced " Galileo's labours. (Salviati, Galileo's spokesman in the *Dialogues*, said that he proffered " a key that openeth the door to a path never yet trodden by any.")[1] Again, it had been left to the Englishman, Harvey (I, viii), ably assisted by physicians, " the only true natural philosophers " in these matters, to discover an intelligible *science* of the human body.

[1] Translated Salusbury, 1661 (=Gal.), p. 381.

What, then, was left for Hobbes ? Partly, no doubt, to consolidate the advance, but largely also to apply the new theory, with rigorous solicitude, to human psychology and its social consequences. Aristotelians like Suarez, and some like Telesio, who were not Aristotelians, had written great tomes *On the Nature of Things*, where man and his affairs loomed large at the end. Hobbes, who agreed with none of them, set himself to apply the new theory of motion over this whole gigantic territory.

Again, if Hobbes's disrespect for the ancients (except in geometry), and especially for Aristotle, was a trifle old-fangled in 1655, it is not to be supposed that Hobbes, himself no youngster, was dancing on a corpse. Oxford might possibly have ceased to confound Aristotelity with philosophy (III, 670), although John Locke, then an undergraduate, did not think it had. But Aristotle's reign had been almost uninterrupted in European academies since 1254, when he had been officially accepted by the University of Paris, and this " precursor of Christ in natural things " took an unconscionable time in dying. Aristotelianism had been scarcely perturbed by attacks like Petrarch's and Ramus's ; it withstood Telesio and Bacon ; Gassendi, in 1624, became famous through his prolix *Exercitationes* against it, and it did not really begin to sag at the knees before Galileo's *Dialogues* overwhelmed its physics in 1632. Indeed, in the last quarter of the century, Malebranche and other Cartesians inveighed against the Aristotelians, and their master, with an asperity and petulant invective from which both Hobbes and Galileo refrained. " Aristotle," said Galileo (Gal. 94), " had he but seen the novelties described in the heavens, would have changed his opinions." Aristotle, said Hobbes, was one of the very few who had studied philosophy for curiosity's sake (VII, 72), and, like Pythagoras, Plato, Zeno, and Epicurus, was " a man of deep and laborious meditation " (VI, 98). While Hobbes had a Lucian-like contempt for *schools* of philosophy, and for the sciolists and rhetoricians who " prated and loitered " (III, 667), he respected the masters.

Indeed, we may reasonably ask at the present day, when there is little excuse for passion,[1] whether Hobbes's attitude towards Aristotelianism was either unjustifiable or unhistorical. He held that while Platonists " founded their doctrine upon the conceptions and ideas of things," Aristotelians " reasoned only from the names of things according to the scale of the categories " (VI, 100 ; cf. Bacon, E.S. III, 394) ; that all Greek physics, more particularly Aristotle's, was " rather a dream than science " (III, 668) ; that Aristotle's logic was embrangled in verbal puzzles (III, 669) and (*ibid.*) his ethics a " description of passions." Hobbes may have been a little too nervous about sedition when he said (III, 203) : " I think I may truly say there was never any thing so dearly bought as these Western parts have bought the learning of the Greek and Latin tongues ; " but there was substance in his complaint that " school divinity " had turned Aristotelian metaphysics into " supernatural philosophy " (III, 671), and that (III, 680), " if such metaphysics and physics as this be not *vain philosophy*, there was never any ; nor needed St. Paul to give us warning to avoid it." Nevertheless, as we shall see, there was much incidental Aristotelianism in Hobbes's pages.

(2) FIRST PHILOSOPHY [2]

In the *Leviathan* (III, 73), Hobbes, having defined philosophy, rather awkwardly, as " knowledge of con-

---

[1] Some of our contemporary Platonists, if not passionate, are very severe. Thus, according to Mr. A. E. Taylor (*Commentary on Plato's Timœus*, p. 408), " Of all the considerable Greek philosophers Aristotle was far the most incompetent as a physicist," and his *Physics* are " a curse to science." He was (*ibid.* p. 443) " about the *worst* of physicists."

[2] *i.e.* the Aristotelian and Baconian *philosophia prima*, or, as Bacon said, " summary philosophy."

sequences," said that " first philosophy," *i.e.* " the principles or first foundation of philosophy," consisted of
consequences " from quantity and motion indeterminate."
Clearly, however, " the seeds or the grounds of philosophy "
(VII, 226) were premisses, not conclusions, and elsewhere
in the *Leviathan* (III, 671) first philosophy was said to
" consist principally " of " the *definitions* of body, time,
place, matter, form, essence, subject, substance, accident,
power, act, finite, infinite, quantity, quality, motion,
passion, and divers others." If these definitions went
astray, philosophers, like puzzled accountants, would spend
their time " in fluttering over their books " (III, 24).

While Hobbes was prepared to deploy the Aristotelian
" forms of the predicaments of Body, Quantity, Quality,
and Relation " (I, 25 *sqq.*), he " confessed that he had not
yet seen any great use " of them (I, 28). We should
therefore pay most attention to the categories he habitually
used, and principally to Substance (or Body) on the one
hand, and Cause and Effect on the other.

Objecting to Descartes (L. V, 253), Hobbes argued that
" I am " could certainly be inferred from " I think," since
thinking was an act and every act implied a subject or
substance. " Hence," he said, " it *follows* that a thinking
thing is of a corporeal nature ; for the subjects of all acts
seem to be intelligible *only* as corporeal or material."
Sometimes, it is true, Hobbes jibbed at the *word* " substance." " Do you understand the connection of *substance*
and *incorporeal* ? " he asked (IV, 427). " If you do,
explain it in English ; for the words are Latin. It is
something, you will say, that being *without body, stands
under*—Stands under what ? " Yet Hobbes accepted the
category of substance, provided that substance was identified with body. " Everything is either Substance or
Accident," he wrote in the *Short Tract* (E.L. 153) ; and,
later (IV, 308 ; cf. L. III, 529), " the word substance, in
Greek ὑπόστασις . . . signifies . . . a ground, a base, any-

thing that has existence or subsistence *in itself*, any thing
that upholdeth that which else would fall."[1]

Certainly, substance did not, as the " common people "
supposed, need to be visible or sensibly pressing (III, 381).
It was discerned with the eye of reason. " Substance,"
Hobbes said, speaking quite generally, although arguing
with Descartes about God, " being matter subject to
accidents and mutations, is revealed to ratiocination alone,
and is not conceived or shown to us in any idea " (L. V.
264). Or again : " The word *body*, in the most general
acceptation, signifieth that which filleth, or occupieth,
some certain room, or imagined place ; and dependeth not
on the imagination, but is a real part of what we call
the *universe*. For the *universe*, being the aggregate of all
bodies, there is no real part thereof that is not also *body* ;
nor anything properly a *body* that is not also part of that
aggregate of all *bodies*, the *universe*. The same also,
because bodies are subject to change, that is to say, to
variety of apparence to the sense of living creatures, is
called *substance*, that is to say, *subject* to various accidents.
... And, according to this acceptation of the word,
substance and *body* signify the same thing " (III, 381).

Thus " immaterial substance," despite Descartes (L. V,
255), was " a senseless speech "[2] (III, 32). " Substance
without dimension " was " a flat contradiction " (IV, 61) ;
and school-divines should really learn to talk sense. Did
they speak of the soul ? Body and soul meant the body
alive (III, 615) ; it was the *bodies* of the faithful that, after
the resurrection, were spiritual and eternal (*e.g.* III, 460).
Was spirit their theme ? " By the name of *spirit* we
understand a *body natural*, but of such *subtilty* that it
worketh not upon the senses " (IV, 60 *sq.*). Were they

---

[1] Cf. Aristotle, *Met.* 1029 a 1.
[2] Aristotle had held, sometimes, that space, time, and movement were
common to everything (*Physics*, III, ch. 1), and (*ibid.* IV, ch. 1) that
" everyone admits that whatever is, is somewhere." This included the
soul (*ibid.* IV, 7, § 8. Cf. *De An.* I, 414 a and 424 a).

speaking about angels ? If they persisted in " the labour of supposing permanent ghosts " (III, 390), how could they prove, from Scripture or elsewhere, that heavenly " messengers " were incorporeal ? Or were they trying to describe the indescribable Godhead ? God had the being " of a spirit not of a spright " (IV, 313), and was (*ibid.*) " a most pure, simple, invisible spirit *corporeal.*"

Of " first matter," *i.e.* " body in general, that is, body considered universally," Hobbes said (I, 118 *sq.*) that while in one sense a mere name, it was yet " a name which is not of vain use," since we often had to consider " that matter which is common to all things " and persisted " in all generation and mutation." A body, on the other hand, *i.e.* a " singular thing," was defined (I, 102) as " that which having no dependence upon our thought, is co-incident or co-extended with some part of space," and the definition (*ibid.*) was said to imply that it was body because extended, self-existent because outside us, and a subject because it could be understood by reason to be subjected to imaginary space.

This attempt to combine the traditional Aristotelian. subject of properties with extension was not very convincing. Descartes (*loc. cit.*) was obviously right in saying that only " metaphysical matter," not corporeal thinghood, followed from the traditional definition of " substance," and the other important meaning of " substance " (that is to say, the persistent *subject of change*) has no self-evident connection with extension. We may suspect, indeed, that while Hobbes *said* the thing was self-evident, what he *meant* was a doctrine of the modern kind, viz. that " substance," so interpreted, was amenable to scientific method, and was otherwise only an excuse for rhetoric. Hobbes's own theory, had he made it clear, should have been deduced from his principle that all change was local motion ; but in that case he might have been wiser to do what Leibniz and Boscovich later did, and attempt to explain matter itself as a set of centres of force. As things were, he made a hasty match between the traditional view that all attributes must be attributes *of something* and his own new theory of motion, leaving the relations between kinematics and dynamics quite obscure.

Again, his account of the spatial magnitude of bodies was thoroughly puzzling. One of his difficulties, the relation between "imaginary" and "real" space, will concern us later, and, for the moment, it may suffice to say that Hobbes never wavered in his belief that real bodies had real spatial magnitude (*e.g.* I, 105, and IV, 393). Another difficulty may serve as an introduction to Hobbes's account of "accidents." Believing in the category of substance and accident, Hobbes said pithily that " bodies are things and not generated ; accidents are generated and not things " (I, 117). He had also said, however (I, 116), that " that magnitude for which we give to any thing the name of body is neither generated nor destroyed." And magnitude *was* an accident or property.

Let us turn to "accidents." These, according to Hobbes, inhered in bodies (I, 68), and certain accidents collectively constituted the whole *nature* of a thing, although not the thing itself (I, 67). If we asked, "What is an accident ? " we made " an enquiry after that which we know already, and not that which we should enquire after. For who does not always and in the same manner understand him that says any thing is extended, or moved, or not moved ? " (I, 102 *sq.*).

Unfortunately Hobbes set himself to derive the ultimate (or what he had called so) and to explain the intelligible. He argued (*a*) that an accident was an abstract name, and that such a name (I, 103) was " the cause why a thing appears so or so." " Wherefore I define an accident to be the manner of our conception of body " (I, 104). In addition to its vagueness this explanation confused an abstract name with that *of which* it was the name, and was clearly circular, since it stated that the " property " of a body *meant* the " property " that gave the body a certain look. Moreover (*e.g.* I, 75), Hobbes was quite capable of confusing between the property of a body that caused an appearance and that appearance itself.

He also argued (*b*) that Aristotle's account of the *inherence* of accidents—" an accident is in its subject not as any part thereof, but so as it may be away, the subject still remaining " (I, 104)—was " right," except that it was largely wrong, the truth being that extension and figure " can never perish except the body perish also," but that " all other accidents, which are not common to all bodies, but peculiar to some only, as *to be at rest, to be moved, colour, hardness*, and the like, do perish continually and are succeeded by others ; yet so as that the body never perisheth " (I, 104, cf. 33 and 116).

Defective or not, these explanations had a purpose. In the first place Hobbes contended that all accidents belonged to a single class, since they all described *motions* in bodies " either of the mind or of the perceiver or of the bodies themselves which are perceived." (I, 105), in such wise that " colour, heat, odour, virtue, vice, and the like " (I, 104) had *some* physical habitat, if only in men's brains. Secondly, he denied that accidents were themselves bodies or parts of bodies, and professed to discern this error in the entire scholastic apparatus of " forms," " essences," and " species." In reality there were no such quasi-bodies. Essence itself simply meant " the *is-ness* of the thing that is " (IV, 394). Again (I, 104), " when an accident is said *to be in a body*, it is not so to be understood as if any thing were contained in that body ; as if, for example, redness were in blood, in the same manner as blood is in a bloody cloth . . . for so an accident would be a body also."

Nevertheless, although accidents were not *parts* of bodies, certain accidents or " universal things," Hobbes maintained (cf. I, 117), constituted the real *nature* of a real body. All bodies had at least the property of extension, and a body unpropertied would not be a body at all. Accordingly, Hobbes had no genuine reply to the criticism that the real characters of real things could not possibly be nonentities, abstract names, or merely a "manner of conceiving." Without such real characters of real things, Hobbes's philosophy could not set out from port.

Postponing this question for the time being, we may here remark that Hobbes's philosophy of the διότι depended on the analysis of a thing's *nature*, and that, in this matter, he tried to coax two distinctions into doing the work of three. When dealing with conceptual analysis, he was fond of the illustration (*e.g.* I, 4) that we first perceived a body vaguely, then, coming nearer, perceived it to be animate, and, coming nearer still, perceived it to be a man.[1] This clarification of the vague was certainly different from physical composition, but it was also different from conceptual analysis, where general terms should be just as clear as specific or determinate ones. Where there is intellectual articulation every incision should be made with a scalpel.

After Body, Cause was the great first principle of the Hobbian philosophy. All causes, Hobbes said (I, 132, cf. VII, 82), were efficient causes, or, more accurately, the " entire cause " consisted of the efficient and the material cause (I, 121). Of the other Aristotelian causes, he said that a " final " cause " has no place but in such things as have sense and will ; and this also I shall prove hereafter to be an efficient cause" (I, 132), and that a "formal" cause (*ibid.*, cf. I, 43 *sq.*) could only be " a cause of our knowledge," since, Aristotle notwithstanding[2] (I, 63), it was not intelligible to say that the *definition* of anything could *cause* that thing (I, 131). It is to be feared, however,

---

[1] A favourite example of Campanella's; see Levi, *Il pensiero di F. Bacone*, p. 23.

[2] *Physics*, II, ch. 3. For Aristotle (*ibid.* II, ch. 3, earlier) an efficient cause was a " principle of motion or rest."

that Hobbes sinned with Aristotle, since the principles he reached by philosophical analysis were no more efficient causes than they were physical parts. (Hobbes partially parried this criticism, however, by affirming, *e.g.* that geometrical figure was *made* by geometrical construction.)

Hobbes's account of efficient causation referred, as was customary in his age, to things generated *only*. It did not apply to the First Mover, in whose existence, he said (III, 92), any one who made " any profound enquiry into natural causes " was " inclined to believe." Reason decreed that whatever *had a beginning* had a cause ; and Hobbes, generalising Galileo (Gal. 11), tried to clinch the matter by the argument[1] that Hume (*Treatise*, I, Pt. III, iii) later showed to be question-begging. " The point that a man cannot imagine any thing to begin *without a cause*, can no other way be made known but by trying how he can imagine it ; but, if he try, he shall find as much reason, if there be no cause of the thing, to conceive it should begin at one time as another, that he hath equal reason to think it should begin at all times, which is impossible ; and therefore he must think there was some special cause why it should begin then rather sooner or later ; or else that it began never, but was *eternal* " (IV, 276, cf. I, 115).

Developing this principle to the extreme of his logical bent, Hobbes declared that " in respect of their causes, all things come to pass with equal necessity ; for otherwise they would have no causes at all, which of things generated is not intelligible " (I, 127).

It will be convenient to postpone discussion of Hobbes's determinism until we have to deal with his controversy with Bishop Bramhall. Here we should note that Hobbes never denied that there might have to be much conjecture and unconscionable complication in man's inquiry into causes. " The doctrine of natural causes," he said (VII, 3),

---

[1] The argument was Aristotelian; see *Physics*, III, ch. 7, and IV, ch. 11.

" hath not infallible and evident principles. For there is no effect which the power of God cannot produce by many several ways." Again he remarked (VII, 78) : " You enquire not so much, when you see the change of any thing, what may be said to be the cause of it, as how the same is generated ; which generation is the entire progress of nature from the efficient cause to the effect produced. Which is always a hard question, and for the most part impossible for a man to answer to." (The " man " in question had, of course, to be a *man of science*. Hobbes, speaking as a philosopher, was not concerned with what " almost all men " called causes (III, 97), that is to say, with custom-bred expectations.)

What, then, did Hobbes mean by an efficient cause in its scientific sense ?

" A body," he said, " is said to work upon or to *act*, that is to say, *do* something to another body when it either generates or destroys some accident in it. . . . That accident which is generated in the patient is called the effect " (I, 120). Thus " power " and " efficient cause " were the same thing ; but the *generation* of accidents was not to be regarded as the *transmission* of anything. " It is not to be thought that an accident goes out of one subject into another " (I, 117). Again, causes were the antecedents in a succession, usually, although perhaps not always (*e.g.* III, 677), regarded as temporal, not logical. " Causation and the production of effects consist in a certain continual progress " (I, 123) ; and (*ibid.*) " in whatsoever instant the cause is entire, in the same instant the effect is produced."

Clearly, an agent implied a patient. Therefore, said Hobbes, the *entire* cause consisted of the efficient *and* the material cause. The plenary " power " in any causal transaction was the active and passive powers taken together (I, 128), and the separate threads in the web had to be teased apart. " The agent hath its effect precisely such, not because it is *a* body, but because [it is] *such* a body; or *so* moved. . . . The fire, for example, does not warm because it is a body, but because it is hot" (I, 121).

Again, the *entire* cause should be defined as "the aggregate of all such accidents, both in the agents and the patient, as concur to the producing of the effect (I, 77 ; cf. I, 121 *sq*., and V, 105) ; and Hobbes asserted that an *entire* cause was identical with a *sufficient* cause ; for "no man will say that that is *cause enough* to produce an effect, to which any thing is wanting needful to the production of it " (V, 382 *sq*.) ; and the entire cause, by definition (I, 128), included just the requisites needed. He even argued, in Epicurean vein (I, 129), that every possible act " shall at some time be produced," since an event would be impossible " if the power shall never be plenary."

What he most desired, however, was to connect these general propositions concerning causality with the new doctrines[1] that all mutation was motion, and (III, 2) that nothing but motion could cause a motion. He therefore declared (*a*) that a finite body at rest in empty space would have to move itself " alike all ways at once," if, *per impossibile*, it began to move without an external cause (I, 115), and (*b*) that if a body were at rest and not in contact with another body, " we may conceive that it will continue so till it be touched by some other body " (I, 124). He added the explanations that " rest " did not resist motion (I, 125), that empty space was wholly inoperative (*ibid*.), and that it was "manifest of itself" that processes " not differing in any thing besides time " must be " equal and like " (I, 126).

Of these arguments, the first (*a*) was obviously question-

---

[1] " New" at least in their application and great development. Aristotle had held (*Physics*, VIII, ch. 14) that all " motion " (including alteration of quality and increase or diminution of bulk) implied *local* motion. Thus (*ibid*. V, ch. 1) " whitening " was a movement; and Nature itself, for the physicist, *was* movement (*ibid*. VIII, ch. 3).

begging. For if all bodies were self-moving, there might, *ex hypothesi*, be sufficient *internal* reasons for determinate movements, and if, in the fashion of Leibnizian monads, all bodies moved under their own power because they had some sort of " soul," they might very well rest or move for their souls' sake, or, when they moved, prefer walking to running. Again, the second argument (*b*) was so beautiful an example of a logical circle that any commentary would be inartistic. Speaking clumsily, however, one might suggest that believers in *actio in distans* need not be fools, and that Hobbes never even began to prove that all *mutation* must be motion. His argument was that " we do not say anything is changed but that which appears to our senses otherwise than it appeared formerly " (I, 126), *i.e.* that since sensible appearances were motions *in us*, their changes must be due to other motions. But this conclusion followed only if it was certain that all changes *were* changes of motion, and consequently could not be used in support of that important principle.

Summing up, we may say that Hobbes's interpretation of Body and Accident, together with his interpretation of Cause, defined his materialism. There was nothing except Body with the ingenerable accident of spatial magnitude and the generable accidents of motion, than which there were no other accidents. Every natural appearance was an *instance* of the motion of bodies.

Hobbes's account of two other important categories, however, may be briefly considered here, if only for the historical reason that it probably influenced the subsequent discussions of Locke and of Hume.

Regarding " relation " (*i.e.* correlation) Hobbes remarked (I, 133) that the category applied to likeness or unlikeness, equality or inequality, and that it led to propositions concerning proportion. More generally he said (I, 23) that relative names were " imposed for some comparison," and so included master-servant or father-son. He also said, in effect (I, 135), that correlatives had an identical *fundamentum relationis*. "The likeness of one white to another white, or its unlikeness to black is the same accident with its whiteness."

Regarding the individuality or identity of things, Hobbes said that " two bodies are said to *differ* from one another when something may be said of one of them which cannot be said of the other at the same time " (I, 132), and he inferred (I, 133) that " all bodies differ from one another in *number*, namely, as one and another " although ultimately (*e.g.* VII, 83) variety of motion was the efficient cause of all bodily diversity. There were, however, further problems. Was individuity " unity of matter "? Then, strictly, the same culprit could never be punished, since his body continually altered, and yet we spoke of the " same " wax when a lump was melted. Should we say that Socrates retained the same " form " although the matter of him changed ? If so, we might intelligibly define an individual thing by the " form " that persisted after some " beginning of motion " (I, 137), and say that a river remained the " same " if it flowed from the same fountain. If, however, we tried to define individuity by the aggregate of its accidents : (*a*) every new accident would imply the existence of a new thing, " so that a man standing would not be the same he [that] was sitting " (*ibid.*) ; and (*b*), since accidents were accidents *of matter*, the same numerical accident could not belong to different things.

(3) QUANTITY, MEASURE, AND GEOMETRY

One of the lessons that Hobbes read to the egregious professors was that the definitions of magnitude, quantity, and other such " accidents of body " " proceeded from the common understanding " (VII, 226), and so pertained to general, not to departmental, science. It was the *demonstrations*, drawn out by a proper method (L. IV, 23), that were the field of technical mathematics. Mathematical principles were a philosopher's affair.

The magnitude of a body, Hobbes affirmed, was its "extension" or "real space" (I, 105), and every body had "always the same magnitude" (*ibid*.), which was therefore "the peculiar accident of every body." He also held that it was intelligible and convenient, although "improper" (VII, 227), to say in the abstract that "when bodies are equal their magnitudes are also called equal."

Quantity, Hobbes said, was really *tantity* or *so-muchness*. "Wheresoever there is *more* or *less*, there is one kind of quantity or another" (VII, 193). He did not, however, use the term quite so widely, or examine the greater difference in rank between a lance-corporal and a sergeant than between a corporal and a sergeant. On the contrary, he limited his treatment to length, velocity, etc., and maintained that the methodical deduction of quantities was *geometry*, to which even arithmetic—an affair of small discrete points or lengths (I, 141)—was subordinate. Therefore "as quantity may be considered in all the operations of nature, so also doth geometry run quite through the whole body of natural philosophy" (VII, 196). Geometry could be defined most precisely as "the science of determining the magnitude of a body, of a time, or of anything else *unmeasured* by comparison with some other *measured* magnitude or magnitudes" (L. IV, 28).

Natural good sense (L. IV, 295) could tell what a straight line was, but it was quite another thing to discover a method of deduction that would be fertile in consequences. On this point Hobbes said several (not necessarily inconsistent) things. Firstly, he remarked that a geometer had to *expose* his quantities either "to the eyes" or to "memory" (I, 139), *i.e.* in a way "revocable to sense" (I, 140); and, admitting "coincidence," Hobbes challenged the legitimacy of many proofs by superposition

(VII, 197). Secondly, he admitted *apposition* (of very short lines or very thin solids) and *section* as methods of " exposition " (I, 140) ; and he allowed, thirdly, that it was possible, in some cases, to compute by •ndivisibles and by powers (I, 314). He held, however, that by far the best method was exposition by motion (*e.g.* I, 140 and 314).

This method included, and very largely *was*, " construction by the rule and compass " (I, 316),[1] which left permanent marks (I, 140 ; VII, 219). Hobbian geometry, however, was not an affair of diagrams, being a thing of reason, not of sense and experience (I, 217). The compass was only approximately precise (L. V, 159), and proper attention had to be paid to what was, and to what was not," reckoned " in the diagram (cf. VII, 382). Ultimately, Hobbes's view was " that the science of every subject is derived from a precognition of the causes, generation and construction of the same ; and consequently where the causes are known, there is place for demonstration, but not where the causes are to seek for. Geometry therefore is demonstrable, for the lines and figures from which we reason are drawn and described by ourselves " (VII, 184).[2]

These reasons may not sound very convincing. A child, scribbling with a pencil, draws and describes *by himself*. If he knew what he was doing in a geometrical way, he must have acquired an insight into the nature of the space within which he drew and described. Hobbes had no sympathy with such criticisms (VII, 215 *sq.*), and was fond of pointing out that Euclid's definition of a circle (VII, 205) and of a sphere (VII, 214) were Hobbian. Indeed, he believed himself to be a geometer after the manner of Euclid, Archimedes,[3] and Apollonius (I, 204)—which was

---

[1] Cf. a letter from Wallis to Huygens, quoted in Brockdorff's *Hobbes*, p. 157.

[2] Cf. Gassendi, *Works*, Florentine ed. (=Gas.), I, 29, where Gassendi distinguished the inquiry into the *being* from the inquiry into the *generation* of things, and held that the latter, if rational, depended *on us*.

[3] In whom, however, Hobbes suspected a tendency towards what is now called the " arithmetising of geometry " (VII, 67 *sq.*).

the only true manner—but to have been " the first that hath made the grounds of geometry firm and coherent " (VII, 242) by consistently applying the method of the generation of motion, and so uniting geometry with kinematics (I, 204). " To imagine motions with their times and ways," said he, " is a new business, and requires a steady brain, and a man that can constantly read in his own thoughts, without being diverted by the noise of words " (VII, 272).

Hobbes was therefore very anxious indeed to repudiate the suggestion that Roberval had anticipated him in the case of the Archimedean problem of the equality of a spiral to a certain semi-parabola (VII, 343), and cited a witness to prove (L. IV, 190) that he had indicated the method to Roberval, and that Roberval, pointing out Hobbes's failure to discriminate between uniform and accelerated motion, had produced the correct demonstration next day. (This anecdote was instructive in more ways than Hobbes supposed.)

In much of his work, the Greek methods that Hobbes believed himself to be pursuing and improving were those of their " geometrical algebra,"[1] according to which the relations between curved and rectilinear figures were treated by the application of areas, and by the method of proportionals. Hobbes therefore challenged the new algebraic methods in geometry of Descartes, Oughtred, and Wallis, although it is significant enough that he once " lamented [to Sir William Petty] that he had not taken the art of algebra more into his studies."[2] Apart from this unusual lamentation, Hobbes's argument was that while " logistic "[3] or the art of geometry (I, 89 sq.) included both analysis and synthesis—which, in a sense, were complementary (I, 310)—it was *synthesis* that " made a geo-

---

[1] See especially I, 246 sqq.
[2] The Petty-Southwell Correspondence, p. 322.
[3] Λογιστική, usually translated " the art of calculating."

metrician " (I, 314). Therefore Hobbes's methods were not only " more natural, more geometrical, and more perspicuous " (VII, 326) than those of Wallis, but it was also true that Wallis, as well as Oughtred, Vieta, Regiomontanus, Copernicus, and even Archimedes (L. V, 149) had sinned against the natural light by attempting to describe the properties of figures in numbers.

According to Hobbes (*e.g.* I, 141) numbers exposed discrete magnitudes, and were empty names unless they exposed *bodies* (VII, 67). Therefore arithmetic was spatial, and the attempt to algebrise geometry was bound to fail. Again all numbers were whole numbers (L. IV, 18). Therefore surds (L. IV, 11) pertained to geometry, not to arithmetic. The root of a square number was *not* the side of a square figure (L. V, 161), any more than the root of 100 soldiers could be anything except 10 soldiers (VII, 436) ; and when lines were multiplied by numbers, the product remained in one dimension (VII, 67). The algebrists completely forgot that if their numbers did not designate *homogeneous* quanta (VII, 198) they simply disfigured their pages with " a scab of symbols " (VII, 316), " as if a hen had been scraping there " (VII, 330). Thus solids were homogeneous with solids, not with superficies, and so on. (But kind persons like Aubrey (at I, 332), and unkind persons like Wallis (H.H. 35) thought (rather too glibly) that Hobbes did not understand such matters, having begun to study mathematics too late.)

Again, following (as he believed) the Greek tradition,[1] Hobbes held that the infinite divisibility of continuous quantity simply meant its *indefinite* divisibility. A " point," therefore, was simply that *undivided* body " whose quantity was not considered "[2] (VII, 201) ; and Wallis's " indivisibles " were entirely spurious entities

---

[1] Cf. T. L. Heath's *Archimedes*, p. cxlii.
[2] On the general doctrine of "considering" or "neglecting" in mathematics see Aristotle, *Met.* M. 1077 b 24.

(VII, 301) even if he could be forgiven for saying, un-geometrically (VII, 308), that a parallelogram of "infinitely little" altitude was " *scarce* anything else but a line," or that an infinitely little line could be equal to an infinitely little square or cube (L. IV, 392).

Hobbes lived at the wrong time for these contentions. It is now freely admitted[1] that Wallis's logical exposition of his governing conceptions was defective ; but Wallis was the first mathematician of his time in England, and his advances upon the work of Descartes and of Cavalieri retains an honoured place in the histories of mathematics, partly because, as Montucla[2] said, Wallis greatly extended the range of geometry, partly because of his pioneer work in the discovery of the calculus. The task of tidying up was left to later ages. Hobbes was rowing against the stream, and since he did not himself row very well (at any rate not evenly) his name has disappeared from the histories of mathematics, and is not to be found, for example, in the index to Cantor's *Geschichte*. Montucla, it is true (*ibid*. II, 187), remarked, with some surprise, that Hobbes's criticisms of Descartes' " inclination to motion " were " better than we should be disposed to expect from a man who subsequently discovered the quadrature of the circle and undertook to reform geometry even in its axioms." To some extent time has brought its revenge, since the " logistical " examination of geometrical axioms is now regarded as indispensable, not absurd. Still, if Hobbes is no longer in the wilderness, his cries are very seldom heard. It was always false to claim, as Hobbes did, that *he* was read on the Continent, Wallis only in England (L. V, 146) ; and the claim soon became ludicrous.

Let us attempt a little greater detail.

In addition to his crusader's zeal for true geometrical method, Hobbes hoped to produce a " little " that was

---

[1] *e.g.* by Rouse Ball, *History of Mathematics*, p. 289.
[2] *Histoire des Mathématiques*, II, 299.

" new " in the science of geometry (I, 204), and, in his modest way, to square the circle, duplicate the cube, and trisect angles. He was therefore specially concerned with the nature of angles and with the theory of proportion, since, *e.g.*, the Greek " geometrical algebrists " had to find two mean proportionals between two unequal straight lines if they tried to " double " the cube.

Angles, Hobbes said, differed in kind, according as they were the " quantity of a revolution " or the " quantity of flexion " (VII, 261). The first, or an angle " simply so called " (I, 184), was obtained by " pulling open " straight lines that concurred in a point, the latter by " continual flexion or curvation " (*ibid.*). In the former case (I, 186), " the quantity of an angle was an arch or circumference of a circle " ; but angles might also be obtained by flexing a straight into a continuously crooked line, or by altering the curvature of a curve (VII, 260). Hence Hobbes concluded (VII, 253) that " the same angle computed in the tangent is rectilineal, but computed in the circumference not rectilineal, but mixed ; or if two circles cut one another, curvilineal."

Proportion, ratio or analogism, Hobbes maintained, was essentially a geometrical matter, and was grossly misrepresented by Wallis (L. IV, 103) when he treated it as a fraction. For unity could not be divided into parts. Proportion measured " quantity of inequality " (VII, 238), and was arithmetical proportion when one magnitude exceeded another by so many unities, geometrical proportion when the excess was in degree of inequality (I, 144 *sqq.*). Thus (VII, 298) 4 to 1 was double 2 to 1, but although the number 2 was double the number 1, 2 to 1 was not, in itself, a double proportion.

I do not propose to examine Hobbes's attempts at circle-squaring. There were too many. " Of all his twelve quadratures," said Wallis " (the ninth and eleventh only excepted), there are not any two agreed upon the same verdict " (H.H. 117) ; and the round dozen (in the *De Corpore*) had a troop of followers. Montucla, in the best of the histories of circle-squaring,[1] said that Hobbes " surpassed all his predecessors in absurdity." Hobbes's conception of the problem, however, may be indicated briefly.

It was easy, he said, to obtain an approximate value for π " mechanically " " by winding a small thread about a given cylinder " (I, 288), but Hobbes proceeded by *geometrical* construction, and held that it was an open question whether geometrical methods might not succeed where arithmetical methods (as he admitted) necessarily failed (I, 288). " Archimedes, Apollonius and, in our own time, Bonaventura," had supposed so, and Kepler (L. V, 11) had admitted that the thing might be done " by chance." (We should remember to-day that De Morgan, in the nineteenth century, said that the *geometrical* quadrature was " not fully demonstrated to be impossible.")[2]

Reverting to wider topics, we may note that Hobbes's actual procedure, on the score of mathematical method, involved a certain revision of his ostensible starting-point. Ostensibly he distinguished " principles of demonstration " from " principles of construction " (VII, 199) or of " operation " ; and he declared (L. IV, 67) that Euclid's axioms[3] might be deduced from the latter. Since, however, according to Hobbes (*e.g.* L. IV, 107), the operation itself supplied the demonstration (the *definition* (*e.g.* L. V, 204) being only an account of the generation of lines and figures by motion), it seems clear that Hobbes's initial distinction between " true definitions " on the one hand, and, on the other, " petitions " or " postulates " of construction, (VII, 210) had, as nearly as possible, vanished away.

---

[1] Paris, 1754. I quote from the reprint of 1831, pp. 208 *sq.*
[2] *A Budget of Paradoxes*, 2nd ed. II, 214.
[3] Ellis showed (E.S. I, 47) that Bacon used the word " axiom " widely, probably following Ramus.

(4) PHYSICS

By physics Hobbes himself meant the attempt rationally to explain the phenomena of nature (I, 386), or, in classical phrase, to " salve the appearances " (I, 437). It dealt largely with bodies " in special," and so was distinct from " motion and magnitude by themselves in the abstract " (I, 386). I have, however, to say something more about the general theme.

As we saw, Hobbes's fundamental premiss was that " all mutation consists in motion " (*e.g.* I, 70), and the development of his thought in this particular deserves a short inquiry. In the *Short Tract* (E.L. 152) Hobbes admitted the possibility of motion by " inherent power " as well as " received " local motion (cf. P.P. 128), and also held that " some inherent form " might be produced as well as motion (*ibid.*). In *Tractatus Opticus II* he seems to have used the principle that " all action is local motion in the agent" simply as a scientific *hypothesis* (E.L. 169). In *De Corpore*, on the other hand, the principle was said to be " manifest of itself " (I, 69), although " many cannot understand till it be in some sort demonstrated to them " (I, 70). Not unnaturally, the quasi-demonstration was circular (I, 124 *sqq.*).

Later (VII, 83 *sqq.*) Hobbes *defined* motion as change of place, and deduced the " axioms " that " nothing can begin, change, or put an end to, its own motion," and that " whatsoever body, being at rest, is afterwards moved, hath for its immediate movent[1] some other body which is in motion and toucheth it." He imperilled his self-evident proposition, however, by admitting a First Mover, although he explained that the eternal cause or causes might be " eternally moved " (I, 412).

Hobbes defined (local) motion as " a *continual* relinquishing of one place and acquiring another " (I, 109, cf. 81),

---

[1] Molesworth reads " movement," obviously an error.

and deduced a general principle of inertia (I, 125), that " whatsoever is moved will always be moved on in the same way and with the same velocity except it be hindered by some other contiguous and moved body." Such continuity implied the potency of unending divisibility (I, 98), and Hobbes explained (I, 110 *sq.*) that the ancient puzzle about the flying arrow was a mere sophism. " That which is moved," he said, " is neither moved *in* the place where it is, nor *in* the place where it is not, but *from* the place where it is *to* the place where it is not." In Mr. Whitehead's language, motion was continuous *passage*.

If the motion were " simple " or uniform, this doctrine described geometry (in Hobbes's sense) as well as (abstract) physics ; but Hobbes also dealt (I, 71) with " what effects one body moved worketh upon another."

He gave general definitions of velocity, acceleration, force (or " magnitude of motion ") and the like, as well as of their " computation," in two passages (I, 110 *sqq.* and 204 *sqq.*), and explained how they could be " exposed " in geometrical diagrams (I, 142). Here he expressed rather than advanced the new mechanical theory, and, especially with regard to " magnitude of motion," showed some of the uncertainty that accompanied the great achievements of his age. Although he held that the magnitude of the motion of a solid must be " computed in all the parts " of the solid (I, 112), and explained that " when two horses draw abreast, the motion [although not the swiftness] of both is greater than the motion of either of them singly " (I, 205), he *defined* force (I, 212) as " the impetus or quickness of motion multiplied either into itself or into the magnitude of the movent." In other words, he vacillated between v and mv, and, as Lasswitz[1] remarks, would have reached Leibniz's position had he substituted " and " for " either—or " (*i.e.* mv^2).

Some other matters should be mentioned. Firstly,

[1] *Geschicte der Atomistik*, II, 218 n.

Hobbes maintained that the beginning of motion was always propagated *in an instant*[1] to infinite distance (I, 216, cf. VII, 268), although it grew "weaker and weaker by proceeding " (I, 217). Such instantaneousness he seems to have thought self-evident (as many of his contemporaries also did), although in one (unpublished) passage (E.L. 170) he held that the *velocity* in such cases grew more sluggish.

Secondly, Hobbes loved motion so well that he could say little to the purpose about rest. He repudiated the Cartesian "inclination " (L. V, 296), and maintained that nothing but motion could resist motion (I, 125). If, however, all motion was actual local motion, and if (V, 305) "there cannot be a motion in one part of the world, but the same must also be communicated to all the rest of the world," it is not clear how rest could be more than apparent.

Thirdly, as Mr. Brandt has shown (Br. 282 *sqq.*), doubt may be cast upon Hobbes's grasp of the principle of inertia itself. He may have remained half Aristotelian. Galileo (Gal. 10) had held with Aristotle that circular motion, being "perfect," could alone be "natural." It was Cavalieri and other pupils of Galileo who analysed the principle of inertia into persistence at rest or in a straight line. When Hobbes, however, enunciated his general formula, for whatever "is moved on in the same way and with the same velocity " (I, 125), he did not interpret the "way " as necessarily a straight line, for he later argued (I, 215) that " if a moved body have direct motion, its first endeavour will be in a straight line ; if it have circular motion, its first endeavour will be in the circumference of a circle ; " and there is not sufficient evidence that he ever interpreted the principle otherwise.

The general abstract conceptions that Hobbes took most trouble to express were those of " endeavour " (*conatus*)

---

[1] Cf. Aristotle, *Physics*, VI, ch. 7.

and *impetus*. The former he defined as " motion made in less space and time than can be given, that is, less than can be assigned . . . by exposition or number ; that is motion made through the length of a point, and in an instant or point of time " (I, 206). The second, a favourite term of Galileo's, was designed to measure acceleration. Hobbes defined it, generally, as " quantity or velocity of endeavour " (I, 207) considered in the several points of the time during which an accelerated motion occurred.[1]

The doctrine of *conatus* seems to have been a resolute attempt on Hobbes's part to elucidate the transition from the mere geometry of local motion to a fundamental unit of *action*, philosophically conceived as involved in *continuous* movement, yet without implying any actual infinitesimal. Moreover, Hobbes seems to have tried to interpret his conception, not (in his usual way) in terms of vision, but in terms of volition. It was no accident that he defined *conscious* " endeavour " as the " first beginning " of voluntary motion (*e.g.* I, 408) ; and he seems to have meant that these first beginnings of appetite were something more than mere inclination. In them we caught without arresting the very act of passage. They were beginnings of *motion* and yet *almost* as nothing in comparison with any completed appetite.

These general conceptions were regarded as logical or rather as " logistical " deductions from the nature of moving bodies, and so had to be distinguished from specialised inquiries, deductive but largely guess-work, into the tides, the precession of the equinoxes, the barometer, or " circles of confusion " in optics. The fourth part of *De Corpore* dealt with special problems such as these ; but I shall confine my attention to more general issues.

Some commentators, for example Robertson (R. 114),

---

[1] It is possible that neither Galileo, Hobbes, nor Newton effectively contemplated a *genuine* continuity of acceleration.

have objected that Hobbes should not have included a chapter upon sensation and its stimuli at this stage of his discussion. The censure, however, was mistaken. According to Hobbes (*e.g.* L. V, 309) all sensations were literally motions in a man's body. He was therefore entitled to preface his account of the " salving " of particular appearances by a general explanation of the way in which these appearances themselves came about ; and although, for convenience' sake, I propose to postpone consideration of Hobbes's theory of sensation, I do not think that Hobbes here overstepped the boundaries that he himself drew in this matter, viz. that the sensations and appetites common to man and beast pertained to (animal) " physics,"[1] while the " passions and perturbations of mind " that were peculiar to men were properly the subject of a separate treatise, *De Homine*.

Having tried to explain, then, what the sensory appearances in any animal organism essentially were, Hobbes gave two other explanations of a general kind before he passed from the physical universe (or the " world ") to intersidereal and thence to sublunary fact. Both of these explanations dealt with the limits of natural knowledge, for the first concerned the magnitude, infinity, and ultimate beginning of the " world," and the second had to do with the problem of the possibility of vacuum in nature.

Regarding the first of these, Hobbes argued that the infinite magnitude and the eternity of the " world " was not a scientific question at all, but should be decided by Scripture and the established church (I, 414). (Galileo had said (Gal. 324) : " Let us reverence then the Sacred Leaves and pass on to natural and human reasons.") Rash geometers might indeed have intoxicated themselves into the contrary opinion ; but, in fact (I, 412), " whether we suppose the world to be finite or infinite, no absurdity will follow," and " the knowledge of what is infinite can never

[1] Cf. Kenelm Digby, *The Nature of Bodies* (1644), p. 242.

be attained by a finite enquirer " (I, 411). (Although Seth
Ward (*Exercitatio Epistolica*,[1] 116 *sqq*.) strongly resented
these contentions, Hobbes's position in this place, while
it may have damaged a prop in his ostensible theism, was
not unorthodox.)

The second question was equally general, because it
asked whether the entire universe must be *full*. The
Middle Ages, following Aristotle's lead, had decided, almost
without exception, in favour of plenism ; and Descartes,
who identified body and space by definition, could not, of
course, admit the existence of vacuum in any of the
traditional senses, viz. *vacua* or *vacuola disseminata* (*i.e.*
tiny nooks between the atoms), *vacua coacervata* (of greater
dimensions), and a vast inane in which, according to some,
the universe might be enclosed. On the other hand, the
revival of atomism in Hobbes's day, and just before it, had
made the existence of *vacua disseminata* a very burning
question ; and while Bacon had held (N.O. II, 48) that
although there might be vacua the arguments of
Democritus and Leucippus were certainly wrong, Gassendi
and others had revived and popularised the atomistic
theory with eloquent and elegant seriousness. Again, the
middle seventeenth century, and more especially Mersenne's
circle,[2] had been stirred by the experimental evidence of
Torricelli and Pascal ; and, later, the Royal Society in
England eagerly followed the researches of Robert Boyle.

Hobbes himself held in 1648 (A.G. XIX, 172) that there
were tiny spaces destitute of body, and asserted, during
the period of his Parisian exile (A.G. XVI, 72), that he
found " no impossibility, nor absurdity, nor so much as
an improbability in admitting vacuity" except upon
(absurd) Cartesian suppositions. In *De Corpore*, however,
and consistently after it, he became an enthusiastic plenist,
and set himself to refute both the classical arguments of

[1] =E.E.
[2] Lasswitz, *op. cit.*, II, 135.

Lucretius (I, 416 *sqq.*) and "the experiments of later writers" (I, 420). He did so (I, 414) by deduction from a common or garden experiment (with a gardener's hose), but thought another experiment (VII, 90 *sq.*) with pieces of marble would do just as well.

This reliance upon (vulgar) experiment was not without interest. Hobbes did not despise experimental investigations. On the contrary, he shared the interests of the house of Cavendish regarding telescopes (A.G. XVII, 312), noted the effect of wind upon a contrivance he had rigged up with boards (VII, 45), and was interested in the recoil of guns (I, 492). Indeed he seems to have taken a catholic pleasure in all ingenious attempts to account for particular facts, as when (VII, 136) he welcomed Descartes' suggestion that the infection of the plague was due to "little flies," and, after defending it with spirit, remarked that he " would we knew the palate of those little animals ; we might perhaps find some medicine to fright them from mingling with our breath." But he was no experimentalist, and never sufficiently pondered Galileo's question (Gal.420): " Who shall be able, unless after very *long* observations, and very *certain* relations, to frame so *expeditious histories* thereof, as that they may serve for hypotheses ? " (Italics mine.)

Except, perhaps, in his circle-squaring, Hobbes never carried his large generalisations concerning motion into great mathematical detail, and although he never claimed that his abstract definitions could explain *special* physical phenomena, he was oddly content with guess-work. All we could do in such special inquiries, he said, was to *suppose* a possible cause (I, 425), that is to say (*ibid.*), a cause that did not conflict with " the most general hypotheses of natural philosophy." He even said, regarding one of his favourite theories, that he " thought best . . . from it to derive as many of the phenomena as I could, and to let alone such as I could not deduce from thence " (I, 431).

The experimentalists, with some justification, resented Hobbes's strictures; and Boyle's *Examen* of Hobbes's views on vacuum, with special reference to "the engines at Gresham College"—Hobbes, later (VII, 19), called them "pop-guns"—is a good example of a dignified rejoinder, even granting that its design was to defend "orthodox Christian naturalists" (the Preface) as well as "Experimentarian Philosophers." *No* particular experiment, Boyle showed, could prove the plenists' case. For that, as with Descartes, a metaphysics was required (5). Again, no particular experiment, such as that of the gardener's hose, could disprove *other* experimental evidence, such as Pascal's on the Puy de Dôme (24) ; and if Hobbes believed that "air" could enter into the "engines" in ways that the experimentalists believed they had prevented, he should have produced experimental evidence for his criticism, although, in fact, "he did not pretend by any *phenomenon* to countenance his bold assertion" (33).

What could really be inferred from this particular controversy was that Hobbes and his opponents were talking about different things. Hobbes was a plenist because he postulated a "pure" air (or ether) to explain the phenomena. Boyle and the experimentarians were talking about, and were learning about, "common air" (*Examen*, 32). On the other hand, the essential justice of Boyle's criticisms shows, I think, that it would be unprofitable to examine much of Hobbian special physics in detail, and I shall conclude this discussion by mentioning (*a*) and (*b*), two of Hobbes's wider physical suppositions, and then (*c*) by giving a brief account of his views on optics.

(*a*) There was at least one important respect in which Hobbes's physical theory introduced a unity into the conception of nature that was absent from the speculative atomism on which Boyle and others (*Examen*, 49) ultimately relied. His plenism, rejecting the dualism of atoms and the void, was accompanied by a doctrine of the unity of all matter based upon its universal fluidity. Matter, he said (I, 426), was analogous, not to dust, but to water ; hardness and softness were differences of degree, not of kind (*ibid*.), and the " consistency " or cohesion of particles (together with their density and gravity) was to be inferred from their motions. While it may be true (as Leibniz, who commended this view of Hobbes's, later declared[1]) that neither Hobbes nor anyone else had intelligibly explained the " subtle motion " that such a theory presupposed, there can be no doubt that Hobbes was a leader in the various attempts made to unify the dynamics of cosmic theory.

(*b*) In all his physical arguments Hobbes preferred something like wave-motion to the migration of particles, but in his earlier writings he advocated a motion of dilation and contraction (or of systole and diastole). In *Tractatus Opticus II*, however (E.L. 172), we hear, for the first time, of the possibility of a " sieve-like " motion ; and in *De Corpore* and its successors this motion " of a basin or a sieve " (VII, 8), usually described (*e.g.* I, 448) as " simple circular motion," entirely supplanted its predecessor.

Hobbes said he had taken the notion from Copernicus (L. IV, 251), but he might also have found it in Galileo, who said (Gal. 362 *sq.*) : " As to the annual motions assigned [to the earth] by Copernicus . . . I will tell you a thing worthy of great consideration, namely . . . that naturally and without any moving cause, it agreeth to any whatsoever suspended and librated body, which if it shall be carried round in the circumference of a circle, immediate of itself it acquireth a conversion about its own centre, contrary to that which carrieth it about, and of such velocity that they both finish one revolution in the same time precisely," and illustrated by the behaviour of a ball floating freely in a basin when " you turn upon your toe." Hobbes's single-minded devotion in his later

---

[1] In a letter to Oldenburg, quoted Brockdorff, p. 160.

years to this hypothesis, and his attempt to unite sidereal and sublunary motions by its means, may have deserved Wallis's gibe about " vertigo Hobbiana " (H.H. 157) or Ward's " Euge Thoma! " (E.E. 148) and his references to a philosophers' stone, or to a catholicon for mechanics and perpetual motion (*ibid*. 156). But Hobbes's enthusiasm was not entirely senile.[1]

(c) While Hobbes employed this catholicon in his astronomy, in his account of " fermentation " (I, 449), and indeed everywhere, he came upon it in connection with optics.

Hobbes tended to treat most phenomena in visual terms, and the work of Kepler and Descartes, in the age of the invention of telescopes, spurred him on to deal with problems of vision. Indeed, it seems clear that he regarded optics as pre-eminently the forge in which his natural philosophy was fashioned. In any case, he was very confident indeed about the importance of his optical discoveries. He was, he said (VII, 468 *sqq*.), the first to make the science solid, incontestable, and perspicuous, as well as to free it from the rubbish collected by others (*e.g.* (*ibid*.) " millions of strings in the optic nerve[2] . . . and other innumerable such trash ").

Even a reader who thinks highly (as he should) of Hobbes's optical treatises can hardly take Hobbes at his own rating, in view of the extent and excellence of the work on optics done in Hobbes's time. It should be remembered, however, that, according to Hobbes, all emanation or corpuscular theories of light were tainted

---

[1] The sieve-like motion of a δίνη was not a new idea. See A. E. Taylor (*Commentary on the Timæus*, p. 355), who refers to Democritus and Leucippus. The circular movement (*op. cit.*, p. 423) of περίωσις or ἀντιπερίστασις was commonly held, in ancient times, to be the only movement possible in a plenum. It is probable that Hobbes's conversion to plenism had some connection with the attractions of his new darling hypothesis. It should also be noted (*op. cit.*, p. 558) that such circular motion in a plenum was held in the ancient theories to be instantaneous.

[2] Apparently a reference to Descartes' *Dioptrique*, III.

with the same vice as the scholastic theory of " species " (*e.g.* E.L. 171). A great part of Hobbes's high opinion of his own theories, moreover, may have been due to his pride in the comprehensiveness of his results. He gave, as he believed, a tenable account of optical stimulation, and showed its conformity with an adequate theory of the nature of visual sensation itself. In the optical part of *De Homine* his appeal to physiological phenomena, such as illusions (L. II, 17) and positive after-images (L. II, 28), combined with the range of the rest of his argument (concerning the angle of vision, optical instruments and the like) may even have justified him in saying (VII, 471) that he took *experience*, widely interpreted, as his chief witness.

(5) BIOLOGY

If we compare Hobbes's philosophy of nature with such works as Telesio's *De Rerum Natura* or Gassendi's *Syntagma Philosophicum*, and if we compare his psychology with the treatises *De Anima* of Aristotle, Melanchthon, and Suarez, we notice that, while these authors made an elaborate biological transition from inanimate objects to the mind of man, Hobbes passed very abruptly indeed from physics to introspection. He had much to say, it is true, about sensation as a physical motion, and he paid vague deference to cerebral physiology, but he had very little indeed to say about biology in general. This may seem strange on the part of a man who held that the " soul " was just " life " (L. III, 522), and that when a man thought, an *animal* thought (L. III, 526).

Some may think that Hobbes simply regarded a living being as a natural automaton (III, ix), and accepted Harvey's discoveries concerning the motion of the blood and the generation of living creatures (I, viii and VII, 338) as the final demonstration of the mechanical theory of life. Certainly Hobbes was an enthusiastic Harveian. " Vital motion," he said, " is the motion of the blood, perpetually circulating (as has been shown by many infallible signs and marks by Doctor Harvey, the first observer of it) in the veins and arteries " (I, 407, cf. L. II, 3). I think, however, that the principal reason why Hobbes said so little about biology was that he never had time to study the subject. He " left the matter to others " (L. II, 6), and at the end of his life he remarked regarding the generation of animals : " How should I know that never had so much leisure as to make any observation which might conduce to that ? " (VII, 158).

Since Hobbes held that the *matter* of the fœtus was contributed entirely by the female, while the " prolific humor " of both parents " formed " it into the human species, it seems clear that his notions in this affair were scholastic ; and although he was certainly a mechanist in all his philosophy, there are two curious passages that deserve a passing mention. The first states that philosophers " would themselves be without a mind if they thought that the machinery (*machinæ*) of generation and of nutrition could have been established and ordered for its functions except by some kind of mind " (L. II, 6). The second states (perhaps without reference to man) that although God gave earth the virtue of bringing forth living creatures (at least when it was soft), it was " no harm " to think that God " worketh still " (*i.e.* after the Creation), because, among other reasons, " It is very hard to believe, that to produce male and female, and all that belongs thereto, as also the several and curious organs of sense and memory, could be the work of anything that had not understanding " (VII, 175 *sqq*.).

Hobbes did not believe (*ibid.*) that all present-day species had been represented in the Ark, but he professed his allegiance to the Mosaic story generally (L. II, 2), after giving some account of the more liberal speculations of Diodorus Siculus. He also briefly examined certain prior conditions of the circulation of the blood. The blood itself, he said, was moved by the air which moved the heart like any other muscle (L. II, 4). But not by " pure air." Certain invisible corpuscles in the air, as of salt or nitre, which were a cause of fermentation according to his beloved hypothesis of simple circular motion, were here the cause. Similarly, disease or death was due to aerial corpuscles which obstructed the motion of the blood (*ibid.*). And Hobbes (L. II, 2 *sq.*) gave a sketchy exposition of the nutrition of the blood, of its capacity for forming flesh, and of its alliance with the nerves.

IV

PHENOMENALISM

(1) SENSE

In the previous chapter I have maintained that Hobbes, although he was sometimes a realist and frequently a naïve rationalist in his philosophising, was fundamentally a materialist, since he maintained that nothing existed except body, and that all mutations in bodies were motions. I have now to describe what I shall call his phenomenalism, and should first explain what I mean by that word.

" Phenomenalism," I think, is variously interpreted by modern philosophers, but seems to me to mean, most precisely, the theory that phenomena *are* reality ; with the consequence that phenomenal appearances are neither a screen that real things project, nor in their essence symbols for things, nor the mere surface as opposed to the depth of things. In this sense a phenomenalist insists that if only we trace phenomena with sufficient persistence we shall describe all that there is to describe, and that there is no occasion even to dream of anything else.

Even so, however, there may be much argument concerning what really appears, as opposed to what is said to appear but does not ; and the pure phenomenalism I have attempted to describe frequently maintains that sensory phenomena are either the only genuine phenomena, or else that they are the beginning and end of reality, although there is a middle region in which certain derivatives from the senses, namely, images, play a part. Such a doctrine I should call " sensory phenomenalism."

Since Hobbes was a materialist, he firmly believed that our senses might represent, and frequently did represent, *matter* that need not be sensed. In a larger sense of the term, however, a very pronounced vein of phenomenalism pervaded his philosophy. " If the appearances," he said (I, 389), " be the principles by which we know all other things, we must needs acknowledge sense to be the principle by which we know those principles,[1] and that all the knowledge we have is derived from it."

Since I cannot perceive any direct contradiction between the propositions (*a*) that all *knowledge*, and indeed all thought, is (evidentially) derived from sense, and (*b*) that sense itself, and indeed all thought, *is* a material motion among other motions which may be (causally) derived from motions that are not sense or thought, I am not disposed to accept the criticism that Hobbes's " phenomenalism " was directly contradictory to his materialism. He held that the material motion called thought took its place among other material motions. I do not say he succeeded, but I suggest that it was not unreasonable for him to *try*.

Hobbes regarded himself as *the* specialist of his age in the theory of sensation. When he began to study natural philosophy seriously in Paris, he said (L. I, xiv) his first object was to examine what motion it could be that brought about sense, intellect, fancy, and other such animal properties. Again, on an occasion when he was in the company of the learned (L. I, xx *sq*.), one of them remarked, half-contemptuously : " What *is* sensation ? " and Hobbes found to his amazement that none of these learned Parisians dared, or deigned, to reply. Thenceforward, he said, he gave his mind to the problem, and evolved the view that because sensation was a *change* of motion, the causes of everything must be sought in diversity of motions. This was the theme of his preface to Mersenne's *Ballistica*.

[1] Cf. Bacon, N.O. II, 38.

In the opening chapter of the *Leviathan* Hobbes stated very dogmatically (1) that sense was the " original " of all our thoughts ; (2) that sense and its derivatives were *representations* ; (3) that these representations were appearances (or fancies or phantasms) *in us* which nevertheless were (4) representations *of* some motion in bodies *outside* us, these external bodies being (5) the causes of the phantasms that resulted from diverse pressure upon the sense-organs and the nerves, yet (6) appeared to be external to us because the counter-pressure inside us " seemeth to be some matter without."

The chapter ended with a polemic against the scholastic theory of " species " taught in the " universities " (and formerly accepted by Hobbes himself in the *Short Tract*). A visible species, the converted Hobbes now said, was only an " aspect " or a " being seen," and it was absurd to say that an " *intelligible being seen,* coming into the understanding, makes us understand." Historically speaking, the criticism was important, for even if the scholastic theory could be interpreted in ways much less crude, it led to easy acquiescence in explanations that did not explain, and, unlike Hobbes's single canon of " motion," was barren of deductive progeny. On the other hand, the reasonableness of Hobbes's revolt from the academic jargon of " species " did not explain the gaps in Hobbes's own complicated theory.

If we *know* that a phantasm in ourselves is caused by, and represents, an object that is not a phantasm—and Hobbes said (VII, 81) that a physical body was " any thing that hath a being in itself *without the help of sense* "—our thoughts must be capable of transcending such phantasms. If what is given in sense is given *as a representation*, it is something more than a phantasm in any ordinary sense. And much argument was necessary in order to show that, if sense were representative, either initially or at some later stage of its history, it represented its physical cause. The roaring in our ears may be due to ocean waves or to the telegram that preceded a fainting-fit. If it " represents " the sea, does it also " represent " the telegram ?

It must be conceded, I think, that Hobbes's theory was pitted unobtrusively with concealed traps. When he contrasted " mathematical " with " dogmatical " treatment he forgot that there could be such a thing as scientific dogmatism ; and his treatment of sense was a good illustration. Still, it was not a perfect illustration ; for Hobbes, as we shall see, was aware, despite his profession of confidence, that the matter needed delicate handling. Let us, however, pursue his argument.

Despite his phenomenalism, Hobbes was a convinced realist. " Knowledge," he said (IV, 246), " depends on the existence of the things known, and not they on it."[1] This being presumed, he held " that in all the senses the object is the agent ; and that it is, when we hear a preacher, the preacher that we hear ; and that his voice is the same thing with the hearing and a fancy in the hearer, though the motion of the lips and other organs of speech be his that speaketh " (V, 312). This (*ibid.*), he admitted, was a great paradox, and may have been less realistic than another of his statements, viz. " The subject of sense is the *sentient* itself, namely, some living creature ; and we speak more correctly when we say a living creature seeth than when we say the eye seeth. The object is the thing received ; and it is more accurately said that we see the sun than that we see the light " (I, 391, cf. IV, 4 and 8).

Hobbes had little to say about the physiology of sense perception. " The minute and distinct anatomy of the powers of the body," he said in 1640 (IV, 2), was irrelevant to his psychological purposes, and in *De Corpore*, where it *was* relevant, he was content to use vague language, as

[1] Cf. Aristotle, *Met.* 1051 b 7. " It is not because we think truly that you are white that you *are* white; but, because you are white, we who say this have the truth."

when he said (I, 397) that the " fountain " of the animal
spirits was " the cavity either of the brain or of the heart."
His general conception agreed roughly with the modern
doctrine of the sensori-motor arc. The stimulus (*e.g.* of
light) instantaneously propagated by the passage of the
animal spirits through the nerves (I, 403) involved an
equally instantaneous reaction, both sensory and motor
(since motion once begun could not stop). In 1644 (L. V,
309 *sq.*, cf. E.L. 174) Hobbes had convinced himself, with
Aristotle and against Galen, that the heart was the centre
of the sensori-motor system, perhaps because Harvey had
said (*De Motu Cordis*, ch. xvi) that the heart " was made
the first consistent and seems to have in it life, motition,
and sense, before any thing of the rest of the body be
perfected." At an earlier date, however (IV, 7), Hobbes
had believed with Galen that sensation was only a reaction
of the brain, and he seems always to have held that the
special senses had their seat in the brain, although the
" common sensibles " and pleasure-pain (I, 406) pertained
to the heart.[1]

Again, Hobbes emphasised the continuity of the nervous
system. The *pia mater*, he said, was continued, by ramifica-
tion, into nerves and sense organs, and (I, 403) " the
beginning of the medulla spinalis [*i.e.* the spinal cord]
within the scull " was the place where " all the nerves
which are within the head have their roots." Here the
Hobbian theory, in respect of continuity, may be compared with Galen's statement, according to Gassendi
(II, 291), that brain and all nerves were continuous, and
that sensation, like Hobbes's " reaction," was due to
resistance in the brain. Again, the *pia mater* received
what would now be considered undue prominence in the

[1] The latter doctrine was also Harvey's (*ibid.*, ch. xv), and it may be
noted that Melanchthon (*De Anima*, ed. 1540, p. 149) had said that the
" vital spirit " was a " flammula " in the heart, while the " animal
spirits " were refined emanations from this tiny flame, made more lucid
and apter for sensation by the action of the brain.

works of Melanchthon (*De An.* 113 *sq.*) and of Harvey (*op. cit.*, ch. xii) ; but the modern discovery that its functions are chiefly vascular would not affect the ancient doctrine of the " animal spirits," since these themselves were ambiguities of air and blood.

A sufficient number of explicit passages attests that in Hobbes's view mental experiences, *i.e.* phantasms and appetites, were literally internal motions. Thus he said that " conceptions and apparitions are nothing really but motion in some internal substance of the head " (IV, 31, cf. L. V, 258 and 309 *sq.*). His phrasing, it is true (*e.g.* L. V, 310), may sometimes prompt the question whether the motion that was a phantasm merely arose from, or actually *was*, a nervous reaction.[1] In either case, however, the phantasms were held to be physical motions within the sentient's body, although, in all probability, Hobbes frequently thought of them in the same way as Locke thought of " ideas of sense," that is to say, as something generated inside us (I, 389 *sq.*) and appearing external.

Hobbes, of course, regarded phantasms as *mental*, although not as incorporeal. Indeed (IV, 2) he distinguished bodily from mental powers, although not according to the principles professed by school-divines. He believed that knowledge and understanding *were* knowledge and understanding not the less because they were " nothing else but a tumult of the mind raised by external things that press the organical parts of man's body " (III, 352). Moreover, to use modern terms, Hobbes was an introspectionist, not a behaviourist, and so interpreted the maxim, " Know thyself " (IV, 26).

As we have seen, a fundamental step in the new mechanical theory of motion was the alleged discovery that the " secondary " qualities of body, such as heat, sound, or

---

[1] Here it should be remembered that most scholastics held that phantasms were quasi-corporeal—" quid materiale," as Suarez held (*De An.* III, i).

colour, were subjective (*i.e.* mere states of the percipient), and that bodies themselves possessed only the spatio-temporal-dynamical qualities (if they *were* " qualities ") that could be treated by geometry and mechanics. Omitting the question of Hobbes's originality in this matter (since it has been considered earlier—see pp. 7 and 50), we may briefly examine the growth of his opinions about it.

In the *Short Tract*, Hobbes (who then accepted the emission theory of " species ") argued that light, colour, and heat were " the action of external things upon the animal spirits," that they were mere " powers " of such agents "when they were not actually perceived " (E.L. 163), and that " phantasms " (which here meant images as opposed to percepts) were an action of the brain upon the " spirits." The act of sense (164) was " an accident belonging to the agent that useth sense," and was neither an " inherent " (permanent ?) quality of the sentient nor the " bare " presence of the agent (since sensations were intermittent, not permanent, and since there might be stimulation without sensation). " Hence it appears that sense is a passive power of the animal spirits, to be moved by the species of an external object supposed to be present " (165).

From this, so far as I can see, it should not have been inferred that light, colour, " and other proper objects of sense " did *not* qualify objects when they *were* perceived. By 1640, however (and probably much earlier, as we saw), Hobbes was convinced (IV, 7) that " colour is not inherent in the object, but an effect thereof upon us," and similarly (IV, 8) regarding sound, smell, etc. His arguments were of a type now familiar. A man might see double when there was but one physical object. Heat was " manifestly in *us* " (*ibid.*) since it was " our pleasure or pain . . . but in the fire there is no such thing." Or, to quote his last statement of the argument (VII, 117 *sq.*), in a dialogue :

" *A*. It is a fine day, and pleasant walking through the

fields, but that the sun is a little too hot. *B*. How do you know that the sun is hot ? *A*. I feel it. *B*. That is to say you know that yourself but not that the sun is hot. But when you feel yourself hot, what body do you feel ? *A*. None. *B*. How then can you infer your heat from the sense of feeling ? Your walking may have made you hot ; is motion therefore hot ? No. You are to consider the concomitants of your heat ; as, that you are more faint, or more ruddy, or that you sweat, or feel some endeavour of moisture or spirits tending outward ; and when you have found the causes of those accidents, you have found the causes of heat, which in a living creature, and especially in a man, is many times the motion of the parts within him, such as happen in sickness, anger, and other passions of the mind ; which are not in the sun nor in fire."

Since double images are double in shape as well as in colour, it is plain, as Berkeley saw (*e.g. Principles*, § 10), that these arguments should apply to primary as well as to secondary qualities ; and some of Hobbes's critics saw it too, for example, Charles Gildon in *The Deist's Manual* (1705), who wrote (p. 101) : " A blow on the eye presents the image of fire or light where really there is none. . . . He [Hobbes] might have advanced some other paradoxes on this bottom, as surprising as this, by arguing from the different appearances of things in regard to their situation to the eye, as when they are placed too far off or too near, he might have concluded that there was no such thing as round or square, because the eye, viewing a square tower at too great a distance, that is, beyond the power of the eye to judge truly, it seems round, and that round and square are only the different pulsations of the object on them. Many more learned and nice conclusions of this nature might be drawn to confirm what he seems to aim at—a general scepticism." What is more, Hobbes himself sometimes saw the point, for he wrote (E.L. 179) : " Since the whole image or phantasm is a motion in the internal parts of the beholder, and it is agreed that size no less than colour constitutes the image, it necessarily follows that the magnitude or visually conceived space is of the stuff of fancy, and in reality is but motion in the beholder, that is to say, an accident of him and not of the object."

Apart from this statement, Hobbes's account of *space*, by which he meant empty space or a fixed order of externality, is a puzzle to all his commentators, since his official definition of it in *De Corpore* (I, 94) was "the *phantasm* of a thing existing without the mind *simply*," where the phrase, "without the mind" was an inexact way of describing the idea of externality. In our earlier discussion we examined Hobbes's account of the "real space" or *magnitude* presupposed in his materialism, and indeed, in the very definition of "body," but it seems necessary, now (although it is something of a parenthesis), to examine the account of *space* in *De Corpore*.

Hobbes argued that "space" was a phantasm on the following grounds:[1] (1) A man could imagine the world annihilated. In that case (he himself still existing) he would remember and imagine magnitudes, motions, and colours, or, in other words, retain ideas of space with which he could calculate. Indeed, most scientific calculations were made phantasmally, "sitting still in our closets or in the dark" (I, 92). (2) What all men called (empty) space was an imaginary theatre. For it was an order of position. Bodies had always the same definitive magnitude; but they altered their place (*i.e.* their relative position in three dimensions (I, 106)). Since bodies "did not carry their places away with them" (I, 93), we had to distinguish between the fixed order of externality and actual extended bodies. Indeed Hobbes said (I, 105) that

---

[1] He was anxious, incidentally, to criticise Aristotle and Descartes, I, 93.

" place is nothing out of the mind, nor magnitude any thing within it." (3) " Space in general," the subject of the whole debate, must be an idea or phantasm since " nothing is general or universal besides names or signs " (I, 106).

It seems difficult to avoid the conclusion that these arguments present a medley of relevant and sometimes of profound insight, rather than a connected whole. But let us examine them one by one.

(1) This argument certainly proved that " space "—an affair of reason rather than of sense—was commonly reckoned by the currency of ideas. It certainly did not prove, and was not intended to suggest, what idealistic commentators might now be disposed to read into it, viz. that externality was a mere appearance, as on Berkeley's theory. Indeed, according to Hobbes (I, 107)—very possibly inconsistently—" space " (or *feigned* extension) might be *possessed* by a body having magnitude (or " true extension "). And the experiment of feigning annihilation, when compared, say, with Descartes' philosophical doubt, was curiously hesitating, since it presupposed that the memory of real bodies " before their annihilation " (I, 92) was retained.

(2) Much in this second argument may be regarded as an anticipation of a radical distinction between " conceptual " space and perceived contours, or even between a " pure form of intuition " and perceptible things. Much, again, was the attempt of Hobbes, the plenist, to hold that, although there could be no vacuum, it was possible to geometrise without " considering " any properties other than those of an alleged " empty " space. Hobbes himself, however, used language that scarcely marched with such distinctions, as we saw with regard to the first argument. When he said that all space was full (*e.g.* I, 415) he was not, strictly, referring to any " phantasm," although he may have meant that all abstract geometrical relation-

ships had meaning only in their application to the plenum
that was the universe.

(3) As we have seen, and shall see again, Hobbes's
account of universality and of abstraction was either flatly
inconsistent or unequal to the strain his philosophy
required of them. In any case, Hobbes's theory of the
" phantasmal " character of spatial conceptions and com-
putations was not intended to suggest that there was
anything subjective about the orderly externality of real
bodies.

In a similar way, Hobbes said (I, 95) that the complete
definition of *time* was " the phantasm of before and after
in motion." This definition appears to be circular (since
measurable motion implies before and after) ; but, certainly, it was not intended to suggest that either motion
or succession had only a feigned existence. In an alternative statement (*ibid.*) Hobbes affirmed, following Aristotle,[1]
that *time* was " the *number* of motion according to former
and latter "; and he fully accepted the conventional
character of such conceptual measures of time as days,
months, and years (I, 94). Further, in various passages, he
admitted a certain subjectivity regarding the future (I, 17,
and IV, 16), and he declared in the *Leviathan* (III, 15) that
" the present only has a being in nature ; things past have
a being in the memory only, but things to come have no
being at all, the future being but a fiction of the mind."
Hobbes seems, however, to have repented in this matter,
for he said of those who held such views (I, 94) : " they
say that, which they do not mean, that there neither is,
nor has been, nor shall be, any time ; for of whatsoever it
may be said, *it has been* or *it shall be*, of the same also it
might have been said heretofore, or may be said hereafter,
it is."

This parenthesis regarding space and time brings us back
to our earlier question regarding the representative char-

---

[1] *Physics, IV.* ch 16.

acter of sensory phantasms. Hobbes's statement that, because sense was a reaction " it doth always appear as something situate without the organ " (I, 391), was obviously loose, since the same reasoning would show that such a reaction as a knee-jerk appeared *not* to be in the knee. Again, he neglected the significance of the little word " of " in the phrase " representative of " something. " The said image or colour," he remarked (IV, 4), " is but an apparition made unto us *of* the motion, agitation or alteration which the object worketh in the brain or spirits." But why should knowledge of the apparition involve knowledge of its cause ?

Again, commenting upon Descartes (L. V, 251), Hobbes argued that it had been known from very ancient times that there was no infallible criterion for distinguishing dreams from waking ; therefore that waking sensations might be delusive ; therefore that " if we followed our senses without ratiocination, we should properly doubt whether any physical thing existed or not." But how, precisely, did we avoid the doubt *with* ratiocination ? According to Hobbes : " Whatsoever accidents or qualities our senses make us think there be in the world, they be *not* there, but are seemings and apparitions only ; the things that really *are* in the world without us are those motions by which these seemings are caused. And this is the great deception of sense, which also is to be *by sense corrected* ; for as sense telleth me, when I see directly, that the colour seemeth to be in the object, so also sense telleth me, when I see by reflection, that colour is not in the object " (IV, 8 *sq.*). But, again, how could reflection (*i.e.* reason) tell us what *was* in the object ? All that Hobbes could say was that we must compare our phantasm with a *definition*. " If it agree with the properties of matter or body, then it is a body " (I, 75).

The most celebrated passage in Hobbes which suggests something like the great idealistic problem of British philosophy ran as follows (I, 389, cf. L. I, 316) : " Of all the phenomena or appearances which are near us [*prope nos*] the most admirable [*admirabilissimum*] is apparition itself τὸ φαίνεσθαι ; namely, that some natural bodies have in themselves the patterns almost of all things, and others of none at all. So that if the appearances be the principles by which we know all other things, we must needs acknowledge sense to be the principle by which we know those principles, and that the knowledge we have is derived from it. And as for the causes of sense, we cannot begin our search for them from any other phenomenon than that of sense itself."

So far as I can see, however, there were two main thoughts in this passage, namely : (1) that it was very wonderful that some natural bodies (*i.e.* animals) should have sensations at all when others were insentient, with the corollary (I, 393) that sense must be a very special sort of reaction since it contained so many " patterns " ; and (2) that all natural inquiry must start from sensation. There is no evidence that Hobbes thought this " wonderful " thing a *problem* for the theory of knowledge, or that it so much as occurred to him that if we set out from sense we might have great theoretical difficulty in getting back from it to causes that were not sense.

Hobbes had a good deal to say about minor points of some importance. He believed that we could discern nothing by sense unless there were " perpetual *variety* of phantasms," for he held that, " whatsoever others might say," it was " almost all one for a man to be always sensible of one and the same thing, and not to be sensible at all of any thing " (I, 394). In proof of this he mentioned the circumstance that we do not commonly feel our bones, although they " are always and on all sides touched by a most sensible membrane " (*ibid.*). Similarly, he affirmed that, if a single colour or figure were perpetually present to us, we should never notice it.

Again, he held that at any given time we compounded the relevant motions and perceived " but one varied object and not variety of objects " (I, 395), and also combined a doctrine of sub- or un-consciousness with a doctrine of the threshold of sensation. Sensation, he said, occurred only when an " endeavour of the organ outwards " was " by vehemence [1] made stronger and more predominant than the rest, which deprives us of the sense of other phantasms no otherwise than the sun deprives the rest of the stars of light, not by hindering their action, but by obscuring and hiding them with his excess of brightness " (I, 396). All stimuli *might* be sensed, but the predominant one was " contumacious," and, in the later Herbartian language, kept the others below the threshold. Hobbes's illustration that " in reading we see the letters successively one by one, though the whole page be presented to our eye " (I, 395), has not, it is true, been entirely confirmed by later experiment, and the Herbartian subconscious seems to have been replaced by a more exciting monster from Vienna. Nevertheless, Hobbes had a prophetic soul.

With the exception of some of his discussions on optics Hobbes's account of the special senses (I, 445–508) was of smaller account. Colour was " troubled light " (I, 459), sound due to a " stroke," [2] and not, like light, to pressure (I, 486), smell was *not* caused by effluvium of atoms (I, 504), and taste was so various that to make guesses about it " would be to revolt from philosophy to divination " (I, 507). In view of his fondness for prick-song, and of his intimacy with Mersenne, the author of *L'Harmonie Universelle*, Hobbes had surprisingly little to say about music, harmony, and musical instruments ; but he did say something (I, 499 *sqq.* ; IV, 35 *sq.*).

---

[1] Cf. Gassendi, II, 355 : " We attend to the motion that is more vehement than any other."

[2] Cf. Aristotle, *De An.* II, 419 b.

(2) MEMORY

Accepting the view that sensation dealt with what was *present* (I, 396), Hobbes anticipated the modern doctrine of the "specious present." Many things, he said, "are not perceived but by the flux of a point, that is to say, we have no sense of them without time ; and we can have no sense of time without memory "[1] (I, 508). Indeed, he regarded the sense organs as organs of retention, and proposed to distinguish sense from *mere* reaction on that ground (I, 395).

Memory, moreover, was a sort of knowing that one knew. " By what sense shall we take notice of sense ? I answer, by sense itself, namely, by the memory which for some time remains in us of things sensible, though they themselves pass away. For he that perceives that he hath perceived remembers " (I, 389). Again (I, 393) : " By sense we commonly understand the judgment we make of objects by their phantasms ; namely, by comparing and distinguishing these phantasms ; which we could never do if that motion in the organ, by which the phantasm is made, did not remain there for some time, and make

---

[1] Mr. Stocks (*Aristotelianism*, p. 139) says that Hobbes's "more psychological discussions are packed with phrases borrowed without acknowledgment from the *De Anima* and the *Parva Naturalia*," and he has been kind enough to give me references in several places and to refer me to J. Freudenthal's "Ueber den Begriff des Wortes φαντασία bei Aristoteles," 1863.

Most of the passages cited by Freudenthal from the *Parva Naturalia* (usually from *De Somno* or from *De Somniis*) seem to me to show only a vague agreement and to be quite devoid of Hobbes's incisiveness.

In Aristotle's *Rhetoric* (I, xi) φαντασία (imagination) was called "a kind of weak sensation." In *De An.* III, iii, 429 a 1, it was described as "a motion started by actual sensation."

For the question "By what sense, etc.," see *De An.* III, 2, 425 b 11, and cf. Campanella (*Met.* I, iv) ; Herbert of Cherbury, *De Causis Errarum*, 3rd ed. p. 15, "the first condition for the truth of an appearance is that it should linger " ; also two authors mentioned by Bacon (E.S. I, 606), viz. Telesio (*De Rerum Nat.* V, ii, 8, 15), who held that spirit was " commemoratio," and Fracastoro (*Turrius*, 169 D), who argued that a fundamental retentiveness underlay "memory."

the same phantasm return. Wherefore sense, as I here understand it, hath necessarily some memory adhering to it." But a " common organ of sense " was not required for such judgments (I, 399).

Furtner, " memory or decaying sense " referred to the *past*. The thing itself (III, 5 *sq.*) was *imagination* . . . " but when we would express the decay, and signify that the sense is fading, old and past, it is called memory." And Hobbes had a theory of temporal perspective, for he held that the apparent distance of the past depended on its growing vagueness (III, 5 ; I, 398 *sq.*) : " A man that is present in a foreign city, seeth not only whole streets, but . . . particular houses. . . . In process of time the image of the city returneth, but as a mass of building only, which is almost to have forgotten it. Why may not we well think *remembrance*[1] to be nothing else but the missing of parts. . . . To see at a great distance of place, and to remember at a great distance of time, is to have like conceptions of the thing ; for there wanteth distinction of parts in both ; the one conception being weak by operation at distance, the other by decay " (IV, 12 *sq.*).

Hobbes also said that remembrance was " as it were a re-conning " (III, 14) ; and sometimes (IV, 27 ; II, 304) that knowledge was memory.

(3) IMAGINATION

In one passage (III, 3) Hobbes spoke of sensation as " original fancy "—using " fancy " (I, 398) as equivalent to " imagination "—and he regarded conception and understanding as a variety of fancy (*e.g.* III, 11). For the most part, however, " fancy " was " decaying sense " without retrospective reference (I, 398), although Hobbes, like the ancients, also included (III, 96) under the term " reflections on water " or the " ghosts," " imagines,"

---

[1] *i.e.*, more accurately, obliviscence.

and " umbræ " on a looking-glass ; and these were not decaying sense.

Imagination, he said, was due to the persistence of all physical motion (III, 4), although he never proved that there must be such persistence in the brain or heart. The " decay " of sense, in his opinion, was due, not to any inherent tendency to languish, but to the competitive interference of later impressions, which left the former ones sub-conscious[1] (III, 5). What are now called " after-images " he regarded as an anomaly that " had no particular name " (III, 6), instancing the tired geometer, who " in the dark, though awake, had the images of lines and angles before his eyes " (*ibid.*).

Hobbes thought that the " silence of sense " (III, 7) when we were " benumbed in sleep " (cf. I, 396 ; IV, 9) supported his theory, and he investigated dreaming with his usual active curiosity. Dream and waking, he held, were usually distinguishable, unless, indeed, a man were nodding fitfully in his chair (III, 8). In dreams there was " commonly no coherence " (IV, 11), and when there was partial coherence, " our thoughts appear like the stars between the flying clouds . . . as the uncertain flight of broken clouds permits " (*ibid.*). Again, waking, we perceived .the absurdity of dreams, although, sleeping, we did not perceive the absurdity of waking life (III, 7). A dreamer might doubt whether he were dreaming or no (IV, 13), but could not know he was dreaming because his dream-apparitions, because of their clearness, seemed always to be present (IV, 14). (One wonders how Hobbes *knew* dreams were always so clear.) Hobbes further observed that the cause of dreams reversed the causal order of waking life. In waking life the sight of some terrible thing caused fear and chilled us. In dreams the chill aroused the fear, and the fear some terrifying phantasm (III, 8 ; IV, 10).

[1] Cf. Aristotle, *De Somniis*, 461 a.

(4) TRAINS OF IMAGINATION

Hobbes distinguished between " simple " and " compounded imagination " (III, 6)—compounded as a golden mountain—but very perfunctorily, and busied himself chiefly with imaginative reproduction. This he traced sketchily to physiology. " In the motion of any continued body, one part follows another by cohesion " (I, 398). Trains of fancy were relics of sensory *transition* and succession, since (III, 11) " those motions that immediately succeed one another in the sense, continue also together after sense . . . in such manner as water upon a plane table is drawn which way any one part of it is guided by the finger."

Hobbes saw very clearly that such associations[1] (to use a later term that was not his) might become a strange jumble, as when there were too many parentheses (IV, 56) or in the chance sequence (IV, 15) : Andrew, Peter, stone, foundation, church, people, tumult. " There is no certainty what we shall imagine next ; only this is certain, it shall be something that succeeded the same before, at one time or another " (III, 12, cf. I, 398).

Nevertheless (III, 12), even in an apparently " wild ranging " of the mind, there might be genuine " dependance of one thought upon another." The malicious questioner

---

[1] Sir W. Hamilton, in his edition of Reid (pp. 890 and 898), denied the assertion of Mackintosh and many others that Hobbes should be regarded as the founder of the great Association Theory. Hobbes, he said, was " essentially an eclectic " and in this matter was " simply a silent follower of the Stagirite " (see *De Memoria*, ch. ii). He further stated that Bérigard, Kenelm Digby, and Thomas White described association in 1643 (*Circulus Pisanus*, VI, 19), 1644 (*Treatise of Bodies*, 33, § 3), and 1647 (*Inst. Perpat.* II, 20, § 6) respectively, these dates being prior to the publication of the *Leviathan* or of the *Human Nature*. The *Human Nature*, however, was circulated in manuscript in 1640, and its account of association (IV, 14 *sqq.*) was one of Hobbes's clearest. The perfectly true statements, therefore, that Digby and White knew Hobbes very well, and that Bérigard, by a reference to *De Cive*, went out of his way to express personal friendship and regard for Hobbes, certainly do not tell against Hobbes's priority.

who, when the Civil War was mentioned, inquired about
the value of a Roman penny " in a moment of time, for
thought is quick,"[1] had the King's betrayal in his mind
and Iscariot's pieces of silver.

Accordingly Hobbes went about to explain mental
" discursion "—a more accurate term, he thought (IV, 14),
than " discourse "—but without assuming the alleged
" psychical atomism " of the later associationist theory.
He believed that " decaying sense " was *somehow* old, not
that it was composed of unmodifiable " atoms " ; he
thought, not of atoms, but of short transitions ; and his
account of the affair was at least semi-logical.

One of his favourite names for the process was the
" ranging of the mind." This might, but need not, be
" wild " (*i.e.* illogical), and was generally half-directed
like " hounds casting about at a fault in hunting, and the
ranging of spaniels " (IV, 15). Indeed, Hobbes's principal
aim was to examine the *regulated* or *guided* type of discursion (III, 13).

Discursion of the regulated kind was " design " based
upon " desire " (III, 13 ; IV, 15 *sq.*), but although fear
or desire decreed the end (cf. Bacon, E.S. III, 10), the
means had to be discovered by a logical or quasi-logical
search, having two kinds (III, 13 *sq.*), " one when of an
effect imagined we seek the causes, or means that produce
it ; and this is common to man and beast. The other is,
when imagining any thing whatsoever, we seek all the
possible effects, that can by it be produced ; that is to
say, we imagine what we can do with it, when we have it.
Of which I have not at any time seen any sign, but in
man only. . . . In sum, the discourse of the mind when it is
governed by design, is nothing but *seeking*, or the faculty
of invention, which the Latins called *sagacitas* and *solertia* ;
a hunting out of the causes of some effect, present or past ;
or of the effects of some present or past cause."

[1] A remark of Thales, according to Diogenes Laertius (q. Gas. II, 347).

In another passage Hobbes described regulated discursion of the second type as " experiment " and added
with Aristotle[1] that " experience " was " to have had
many experiments " (IV, 16). In the main, however, his
considered view of these matters was that " causes "
belonged to *science* and that " prudence "[2] or " experience " were makeshift expectations that animals and " men
that know not what it is that we call *causing*, that is,
almost all men " (III, 97), had to live by. Indeed, he gave
(*ibid.*) a brilliant short exposition of the custom-bred, unscientific horse-sense that Hume, in the next century,
described as the proper meaning of causality.

There was, however, a certain difference between experience and prudence. Men contented with daily experience,
Hobbes said (I, 2), were commonly " of sounder judgment "
than those who fed upon opinions, and such experience
(I, 1) was part of the " natural reason . . . that every man
brought into the world with him." Indeed, Hobbes once
said (IV, 27) that " all knowledge was experience " ; but
for the most part he interpreted experience much more
narrowly. It was " nothing but memory " (I, 3). It was
" much memory "[3] (III, 6, 664). It was " store of
phantasms arising from the sense of very many things "
(I, 398). And it was always personal. " Experience and
matter of fact are not verified by other men's arguments,
but by every man's own sense and memory " (IV, 276).

Prudence, on the other hand, was the use of experience
for guidance in the future. Being " expectation of such
things as we have already had experience of," it was
" prospect " (I, 3), " foresight and providence " (III, 15),

---

[1] *Met.* A. 980 b, 28. Cf. 980 a, " From memory experience is produced
in man."

[2] In general the distinction between " prudence " and " science " was
Aristotelian. Thus, Suarez, *Tractatus Quinque* (=T.Q.), p. 347, referred
to Aristotle's *Ethics*, III, 5. Hobbes, however, seems to have been
thinking of the sense of prudence defined in Aristotle's *De An.* III, 427 b.

[3] Aristotle's statement, *Post. Anal.*, 100 a 4.

" prevision " (IV, 17), and "presumption of the future " (*ibid.*). Since it was " not attained by reasoning, Hobbes called it " original" (III, 664) ; but it had to be acquired, and was usually " attained while we look after somewhat else " (III, 110).

Hobbes sometimes suggested that the efficacy of prudence depended upon the amount of experience. "When a man," he said, " hath *so often* observed like antecedents to be followed by like consequents that *whensoever* he seeth the antecedent he looketh again for the consequent . . . then he calleth both the antecedent and the consequent *signs* of one another, as clouds are signs of rain to come, and rain of clouds past" (IV, 17). "We esteem the future by what is past, seldom expecting what seldom happens " (II, 181). " The experience of men equal in age is not much unequal as to the quantity " (III, 60) ; and therefore the old were more prudent than the young.

It is possible, however, that Hobbes meant to assert that our innate tendency to project the past into the future was gradually *limited* by the frustration of rash conjectures, and therefore became restricted to what had been *uniformly* conjoined in the past. At any rate, he said (IV, 18, cf. III, 15) that prudence was the " taking of signs from experience *warily*, that is, that the experiments from which we take such signs be *all* remembered ; for else the cases are not alike that seem so." Such wariness could scarcely be amount of experience and nothing more ; and when Hobbes noted with glee that a one-year-old beast was often more prudent than a child of ten (III, 16), the reason was scarcely that the beast had more experience in its single year. He also said (IV, 18) that a certain quickness " to observe more in less time " pertained to prudence ; and such quickness, to use modern jargon, denoted a high I.Q. rather than a large amount of experience.

I submit, then, that Hobbes developed his doctrine of

regulated ranging or discursion upon what I may call sub-logical lines rather than upon lines of mechanical association, as later associationists like Hartley and James Mill were supposed to do ; and I shall linger a little longer upon the relations between logical and sub-logical in this matter.

There is some interest in the historical question how far Hobbes's insistence upon the *unscientific* character of "prudence" was original. His statement that "experience concludeth nothing universally " (IV, 18) was Aristotle's,[1] and the example (*ibid.*), that " though a man have always seen the day and night to follow one another hitherto, yet can he not thence conclude they shall do so, or that they have done so eternally," may have emanated from Magdalen-hall. Again, as the late J.M. Robertson showed,[2] Hobbes might have been thinking of the preface to Raleigh's *History of the World*, where it was written " That those and these be the causes of these effects, time hath taught us and not reason ; and so hath experience without art. The cheese-wife knoweth as well as the philosopher that sour ruanet doth coagulate her milk into a curd. But if we ask a reason of this cause, why the sourness doth it, and why it doth it, and the manner how, I think there is nothing in vulgar philosophy to satisfy these and many other like vulgar questions."

Hobbes's reason for the unscientific character of prudence was hardly satisfactory. " Signs of prudence," he said, " are all uncertain, because to observe by experience, and remember all circumstances that may alter the success is impossible " (III, 37). For, how could *science* remove this obstacle ? He suggested, again, that God alone had adequate foresight (III, 15). If so, how was human science better than animal expectation ? He further said that science and prudence were opposed as natural dexterity

---

[1] *Met.* A. 981 a 15.
[2] *Literary Guide*, August 1932.

was opposed to acquired skill in fencing. The trained fencer (III, 37) would *infallibly* pink his man. And that was a very good example of mistaking a difference of degree for one of kind.

Certainly, Hobbes believed that where the vulgar could only guess a " dependence " philosophers could *see* one, rational insight being the " way " by which the mind should travel (III, 36), the road to the arts and to power (III, 75). Science was a thing " which very few have and but in few things " (III, 110) ; but some men had it in some things. He admitted, however, that all scientific demonstration was *conditional*. " No discourse whatsoever can end in absolute knowledge of fact, past or to come. For, as for the knowledge of fact, it is originally sense ; and ever after, memory. And for the knowledge of consequence, which I have said before is called science, it is not absolute but conditional. No man can know by discourse, that this, or that, is, has been, or will be ; which is to know absolutely ; but only, that if this be, that is ; if this has been, that has been ; if this shall be, that shall be ; which is to know conditionally ; and that not the consequences of one thing to another ; but of one name of a thing, to another name of the same thing " (III, 52). All of which introduces " discourse " and " logic."

(5) DISCOURSE : AND NAMING

No man could have had a greater contempt for verbiage than Hobbes had. He ridiculed the rigmarole of noises that, like a beggar's paternoster, paid no regard to meaning (IV, 25), and he was fond of explaining (*e.g.* IV, 22) that names became debased by ambiguity and twisted by men's passions (III, 28 *sq.* ; IV, 26). He wanted (IV, 26) every man to begin *anew* with what he really meant, instead of struggling like a bird belimed (III, 23) in the treacherous regions of common speech.

Nevertheless, Hobbes believed that *naming* transformed mother wit, put in her hands the sceptre of infallible science, and (III, 18) made peace and society possible. Names were not mere " motions of men's tongues " (IV, 25), but were a device that gave our conceptions general significance and delivered our thoughts from what was only momentary and personal (III, 22). Therefore we had to "transfer our mental discourse into verbal" (III, 19), and from perspicuous appellations or definitions build up a demonstrative system. Again, without names, there could not be propositions (IV, 25), or, in consequence, truth or error ; and without propositions there could not be reasoning or syllogism (IV, 24), much less science (IV, 21). Even the Law of Contradiction, " the original and foundation of all ratiocination, that is, of all philosophy " (I, 19), was an affair of contradictory *names*.

In essence, said Hobbes, a name (*vox*) was a mnemonic *mark*,[1] " as men that have passed by a rock at sea set up some mark, thereby to remember their former danger and avoid it " (IV, 20). Such marks might be made for private use, and Hobbes opined (I, 15) that names began so. Soon, however, they were used for communication ; and then they became not only " marks " but also " signs." Moreover, since names out of syntax could not " teach others," it was necessary that these *signs* should be " disposed and ordered in speech as parts of the same " (I, 15).

" Signs " (I, 14) might either be " natural " (as when a dense cloud signified rain) or arbitrary (as when a hanging bush signified a wine-shop) ; and Hobbes had no doubt at all that language had been arbitrary after Babel and before it (I, 16 ; III, 19). Mathematicians did not have to ask anyone's leave for inventing names like " parabola " or " cissœides " (I, 16), and even if the government or an

---

[1] Cf. Gassendi, II, 352 : "ut monimentum, ὡς μνημόνευμα," referring to Aristotle, *De Memoria*, and Bacon (E.S. III, 391), "marks which may excite our mind to return."

academy had to step in (*e.g.* III, 31), their decisions, like other governmental operations, belonged to art, not to nature.

Such names as " tree " or " stone," Hobbes said (I, 17), were " names of things " ; but only indirectly, since names, directly, were signs of our *conceptions* of things. Some names, however, need not signify any *thing*, for we could name images or fictions, and could even speak about " nothing " or " for doctrine's sake " about " less than nothing " (*ibid.*).

A common name (I, 20) was the name of many things taken severally, and was called a " universal," but (*ibid.*) there were no universal *things* in nature and also no universal *ideas* or *phantasms* in our minds.

" Universality," in this sense, described the *extension* of common names, *i.e.* the logical use of " all, every, both, either, or the like " (I, 21), and the rest of Hobbes's doctrine on this part of the subject sounds very familiar, nowadays, to those who have studied Locke, Berkeley, and Hume. Hobbes denied that the world contained " man in general " as well as " Peter, John and all the rest " (IV, 22). And as for general images, how could there be " in the mind an image of a man which were not the image of some one man, but a man simply, which is impossible ; for every idea is one and of one thing " (I, 60).

Since it is quite possible to have a vaguish image, or even, despite Hobbes (IV, 22), an impressionist picture which is *not* of " one thing," the last of these statements seems indefensible, and it is difficult to see how Hobbes avoided self-contradiction in his account of the *intension* of common names, *i.e.* of " the conception itself that we have of man, as shape and motion " (IV, 20). Here Hobbes, contradicting one part of his theory, said that a definition gave " an universal notion of the thing defined, representing a certain universal picture thereof (*pictura universalis*) not to the eye but to the mind " (I, 84 ; L. I, 74) ; and, contradicting another part, that philosophy inquired into "the causes of *universal things*" (I, 68).

Despite a certain repetition, it seems convenient here to enumerate some of the more important peculiarities that Hobbes discerned in the status of universals.

(1) They were not *things* in any ordinary sense. "Any that say the white*ness*, magni*tude*, quali*ty* . . . go out of the wafer, do they not make those *-nesses*, *-tudes*, and *-ties* to be so many spirits possessing his body?" (III, 70).

(2) They were not *parts* of things (I, 33) but parts of their *nature* (I, 67). Manhood was not a part of a man, like one of his legs.

(3) They designated the "faculty" of a body "by which it works in us a conception of itself" (I, 103), that is, they designated, not something simple, but a correlation in which the human intellect was necessarily a partner.

(4) They were said to be "names of names" (I, 21), although Hobbes's explanation (*ibid.*), viz. that they were "significations of what we think of the nature of things," seemed to tell a different story.

(5) They were derived from propositions "from whose copula they proceed" (I, 33), and, in Hobbes's opinion, "truth or verity is not any affection of the thing, but of the proposition concerning it" (I, 35).

(6) They involved "abstraction"; and abstracting was not separating but "considering,"[1] that is, "bringing into account the increasings and decreasings of quantity, heat, and other accidents, without considering their bodies or subjects" (I, 33).

All these statements went to show that universals had a different status from that of certain other cognoscible entities, but none of them, except the third, could be said either to assert or to support the extreme nominalism that Leibniz[2] and others ascribed to Hobbes. Using traditional

---

[1] Cf. Berkeley, *Principles*, Introduction, § 16.
[2] *E.g.* Gerhardt's ed. IV, 158.

terms, I should like to defend the apparent paradox that Hobbes was a nominalist *because* he was a conceptualist, and that he deceived himself into forgetting the circumstance that, after all, he was also a naïve rationalist.

Clearly Hobbes did believe in the existence of conceptions, and he prided himself upon his skill in discerning them introspectively. " Men," he told Bishop Bramhall, " can never be deceived in the conceptions of things, though they may be, and are most often deceived by giving unto them wrong terms or appellations " (V, 299). If, then, we ask what these conceptions were, the correct answer (I submit) is what Hobbes *sometimes* said, viz. (I, 104) that everybody knew (intellectually) what was meant by discerning the properties of things ; that is, that when we deal with things " by reason of their similitude " (I, 18), our intellects discern this similitude in a perfectly straightforward although non-sensory manner (cf. IV, 21).

Hobbes also believed, however (*e.g.* III, 17), that all conceptions were weakened forms of sensation. Therefore he looked for a general or universal *phantasm*, and, looking, frequently (and correctly) professed that he could not find one. What he did find was that when, instead of simply perceiving a man or a triangle, he thought of *every* man or of *any* triangle, the new fact that emerged was the use of *speech*. The name " man " was a visible mark whose existence (unlike the unearthly " universals " of the scholastics) could not be denied, and it directed our thoughts, not to *one* individual Peter, but to Peter, *or* James, *or* John. Therefore Hobbes went so far as to say that " understanding was conception *caused by speech* " (III, 28).

Obviously, however, speech could not *make* the similitudes between Peter, James, and John. As Hobbes said (III, 20), it " *registered* what by cogitation we find to be the cause of any thing." He therefore had a rationalistic and even a " realistic " explanation in reserve, as may be seen, for better measure, from his controversy with Descartes.

Hobbes pointed out (L. V, 257) that there was a great difference between imagining (or having ideas) and conceiving (or " collecting " by reason), as the peripatetics had shown, yet he proceeded to assert that reasoning depended on names, names on imagination, imagination on sense, sense ultimately on internal bodily movement. Descartes replied that he himself had clearly distinguished between imagination and *pure* conception, and, for the rest, that Hobbes's theory was ludicrous, since the words in French and in German were different sounds, and yet might designate the same things.

Here the first point was verbal. Hobbes's " mental " (or intellectual) conception was just what Descartes called *pure* conception, and both of them professed to distinguish between *such* " conception " and imaginative picture-thinking. Consequently, when Hobbes said that we could apprehend God's existence, and, more generally, the existence of substance (L. V, 264) *by reason* although *no* imaginative " ideas " entered, he was, I submit, a naïve rationalist.

Descartes' second objection seems weak. As the example of the beggar's paternoster showed, Hobbes never supposed that names were mere *sounds*. They were marks that signified conceptions, and, through conceptions, things. There was no good reason why different sets of sounds, in different communities, might not be the marks of the same conceptions, just as there was no good reason why navigators from different places should not each have their own different signals to mark some particular danger.[1]

---

[1] There is some interest in comparing Gassendi's views on these matters with Hobbes's. Gassendi held that every idea in the mind arose from sense, and consequently that there could be nothing in the intellect that had not been formerly in sense (at I, 82). Nevertheless, he held that things were either sensibly discerned *or else* discerned by pure intelligence (I, 109), *although* (*ibid.*) they arose " from the occasion of sense as their

Mention should be made of one of Hobbes's most celebrated aphorisms, namely, that " words are wise men's counters, they do but reckon by them, but they are the money of fools " (III, 25). This aphorism—obviously borrowed from Bacon (E.S. III, 400)—would seem, contrary to Hobbes's intention, to indicate that the *nominalists* were the fools, but may be taken, more charitably, to mean that the *sounds* were only counters while *names* were good money. It might, however, have been less misleading to say that words were the money of wise men (*i.e.* an agreed and standard currency), but were the commodities of fools.

(6) LOGIC

Although Hobbes sometimes excused himself from pursuing the " dry discourse " of logic very far (IV, 24 ; I, 64), he was a competent technical logician, and, in *De Corpore*, began with logic in order (I, xiii) to " set up the light of reason."

Here, after dealing with names, he examined propositions (I, 29 *sq.*)—opposing them to interrogations, commands, etc.—and he analysed propositions into subject, predicate, and copula (I, 31), the two former being names, but the copula (usually but not necessarily expressed by " is ") not being a name. The copula signified the *connection* in the proposition itself, for it " made us think of the *cause* " for which the predicate was assigned (I, 31).

---

beginning " (cf. II, 204). He also appears to have believed in the existence of imaginative " conceptions " (I, 29), and held (II, 392) that intellect and imagination were closely allied. Generality, he held (I, 83), was derived " from the agreements of similar things " ; and thought itself (I, 81) was " internal speech " (II, 357), which brutes did not possess. He declared that a name (*vox*) was quite different from a mere sound (II, 457), and, unlike Hobbes, that it need not be wholly arbitrary. For (II, 461), as Epicurus had shown, interjections were natural ; and it should be conjectured that men in a given neighbourhood, hearing and understanding these natural cries of pleasure or pain, decided thereafter by convention, upon the names of the things that pleased or pained them.

A proposition implied speech and was the unit of truth. "These words *true, truth*, and *true proposition* are equivalent to one another, for truth consists in speech and not in the things spoken of " (I, 35). On the other hand, Hobbes admitted that " tacit " errors might arise " in perception and in silent cogitation " (I, 55), although he attempted, not very convincingly, to explain (I, 36) that a brute creature fawning upon the image of a man in a mirror was not deceived regarding the *likeness*, and, with a better argument, that " natural signs " (such as the clouds that were said to " promise " rain) " do not promise any thing which they do not perform," since they " do not promise at all " (I, 57).

According to Hobbes, a proposition expressed complete or partial identity in the application of names regarded from two different points of view. Thus, in the proposition : " Man is a rational animal "—" man " and " rational animal " signified the same set of beings, and the things signified by " rational animal " were either identical with, or included in, the things signified by " man " (I, 30, cf. II, 304). Hobbes held (I, 18) that " positives were before negatives," but (I, 19) accepted negative names (like *not-white*).

The most interesting part of his discussion of propositions concerned the distinctions between necessary and contingent, and, again, between hypothetical and categorical propositions. A contingent proposition, he said, might be true at one time and false at another time, "as *every crow is black* ; which may perhaps be true now, but false hereafter " (I, 38). A necessary proposition, on the other hand, was one in which we *never* could " conceive or feign " that predicate and subject could name different things (I, 37 *sq.*). It was, therefore, " of sempiternal truth " (I, 38). Hobbes inferred that speech, not things, was here in question, since, " if man, then living creature," was a sempiternal truth, although there need be no sempiternity about the existence of men (*ibid.*). (Hence it is plain that he meant by " speech," not the sounds that perish, but their timeless logical implications.)

He went on to say (I, 39) that " philosophers may in most things reason more solidly by hypothetical than categorical propositions," and (III, 52) that " knowledge of consequence " as opposed to " knowledge of fact " was " not absolute but conditional." The historical importance of this distinction, in relation to Hume's primary distinction between " relations of ideas " and " matters of fact," would be hard to exaggerate. Unfortunately, however, Hobbes darkened his theory by denying that " if a crow, then black," could be inferred from " every crow is black," although affirming that " if a man, then a living creature," could be inferred from " every man is a living creature."[1]

Hobbes regarded a proposition (I, 44) as only a *part* of the movement of reasoning. The " complete pace " was a syllogism ; and he examined the logical doctrine of syllogism in detail,[2] but very summarily (I, 44 *sqq.*).

Hobbes's *philosophical* interest in reasoning was limited

---

[1] This distinction was not formal (as Hobbes thought), but, if valid, was due to the circumstance that " every crow " really meant " every observed crow," while " every man " meant " every man, observed or unobserved, past or future."

[2] Hobbes's account of syllogism contained some points of technical interest. He held that two negative premises might validly yield a conclusion (I, 49), showing, by his example, that he neglected to note that the alleged syllogism contained four terms. Again, he allowed himself to substitute any " equipollent " premiss for a traditional syllogistic premiss, and so obtained many more valid moods than are currently admitted, *e.g.* fourteen in the third figure and eighteen in the fourth (I, 53).

He accepted the traditional pre-eminence of the first figure, and (I, 49), by transforming a negative proposition into an affirmation with a negative term for predicate, was willing to reduce all scientific reasoning to the *Barbara* mood. Since he held that conversion was only " reading, like Hebrew, backwards " (I, 51), he had an industrious, rather than a genuine, interest in figures other than the first. But he stated correctly that there were *four* figures, and that traditional wrangles regarding the fourth figure were mere logomachies about the definition of " figure " (I, 53).

to universal premises and conclusions (I, 49) and he offered the following analysis. " First there is conceived a phantasm of the thing named, with that accident or quality thereof, for which it is in the minor proposition called by that name which is the subject ; next the mind has a phantasm of the same thing with that accident or quality for which it hath the name, that in the same proposition is the predicate ; thirdly, the thought returns of the same thing as having that accident in it, for which it is called by the name that is the predicate of the major proposition ; and, lastly, remembering that all those are the accidents of one and the same thing, it concludes that those three names are also names of one and the same thing ; that is to say, the conclusion is true " (I, 49 *sq.*).

In this account, as it seems to me, conception and memory did the work, and the names were only auxiliaries.

The general title of this part of Hobbes's work, *i.e.* " Computation *or* Logic " has sometimes provoked unfavourable comment and deserves consideration. The " computation," of course, was of names ; and the term, according to Hobbes, had etymological support, since the Latins called accounting " ratiocinatio " and the items in an account " nomina " (III, 25). Etymology apart, " when a man reasoneth he does nothing else but conceive a sum total, from addition of parcels ; or conceive a remainder, from substraction of one sum from another ; which, if it be done by words, is conceiving of the consequences of the names of all the parts to the name of the whole ; or from the names of the whole and one part to the name of the other part " (III, 29, cf. I, 3). Therefore logicians " add together two names to make an affirmation, and two affirmations to make a syllogism ; and from the sum or conclusion of a syllogism they substract one proposition to find the other " (III, 30).

Hence Hobbes has been censured for "hinting at a numerical or mechanical system of computation,"[1] and has also been praised for having had a "remote glimpse of some of the points which are put in the light of day by Mr. Boole."[2] Neither praise nor blame, however, should be very pronounced. For by "addition" Hobbes did not properly *mean* addition, nor by "substraction" subtraction. As he explained (I, 66, with express reference to I, 3), "addition" and "composition" were the same, and "substraction" (or "division") was just "resolution." Again (*ibid.*), "composition" was equivalent to "synthesis" and "resolution" to "analysis."

According to Hobbes, the copula integrated the proposition, and he meant what his contemporaries meant when he said that a conclusion followed. I infer, therefore, that his semi-arithmetical terms were almost wholly innocuous. He may have been influenced by Epicurean and Stoic logic, but even an Aristotelian like Suarez (*De An.*, III, 6) maintained that reason proceeded "by compounding and dividing."[3] And the Epicurean Gassendi (at I, 29) said that to syllogise was to "collect skilfully," the Latins describing as "collectio" what the Greeks called syllogism, and a syllogism being "a sort of subduction or computation of reasons by which a total or a residue is collected either by addition or by subtraction" (*ibid.*, cf. at I, 89 and 95).

Hobbes's account of fallacies (I, 55 *sqq.*) included a resolute effort to explain how language (to use modern terms) may be "systematically misleading," especially if "phantasms" were named in language appropriate only to "bodies," or if names were named in language that properly applied either to "bodies" or to "phantasms."

---

[1] Adamson, *Short History of Logic*, 103 n.
[2] De Morgan, *A Budget of Paradoxes*, 2nd ed., II, 80.
[3] Cf. Melanchthon's account of intellect (*De An.*, p. 221); and Aristotle, *Met.* θ 10, 1051 b 3.

(7) KNOWLEDGE, BELIEF, AND OPINION

In the *Leviathan* (III, xi), Hobbes wrote : " There is another saying not of late understood, by which they might learn truly to read one another, if they would take the pains ; that is *nosce teipsum, read thyself.* . . . Whosoever looketh into himself, and considereth what he doth, when he does *think, opine, reason, hope, fear,* &c., and upon what grounds ; he shall thereby read and know what are the thoughts and passions of all other men upon the like occasions."

This passage, even verbally, is so very similar to the programme of Locke's *Essay*, and to the phenomenalism or phenomenology of British philosophy generally in the eighteenth century that it challenges commentary ; and I propose to offer some general reflections before proceeding to the more special inquiries of this section.

In adopting and adapting the Socratic maxim, " Know thyself," Hobbes asserted the primacy of critical introspection in these matters, the emphasis being upon a man's *own* thought : " let your reason move upon the deep of your own cogitations and experience " (I, xii) ; " I find it so by considering my own ratiocination " (V, 401)—and the negative emphasis upon the rejection of bookishness and hearsay—" instead of books reading over orderly one's own conceptions " (IV, 26). Hobbes further assumed that conceptions themselves could not err (V, 299), and was satisfied with the range of the method, although he once said, with some apparent modesty (B. 29) : " I cannot enter into other men's thoughts farther than I am led by the consideration of human nature in general."

It is interesting, but perhaps unprofitable, to consider how Hobbes came to form this view. He might have been thinking of Montaigne's " the greatest thing in the world is to be at home with oneself " or " my consciousness (conscience) does not falsify one iota ; as for my science

I cannot tell."[1] He might have been thinking of what Bacon criticised as a faulty commonplace, viz. that " logic " dealt with things " in notion " or " in appearance," not " in existence " (E.S. III, 347), and Bacon might have been thinking of Fracastoro's doctrine that understanding and intellect were " from " rather than simply " in " the mind,[2] or of Campanella's view that the senses occasioned " passions " which it was the prerogative of the mind to judge from its own resources.[3] Herbert of Cherbury's *De Veritate* (*e.g.* 3rd ed. p. 162) may have given a hint. But I do not know, and shall content myself with quoting a passage from a letter of the very unphilosophical James Howell to Hobbes's friend Kenelm Digby in 1646 : " I have travelled the Isle of Man, I mean this little world which I have carried about me and within me so many years. For, as the wisest of the pagan philosophers said, that the greatest learning was the knowledge of one's self, *to be his own geometrician* ; if one do so he need not gad about to see fashions, he shall find enough at home."[4]

Turning from these wide generalities, we may note that while Hobbes usually regarded sense (*e.g.* IV, 27), memory (III, 35), and history (III, 71) as instances of "knowledge," he sometimes, like Locke and Hume, affirmed that we *knew* only when we had absolutely conclusive evidence, as when he said (IV, 27) that knowledge implied both truth and evidence.

Scientific " knowledge " implied *evident* principles as well as rigorous deduction from the principles by *evident* steps ; and " evidence," Hobbes said, was " the life of truth " and " as the sap to the tree " (IV, 28). If principles were admitted only " for a trial," we had supposition

[1] q. Brunschvicq, *Le Progrès de la conscience*, I, 132.
[2] See Cassirer, *Das Erkenntnisproblem*, I, 231 n.
[3] See Cassirer, *op. cit.*, I, 252 n. and Levi's *Bacon*, p. 30.
[4] *Epistolæ Ho-elianæ*, ed. Jacobs, I, 507.

(IV, 29) ; if admitted upon trust, " we are not said to *know* but to think them to be true " (*ibid.*). They were opinions (cf. III, 53), and opinions accepted out of trust in other men were either belief or faith (IV, 29). Moreover, belief " in many cases is no less free from doubt than perfect or manifest knowledge " (IV, 30). Again, opinions included " probability " (IV, 29)—a term Hobbes did not often use—and " conjecture "—a favourite term. Sometimes " judgment " was also included ; but Hobbes's use of the term was vacillating. In one passage he ascribed " judgment " to scientific knowledge as well as to opinion. " In demonstration, in counsel and all rigorous search of truth," he said (III, 58), " judgment does all, except sometimes the understanding have need to be opened by some apt similitude ; and then there is so much use of fancy." More frequently (*e.g.* III, 52) he regarded it as simply the *last* of " a chain of opinions alternate " in a state of doubt, and, even then (*ibid.*), did not notice the distinction between a " last opinion " and the *decision* implied in " the resolute and final sentence of him that discourseth."

Of opinion Hobbes also said : (1) that it was opposed to knowledge (since (IV, 27) it might be false) ; (2) that it was opposed to science (since (III, 53) it might either be false or inconclusive) ; (3) that it might depend on individual reason (II, 305) and hence included " conscience " (III, 53 ; IV, 30) ; but (4) that it was generally induced " through fear, hope, love, or some other perturbation of mind than true reason " (II, 15, cf. IV, 75) ; (5) that it governed the world because " our wills follow our opinions as our actions follow our wills " (IV, 70) ; (6) that it was " not in our power to change ; but always and necessarily such as the things we see, hear, and consider suggest unto us " (III, 360).

Belief, according to Hobbes, was primarily trust towards a *man* (and his veracity). The phrase " to believe in " was " a singularity of ecclesiastical use " (III, 54) ; and we might trust God without accepting creeds (III, 590). Accordingly, Hobbes usually thought of belief as a thing that sprang from personal authority or testimony, even when the testimony was not very good. Thus the " rash beliefs " of the early theologians regarding spirits (such as St. Bernard's or " our Bede's " views on apparitions) were their beliefs in " reports " that they did not know to be " vain " (III, 687). Sometimes, again, Hobbes took faith and belief to be the same (III, 493).

Hobbes's views about faith were sufficiently indicated in the *De Cive*. Faith (a civic as well as a Christian virtue) was there said (II, 305) to be always " joined with inward assent," but to differ from mere opinion through its dependence on " the good esteem we have of another " (*ibid.*), and to differ from (scientific) " knowledge " because science was analytical, deliberately taking " a proposition broken and chewed " which faith " swallowed down whole and entire " (*ibid.*). The mysteries of religion, he said with the same metaphor (also to be found in Selden's *Table Talk*, the section on Oaths) were like " wholesome pills for the sick ; which swallowed whole have the virtue to cure, but chewed are for the most part cast up again without effect " (III, 360).

" Natural wit," Hobbes said (III, 56) included sense—or " sense and memory " (III, 35)—that was born with us, and also the " prudence " that men and brutes learned from experience. Scientific reasoning, on the other hand, had to be "attained by industry" (III, 35), since it implied " the apt imposing of names " and " a good and orderly method " of inference (*ibid.*). Therefore, said Hobbes, " as for *acquired wit*, I mean acquired by method and instruction, there is none but reason ; which is grounded on the right use of speech and produceth the sciences " (III, 61). Hobbes admitted, however, that reason was just as " natural " as " any other faculty or affection of the mind " (II, 16), since (*ibid.*) it was "no less a part of human nature " ; and he allowed that there was an unscientific and " natural," indeed even a *wordless*, type of " reason " (I, 1 and 3).

Hobbes believed that " all men by nature reason alike and well when they have good principles " (III, 35), and that reason was " the same in all men " (IV, 87). It was God's gift of light (IV, 116), " notwithstanding the opposition and affronts of supernaturalists nowadays to rational and moral conversation." Apparently, however, men were very unequal in their ability to see through shams. " If the minds of men were all of white paper,[1] they would almost equally be disposed to acknowledge whatsoever should be in right method, and by right ratiocination delivered to them ; but when men have once acquiesced in untrue opinions, and registered them as authentical records in their minds, it is no less impossible to speak intelligibly to such men than to write legibly upon a paper already scribbled over " (IV, 57).

In the main, therefore, Hobbes was a joyful rationalist, relying confidently upon individual insight. There was, however, a difficulty. Communicable science required general agreement regarding the meaning of scientific terms ; and Hobbes was alarmed at the unsocial attitude of private men who refused to be silent when their private reason and conscience were active. Consequently, he went so far as to say that *even in arithmetic* " no one man's reason, nor the reason of any number of men makes the certainty . . . and therefore, as when there is controversy in an account, the parties must by their own accord set up, for right reason, the reason of some arbitrator or judge " (III, 31). Accordingly, since arbitration was the sovereign's prerogative (*e.g.* IV, 225), it was the sovereign's business to establish " the use and definition of all names not agreed upon and tending to controversy " (*ibid.*) ; and " disobedience may lawfully be punished in them, that

[1] With this Stoic phrase cf. the " clean paper " of III, 325.

against the laws teach even true philosophy" (III, 688). In another passage, however (III, 164), Hobbes held that no doctrine repugnant to peace could be true.

This view was oddly different from a satirical passage (III, 91) in which Hobbes remarked that ethical questions were "perpetually disputed, both by the pen and the sword ; whereas the doctrine of lines and figures is not so " because it " crossed no man's ambition " ; and added, witheringly, that if the Pythagorean proposition seemed contrary " to the interest of men that have dominion " it would be suppressed " if not disputed, yet by the burning of all books of geometry." And yet there was a difficulty. However confident a mathematician may be that he is right and the other obstinate mathematicians wrong, most mathematicians do, in fact, submit to something like a consensus of experts. Hobbes's view, however, was that the authority of teaching geometry belonged to the throne, whether or not the king were a geometer (II, 247). It was fortunate for him that Charles II—" our great Monarch of the Virtuosi," as Boyle called him (*Examen*, p. 4)—did not officially ban the Hobbian philosophy, as his bishops and perhaps the other virtuosi at Gresham College would have liked him to do.

V

ETHICS AND MORAL PSYCHOLOGY

(1) PLEASURE, APPETITE, AND WILL

As I shall narrate, Hobbes's account of the psychology of human action, on which (together with definitions said to be more precise than the world had known before he wrote) he professed to base his celebrated science of citizenship, had more than a merely official agreement with his materialism and with his phenomenalism, since he was at pains to show that men's appetites were literally physical motions, and habitually assumed that appetite had to be tutored by sense, imagination, or reason. Nevertheless, as he himself asserted (II, xx), it was possible to treat these subjects independently of metaphysics, and to test them simply by experience. In dealing with them now we have, in fact, to enter a new continent in the Hobbian globe.

Following tradition, Hobbes distinguished between " power cognitive or conceptive " and " power motive " (IV, 30).

The latter, which is now our theme, included biological " vital motion " (pulse, breathing, excretion, etc.), but Hobbes was interested, almost exclusively, in voluntary motion where the " mind " or the " fancy " moved our bodies and principally our limbs (IV, 30 ; III, 38).

Here Hobbes's general view was that a stimulus outside the body was sensed in the head, but that its motion, not stopping there, proceeded to the heart, where it either helped or hindered the man's vital motion. When it helped it was pleasure, the Latin term " iucundum " being

so named " a iuvando "[1] (because it helped).   When it
hindered or weakened the vital motion it was pain.   Again
the motion did not stop in the heart, but continued.
Pleasure became a " motion toward " the thing that
pleased, and so was the   " first beginning " of *appetite*.
Pain was an incitement to withdraw, a " motion from-
ward " whose first beginnings were *aversion*, or, even, *fear*
(IV, 31 *sq.*).

This early account agreed in substance with Hobbes's
later views (I, 406 *sqq.* ;   III, 38 *sqq.*) and also with the first
sketch in his *Short Tract* (E.L. 165 *sqq.*), where (" good "
being defined as " attractive ") it was explained that good
things *literally* " drew " us by their local motion, and that
" motion toward " was literal also.[2]

Clearly, the theory was stated very generally.   Aversion,
with clenched fists, might be " motion towards," and pain,
as Hobbes saw (I, 406), may be due to internal or organic
stimuli as well as to external.   Again, the phrase, " such
manner as conduceth most to the preservation and augmentation " of vital motion (I, 407) was almost culpably
vague, and did not distinguish between native instincts
and acquired sagacity.

On this point Hobbes said (III, 40) :   " Of appetites
and aversions, some are born with men ;   as appetite of
food, appetite of excretion, and exoneration, which may
also and more properly be called aversions from somewhat
they feel in their bodies ;   and some other appetites, not
many.   The rest, which are appetites of particular things,
proceed from experience, and trial of their effects upon

---

[1] Apparently in recollection of the pseudo-Apuleius, *De Mundo*.
[2] It is also worth noting that Hooker (E.P. I, 320) had spoken
metaphorically of desire as " motion towards " ;   that Hobbes's
" appetite " and " aversion " were Stoic terms (Diog. VII, 104 ;
Plutarch, *Mor*. 1037 ;   Cicero, *Acad*. II, 24) and corresponded to
Gassendi's *cupiditas* and *fuga* (at II, 429) ; that Melanchthon (*De An*.
202) regarded pain as a motion of the heart ; and that Gassendi (at
II, 420) said that pleasure was " what was accommodated to the body's
substance."

themselves or other men." He had little or no interest in the first class, and habitually regarded man as a cautious, scheming, prospective creature who built upon what he had learnt.

Hobbes was rather vague about the relation of pleasure to desire. " *Pure* pleasure and pain," he admitted (I, 409 *sq.*), " are a certain fruition of good or evil." If so, they should have been distinguished from appetite (which was not a fruition), but Hobbes was anxious to emphasise the continuity of the two in the augmentation of " life " and " vital motion."[1] In short, his pleasure-theory and his political doctrine that self-preservation was the first law of man's conscious nature were intended to be one and the same. So far as I know, he did not discuss the obvious objection that many acute pains need not be dangerous to health, and that many pleasures, such as a stimulating degree of inebriety, do not " preserve " vital motion, even if temporarily and at a price, they " augment " it. Again, he entangled his theory with inconsistent remarks about " bodily " and " mental " pleasures. At an early stage (IV, 34) he explained that sensual or corporeal pleasures " seemed to affect " some organ of sense, while mental pleasures were not peculiar to any part of the body. He proceeded to argue, however (IV, 35, cf. III, 43), that because sense had always a *present* cause, any search for *future* pleasures (of sight, sound, or " onerations and exonerations of the body ") were " of the mind." And that (cf. IV, 55) implied a very odd theory of sensuality.

Appetite and aversion, when distinguished from pleasure-pain, were anticipations of pleasure or pain.[2] When they

---

[1] Cf. Melanchthon (*De An.* 194) : " Our appetites which are not made by contact, but follow thought, are motions of the heart by which we approach objects which thought, rightly or wrongly, represents as advantageous." And Gassendi (at II, 409) : " Appetite is the mind being moved by the knowledge of good or evil."

[2] According to Aristotle (*De An.* II, 414 b 6) ὄρεξις itself was for the agreeable. Again (*ibid.* 434 a 3) there must be ἐπιθυμία where there was pleasure.

were concerned with absent things they were called desire
and fear (IV, 31 *sq.*). Their first beginnings were called
" endeavour," and this, despite the schools, was actual,
not metaphorical motion (III, 40). Continued, the motion
became the muscular reaction of pursuit or avoidance.
Appetites and aversions pertained to volition, and,
since they were prospective, they were " mental." " Endeavour," that " small " or " first " beginning of action,
was a continuation from the pleasure actually felt, and the
mental imaginations that guided the muscular reactions
were relics of sense that mingled with the stimulus actually
experienced. What was operative, therefore, was always
a *present* fact modified by past experience of what, at the
time, might be absent ; and the resultant action, although
forward-looking, was, so to say, pushed from behind.
Therefore " final " causes were " efficient " causes (I, 132).

Many psychologists would say, in their unfortunate
jargon, that Hobbes's account of appetite showed the
" intellectualist's " fallacy and was too little " voluntar-
istic." Certainly he said (III, 39) that it was " evident
that the imagination is the first internal beginning[1] of all
voluntary motion " on the ground that appetite was unintelligible unless it knew its purpose and direction ; and
it may be a fair criticism that instinct knows its way about
before there is experience or imaginative " decaying sense."
On the other hand, Hobbes frequently subordinated " conception " to desire. " The thoughts, he said (III, 61),
" are to the desires as scouts, and spies, to range abroad
and find the way to the things desired " ; and he affirmed
(III, 62) that " to have no desire is to be dead." Again, he
held that the differences between men were principally

[1] Here, as Mr. Stocks has shown me, Hobbes followed Aristotle
(*De An.*, III, 433 b 27). The sense of this passage is that an animal is
capable of self-movement in so far as it is capable of appetite, but that
appetite implies imagination (φαντασία) either calculative (as frequently
in the higher animals) or sensitive (a species of imagination that all
animals possess). Cf. *Met.* 1072 a 29 : " Desire is consequent on opinion
rather than opinion on desire " ; and *De An.* I, 406 b.

due, not to superiority in their senses or in reasoning power, but to the passions and " vital constitution " or temperament (IV, 54 ; III, 57), although (IV, 56 ; III, 56) there were minor differences in the natural celerity of the imagination. Hobbes also knew that (to use modern terms) there was an emotive as well as a referential use of language, and that the two uses often commingled (III, 28 *sq.*; IV, 75).

Although much that Hobbes said about the " will " must be postponed to a later section dealing with the free-will controversy, it is necessary, at this stage, to give some account of what he meant by " will " and of its relation to appetite.

" I always avoid attributing motion to anything but body," he said (V, 313) ; and therefore he avoided saying either that the will was moved or that it moved anything. It was the *man* (V, 295) or, in a certain sense, the "soul"— *i.e.* the living, embodied man—that deliberated and willed. To say that " the will willed " was like saying that " the walk walketh " (I, 58). One might just as well go further and say that " we will will will " (IV, 69). The truth was that " appetite, fear, hope and the rest of the passions . . . proceed not from but *are* the will " (IV, 69). " The will, the willing and the appetite is the same thing " (V, 295).

Hobbes admitted, it is true, that appetite " simply so called " (I, 409) might, because it was undeliberative, be distinguished from " will," but he paid very little attention to this possible distinction, since he held that the " first appetite " in a sudden action (IV, 67) was to be " judged deliberation in such men as can discern good and evil " (IV, 69, cf. III, 291), on the ground that they might have prepared themselves for it beforehand.

Deliberation, he said, was only an " alternate succession of appetites, aversions, hopes and fears " (III, 48), a " propounding of benefits and harms " (IV, 69). The *last* appetite in such a succession was the *act* of willing (III, 48), and " where there is but one appetite, that is the last "

(V, 94). Man and beast, therefore, deliberated in the same sense (III, 48), with the consequence that rationality in willing meant only a calculation subordinate to the pressure of appetite (V, 234).

This analysis seems defective in several respects. A volition is not simply the *last* term in a series of solicitations. It is a *decision*, and therefore analogous to an elected person, not to a mere candidate. Indeed, Hobbes inadvertently admitted this important difference when he pointed out that mere inclination (III, 49) or mere intention in an " interrupted " deliberation (IV, 70) differed from " will." He was unduly "intellectualistic," again, when he explained that the " last appetite " was " the last opinion or judgment immediately preceding the action " (IV, 268) ; for an opinion is not a volition. Moreover, when he explained that the " last appetite " was to be understood in the same sense as the " last feather " that broke the horse's back (IV, 269), or that (III, 48) " the whole sum of desires, aversions, hopes and fears continued till the thing be either done, or thought impossible, is that we call deliberation," he clearly regarded the process as a gradual integration of personality culminating in a settled endeavour (perhaps after some wavering and resolute restraint), and not as a simple succession in which the last member, so to say, exploded into action.

The disease of " intellectualism," again, seems to have taken firm hold of another of Hobbes's characteristic views. " I conceive," he said, " when a man deliberates whether he shall do a thing or not do it, that he does nothing else but consider whether it be *better for himself* to do it or not to do it. And to consider an action is to imagine the consequences of it both good and evil " (IV, 273, cf. I, 8 ; III, 241). His view, therefore, was that a calculation of seeming good (III, 50), *i.e.* of the apparent " overweighting " of selfish good in comparison with evil, *was* the "opinion" that was the "appetite" that was the "will."

Indeed, by uniting determinism with the doctrine of calculating selfishness, Hobbes, in a way that ultimately ruined the consistency of his political theory, maintained roundly that every man *must* choose his own apparent good,[1] that is to say, what seemed to him to be *his own greatest good*.

Regarding the classification of the passions, Hobbes held that " appetite, desire, love, aversion, hate, joy and grief " were the " simple " or root-passions (III, 43) diversified according to a fourfold principle, viz. : (*a*) respecting probability (which distinguished hope from despondency) ; (*b*) respecting the object of the passion (a magnanimous use of riches was liberality) ; (*c*) respecting the " compounding " of appetites (envy was grief plus an endeavour to hinder) ; (*d*) respecting the way in which the appetites might alternate in deliberation. Here many of Hobbes's observations were very acute,[2] as in his statement (III, 47) that shame " in young men is a sign of love of good reputation, and commendable ; in old men it is a sign of the same ; but, because it comes too late, not commendable." In the main, however, he was a little too anxious to invent apophthegms in this part of his discussion ; and we had better return to his doctrine of " good."

In a famous statement Hobbes declared that "whatsoever is the object of any man's appetite or desire, that is it which he for his part calleth good ; and the object of his hate and aversion evil ; and of his contempt, vile and inconsiderable. For these words of evil, good, and contemptible are ever used with relation to the person that useth them : there being nothing simply and absolutely so, nor any common rule of good and evil to be taken from the nature of the objects themselves " (III, 41).

---

[1] Cf. Hooker (E.P. I, 281).

[2] Dilthey (*Gesammelte Schriften*, II, 292 *sqq.*) has shown in convincing detail how much Hobbes was indebted to classical literature for many of these definitions of the passions, particularly to Diogenes, Stobæus, and Cicero (*Tusc. Disp.*).

Here the reference to *desire*, although usual (*e.g.* III,
146 ; II, 196) was not, I think, intended to exclude
pleasure. For Hobbes also said (IV, 32) : " Every man,
for his own part, calleth that which pleaseth and is
delightful to himself good " ; and, again, " What is it to
say any action is good, but to say it is as I would wish ? "
(IV, 255). Indeed, in the very next paragraph to the above
famous statement, he explained that there were three
species of good, viz. " good in the promise " (*pulchrum*),
good in effect as the end desired (*iucundum*), and good as
the means (*utile*). [An Aristotelian trio, N.E. 1104 b 30.]

The statement, however, was intended to deny the
existence of *metaphysical goodness*,[1] that is, a goodness in
the *being* of things " of absolute significance to all men "
(V, 192). Even what was good in God's sight, Hobbes
said (*ibid.*) was simply what pleased God. And he said
elsewhere (IV, 32) that God's goodness was his goodness
to us.

Hobbes affirmed emphatically, then, that goodness was
relative to the variable passions and appetites of particular
men, and it is important to ask how far this view was
" subjective " as well as " relative."

Pleasure and appetite might vary from man to man,
and Hobbes did not say that even pleasure itself was
absolutely good. Good, for him, was the capacity *of an
object* to attract us (*e.g.* V, 192), and in that sense it would
have been meaningless to ask whether the attractiveness
was itself good.

On the other hand, Hobbes clearly assumed that there
was a perfectly objective sense of good and evil, viz.

---

[1] Those who believed in " metaphysical goodness " did not necessarily
regard it as a property of objects. Suarez, for instance (T.Q., p. 210),
explained that the proper analogy was to " certitude " or " clearness "
of truth, that is to say to a metaphysical *relation* between intellect or
intelligible volition and its object. It should also be noted that when
Hobbes spoke of pleasure-pain as the *measure* of good and evil (II, 196,
cf. III, 146) he did not mean to suggest that it was not also the *reality*
of these conditions.

benefit or hurt. When he said (V, 192) that " to speak properly, nothing is good or evil but in regard of the action that proceedeth from it, and also of the person to whom it doth good or hurt," he used the word " good " in a relative sense in the first part of the statement and in an absolute sense in the second part. Evil was actually *molestum* (III, 42), an objective damage or hurt, and pleasure, for Hobbes, was a *physical* occurrence that corroborated vital motion. Again, Hobbes habitually regarded death as the greatest of all evils, not only because *dying* was painful, but also and chiefly because death implied " the loss of all power " (IV, 83). Moreover, by distinguishing between apparent and real good, Hobbes presupposed a certain objectivity. A thing might seem hurtful although in fact it was innocuous, and Hobbes was thoroughly contemptuous of those who " greedily preferred the present good before the future " (II, 48).

The truth of these comments is not impugned by the fact that Hobbes regarded good as a changing, not as a stable condition, and believed, like Bacon, in the priority of active good.[1] There was, said Hobbes, no *utmost* end ; for " while we live we have desires "[2] (IV, 33) ; " There can be no contentment but in proceeding " (*ibid.*) ; " Felicity consisteth not in having prospered but in prospering " (*ibid.*). " There is no such thing as perpetual tranquillity of mind, while we live here ; because life itself is but motion, and can never be without desire, nor without fear, no more than without sense " (III, 51) ; " Felicity is a continual progress of the desire from one object to another " (III, 85).

There was also a certain objectivity in Hobbes's account of " value," although the conception was relative. " The

---

[1] *i.e.* (E.S. III, 424) : " the affection which is natural in man towards variety and proceeding." Here Hobbes opposed the Epicureanism of Gassendi (who (at II, 581) praised " voluptas stabilis ") and also the Stoics and the Peripatetics.
[2] Cf. Aristotle, *Politics*, II, vii : " Desire is in its nature limitless."

value or worth of a man," he said, " is as of all other things
his price, that is to say, so much as would be given for the
use of his power, and therefore is not absolute ; but a
thing dependent on the need and judgment of another "
(III, 76).   The need was objective scarcity ; the judgment,
in part, " esteem " which, although comparative, need
not be subjective.   A man might esteém his own glory
justly (IV, 40), but was likely to be vainglorious unless
others corroborated him (IV, 41) ;   and therefore his
sovereign ought to determine his " dignity " (III, 283).

To be sure, " power " and the " price " of it seem
obviously distinct from pleasure or the rosy shimmer
engendered by mere appetite ;   but Hobbes's moral
psychology was a psychology of " power " and of victory
over " fear," at least as fundamentally as of pleasure, and
we must go on to examine the point.

Assessing human motives, Hobbes said : " In the first
place I put for a general inclination of all mankind a
perpetual and restless desire of power after power, that
ceaseth only in death " (III, 85).

This statement was much more than an account of what
Hobbes had learned by observation.   It was a metaphysical
assertion to the effect that power *had to be* the mainspring
of every man's action ;   and Hobbes connected this metaphysical assertion with his pleasure-theory by saying
(IV, 37) that " whosoever expecteth pleasure to come
must conceive withal some power in himself by which
the same may be attained."

In this general sense " power " included " a man's
preservation of his own life and limbs with all the power
he hath " (IV, 83) ;   and so, in another and in a quite
objective way, Hobbes's pleasure-principle and his reality-
principle were held to come together.   Indeed, Hobbes
seems to have thought that sensuality (III, 86) and the
desire for " conveniences " (II, 5) were opposed to this
restless love of power, but came in indirectly since they

had to be defended against predatory neighbours. Hobbes's
" power " was really competitive. For him not to compete
was to die. " All the mind's pleasure is either glory (or to
have a good opinion of oneself) or refers to glory in the
end ; the rest are sensual or conducing to sensuality,
which may be all comprehended under the word " conveniences." All society, therefore, is either for gain or
glory, that is, not so much for the love of our fellows as
for the love of ourselves " (II, 5). The duellist's pleasure
in having killed his man (IV, 38) was a glorying in greater
skill and strength than was common. Beauty of person
(*ibid.*) was admired because it indicated an unusual degree
of " natural heat and power generative."

Nevertheless, since danger was always present in a
competitive world, the fear of losing power was an even
stronger motive than the positive lust after power. " The
passion to be reckoned upon is fear " (III, 129).

In much scholastic literature (*e.g.* Suarez, T.Q., p. 338)
the word " timor " (fear) included every apprehension of
future evil ; and Hobbes, under pressure of controversy,
explained that he distinguished between " fear " and
" being affrighted." As he said, in what may well be
the most elegant footnote in the English language (II,
6 n.) :

" It is objected : it is so improbable that men should
grow into civil societies out of fear, that if they had been
afraid, they would not have endured each other's looks.
They presume, I believe, that to fear is nothing else than
to be affrighted. I comprehend in this word *fear*, a certain
foresight of future evil ; neither do I conceive flight the sole
property of fear, but to distrust, suspect, take heed,
provide so that they may not fear, is also incident to the
fearful. They who go to sleep, shut their doors ; they
who travel, carry their swords with them, because they
fear thieves. Kingdoms guard their coasts and frontiers

with forts and castles ; cities are compact with walls ; and all for fear of neighbouring kingdoms and towns. Even the strongest armies, and most accomplished for fight, yet sometimes parley for peace, as fearing each other's power, and lest they might be overcome. It is through fear that men secure themselves by flight, indeed, and in corners, if they think they cannot escape otherwise ; but for the most part by arms and defensive weapons ; whence it happens that daring to come forth they know each other's spirits. But then if they fight, civil society ariseth from the victory ; if they agree, from their agreement."

Hence some might infer that Hobbes's theory was but a pallid, precautionary thing. But there was stark fear at the root of it.[1] Those who had a competence had to earn more in order to keep what they had (III, 86) ; lust provoked crime (III, 284) ; even the frugal were apprehensive when there was not enough to go round (II, 8). In short, every minor and petty apprehension or precaution had the fear of death behind it, if not immediately, yet at no very distant remove. For nearly any weakling, given a favourable opportunity, was strong enough to hurt (II, 6), and even to *kill* (IV, 82).

The most striking piece of sustained psychological description in all Hobbes's writings was his attempt (IV, 40 *sqq.*) to show how human nature was compounded of fear and weakness in varying degrees. It ended with the famous comparison of life to a race which " though it hold not in every part, yet it holdeth so well for this our purpose, that we may hereby both see and remember almost all the passions before mentioned. But this race we must suppose to have no other goal, nor other garland, but being foremost ; " and in it :

[1] Therefore legal coercion had to make use of this same fear. Holland (*Jurisprudence*, 13th ed., p. 79) quotes *Decretum* (I, i, c. 1.) : " Factæ sunt autem leges ut earum *metu* humana coerceatur audacia."

To endeavour is appetite.
To be remiss is sensuality.
To consider them behind is glory.
To consider them before is humility.

    .   .   .   .

To be in breath, hope.
To be weary, despair.

    .   .   .   .

To fall on the sudden, is disposition to weep.
To see another fall, is disposition to laugh.

    .   .   .   .

To hurt oneself for haste is shame.
Continually to be out-gone is misery.
Continually to out-go the next before is felicity.
And to forsake the course is to die.

(2) ETHICS IN RELATION TO CIVIL PHILOSOPHY

According to Hobbes, ethics had to do with " good
manners or virtue " (II, 48, cf. II, 234 ; IV, 111) although
not with " small " manners, " as how one should wash his
mouth or pick his teeth before company " (III, 85).   It
was concerned with right and wrong in serious matters
(II, xiii), and with the " dispositions, affections and
manners of men " so far as these led to " civil duty "
(I, 11 *sq.* ; B. 44).   There was a " quality of human nature "
that made it " fit to make up a civil governement " (II, 14),
and " a certain rule and measure of right " that might be
" established " (I, 9).   " Justice," the " laws of nature,"
and also the laws of " honour and profit " were Hobbes's
theme ; and " all writers do agree that the natural law
is the same with the moral " (II, 47).

Hobbes maintained that the science of right and wrong
really was a science, that is to say, a *demonstrative* study,
and he claimed that he had been the first to escape from
the " hermaphrodite " (II, xiii) if eloquent (I, 9) conceptions of the ancients.   This science was " made from
the passions " in the sense that it was " collected by

reason out of the definitions themselves of will, good, honour, profitable " (II, 5) as applied to the introspective evidence readily obtained by " every man that takes the pains to observe these motions [the passions, etc.] within himself " (I, 73). Hobbes thoroughly approved of the title, *Ethics Demonstrated*, that had been given to a French translation of an abstract of his *De Cive* (VII, 333).

In attempting his deduction Hobbes, like Hooker (E.P. I, 353 and 430) first considered " the duties of men as men " (II, ix), *i.e.* in their individual capacity.

Man was concupiscent and also rational (II, vii).   By " a certain impulsion of nature no less than that whereby a stone moves downward " (II, 8) every man sought his own preservation,[1] power and pleasure ; and the lust for power was unlimited since attack was the best, and the only possible, defence.

Accordingly, men " in a state of nature," that is to say, considered as so many units,[2] were a set of competitive egoists.   *In that state*, each private man was " an arrant wolf " to his fellows (II, ii).   The state of nature was a state of war.

Thus Hobbes vigorously opposed the Aristotelian thesis that man was *by nature* a social or political animal.   There might be such " natural concord " in bees, but not in men (IV, 120 *sq.* ; II, 66 *sq.* ; III, 156 *sq.*).   It should be noticed, however, that Hobbes meant by such a " society " a *politically constituted* society, and his point was simply that men *made* themselves " fit for civil governement " by rational artifice and education.   Therefore, although too

---

[1] Cf. *Vindiciæ*, p. 190 : " The law of nature teaches and commands us to maintain and defend our lives, and liberties, without which life is scant worth the enjoying, against all injury and violence.   Nature has imprinted this by instinct in dogs against wolves . . . and yet much more in man against man himself, if man become a beast."   Cf. Leonardo da Vinci, *Frammenti*, p. 119; Telesio, *De Rer. Nat.*, IX, ii ; and a host of others.

[2] In a summary of his theory (III, 343) Hobbes presented the equations : Mere nature = absolute liberty = anarchy = condition of war.

infrequently, Hobbes was prepared to admit a certain natural gregariousness. " Solitude was an enemy " to most men (II, 2 n.). " Even nature compelling " men desired to " come together." Infants needed others' help in order to live at all. But such natural gregariousness led only to " meetings " and not to (political) " society " (*ibid.*).

On the whole, Hobbes's account of the " state of nature " was analytical rather than historical. He *considered* men " as if but even now sprung out of the earth and suddenly, like mushrooms,[1] come to full maturity " (II, 109) without believing in the legend of Cadmus or confusing between *homo sapiens* and *agaricus campestris*. On the other hand, he pointed out that " savage people in many places in America " (III, 114 ; II, 12) had " no governement at all," that separate sovereign states were " in the state and posture of gladiators " (III, 115, cf. II, xv), and that civil war showed very plainly " what manner of life there would be where there were no common power to fear " (III, 114).

Again, Hobbes argued, quite logically, that a " state of war " " consisteth not in battle only, or the act of fighting, but in a tract of time wherein the will to contend by battle is sufficiently known " (III, 113), and, perhaps remembering St. Paul's injunction to Timothy (1 Tim. I, 9) that " the law is not made for a righteous man, but for the lawless and disobedient,"[2] suggested very plausibly that " though the wicked were fewer than the righteous, yet because we cannot distinguish them, there is a necessity of suspecting, heeding, anticipating, subjugating, self-defending, ever incident to the most honest and fairest conditioned " (II, xvi).

Because of each man's weakness, Hobbes said, this " natural " state of war was " perpetual in its own nature, because in regard of the equality of those that strive, it

---

[1] Evelyn nicknamed Hobbes " the mushroom " (A.G. III, 61).
[2] Cf. Hooker, E.P. I, i, § 10.

cannot be ended by victory " (II, 12). Therefore it would
be a state of " continual fear and danger of violent death ;[1]
and the life of man solitary, poor, nasty, brutish and
short " (III, 113, cf. II, 12). Unbridled concupiscence,
therefore, would lead to an intolerable conclusion if no
better way offered ; but any rational being—and every
man was sometimes rational when he was in a quiet
mind (II, 44)—could see that there was a better way.
The rational artifice of a compact for mutual security was
the only and the obvious device for preventing this
deplorable conclusion. Astute concupiscence set to work
obliquely ; and men, by entering into such a compact,
could obtain, not all they wanted, but very much more
than they could get in any other way.

Nevertheless, Hobbes retained a highly peculiar doctrine
of the " right " of nature.

" Right " for Hobbes was opposed to " law " (e.g. IV,
223). Law imposed a duty or obligation that was always a
restriction.[2] " Right " was what the laws did not restrain.
" Law is a fetter, right is freedom ; and they differ like
contraries " (II, 186 ; III, 117).

If so, the proper conclusion surely was that where there
was no law there was no right. Where there was no law,
nothing could be legally permitted ; yet Hobbes, in an
essential part of his argument, held that in the lawless
" state of nature " there was a " right of nature," viz. the
right of self-preservation ; and he usually treated this
" right of nature " as a moral right (e.g. II, 190). Indeed
(what was still more puzzling), he defined it as a " right
to unlimited aggression." The alleged " right of nature "
was men's liberty (in a pre-political or ungoverned condition) " to do all they list "[3] (III, 141), to exploit the

---

[1] Cf. Aristotle (Politics, I, ii) : " The ' clanless, lawless, heartless ' man
so bitterly described by Homer is an instance ; for he is naturally a
citizen of no state and a lover of war."

[2] Cf. Justinian (Inst. III, ix) : " Obligatio est juris vinculum."

[3] One Aristotelian sense of " liberty " (Politics, VII, ii).

lives, bodies, and powers of other men and women (if they could) as well as plants, animals, and inanimate things (III, III ; IV, 84). " Nature hath given to everyone a right to all ; that is, it was lawful for every man, in the bare state of nature, or before such time as men had engaged themselves by any covenants or bonds, to do what he could, and against whom he saw fit, and to possess, use and enjoy all what he would or could get " (II, 9), " *Ius* and *utile*, right and profit " became identical (IV, 84), *i.e.* the most unscrupulous and predatory concupiscence was " lawful " (II, 17).

It was often complained, *e.g.* by Pufendorf,[1] that a man could not have a *right* to anything unless it was the duty of others to abstain from molesting him, but Hobbes, I think, perceived this consequence. No one, he said, could call anything *his own* (II, vi) unless men *obliged* (*i.e.* voluntarily restricted) this " right of nature." It was worth men's while, escaping from " nature," to institute property and security by a compact of mutual forbearance, and if an adequate machinery for enforcing this mutual forbearance were discovered, man, instead of being a *wolf* to his fellows, would become " a kind of God " (II, ii), which, as it happens, Bacon had also said (N.O. I, 129).

Hobbes was greatly exercised over this matter of enforcement ; but he often maintained that an obligation attached to *moral* as well as to *civil* laws. Such laws were divine,[2] but of the sort " which God hath declared to all men by his eternal word born with them, to wit, their natural reason " (II, 186 *sq.*). As we saw, all writers agreed that the " laws of nature " were the same as the moral (cf. Hooker, E.P. I, 482, quoting Aquinas); and covenants (III, 126; II, 24, margin ; cf. IV, 93) obliged *in the state of nature.* Again, there

---

[1] *The Law of Nature and of Nations*, II, v, 3 *sqq.*
[2] The canonist Azo (q. Car. III, 31) had spoken of the " ius naturale decalogi."

was a general, and largely moral, obligation to be law-abiding. " Our obligation to civil obedience by virtue whereof
the civil laws are valid is before all civil law " (II, 200).

Strictly speaking,. these dictates of natural reason were
" conclusions or theorems "[1] rather than " laws" (III, 147),
since " laws " were the commands of a superior ; and
although God commanded natural laws, their substance
was just to declare the ways of peace. Such laws asserted
the only possible way in which security could be attained
in *any* society, and since it was impracticable to define
them in the traditional way[2] as resulting from the consent
of all nations (IV, 87 ; II, 15), they were theorems of
rational insight into " the duties men were necessarily to
perform towards others in order to their own conservation "
(II, 16 n.). In brief, " the sum of virtue is to be sociable
with them that will be sociable, and formidable to them
that will not. And the same is the sum of the law of
nature " (IV, 110 *sq.*, cf. II, 13 ; III, 117 ; IV, 87).

This " sum " was also said (III, 117) to be the " first "
and " fundamental " law of nature, and was succeeded by
the prolonged discussion of a second law (the implications
of contract) and of a third (the keeping of contracts, which
(III, 130) was " the fountain and original of justice ").
And Hobbes enumerated several other laws of nature.
Their precise number[3] is unimportant, however, since he
summed them up in another formula. " They have been
contracted into one easy sum,[4] intelligible even to the

---

[1] Suarez (L.L. II, vi, 3) said that " natural law " was only an " indication," since it contained no " signum voluntatis."

[2] *i.e.* the " ius naturale " was *not* the " ius gentium."

[3] In his first formulation (IV, 87 *sqq.*) Hobbes enumerated eleven
laws and two corollaries. One of the laws (IV, 101) decreed something
very like free trade. In the *De Cive* the total was twenty (II, 44), with
an important addendum (II, 49) to the twentieth. In the *Leviathan* the
list ended with the nineteenth law of the *De Cive*, and the addendum
followed. Later (III, 703) an additional law was mentioned, viz. to
serve in war if protected in peace.

[4] A canonist form of the Golden Rule, derived from imperial rather
than from ecclesiastical sources. See Gratian's *Decretum*, D. i (q. Car.,

meanest capacity; and that is, 'Do not that to another which thou wouldest not have done to thyself'" (III, 144, cf. II, 45, and IV, 107). Hobbes admitted, however, that "a quiet mind" (II, 44) was necessary for the "easy sum," and even said (III, 262) that the law of nature " is now become of all laws the most obscure, and has consequently the greatest need of able interpreters."

Some of Hobbes's "laws of nature" dealt with technicalities such as the safety of envoys and primogeniture; but he *did* include the major Christian virtues among them, viz. "modesty, equity, trust, humanity, mercy" (II, 48). To be grateful (III, 138), to be "sociable" (III, 139), to avoid the arrogance of "natural slavery" or of insatiable acquisitiveness (πλεονεξία) were expressly enjoined.

This has been forgotten by Hobbes's critics. "Strong and low . . . but great in that kind," said the Victorian Masson (*Life of Milton*, VI, 288); and the Georgian Mr. Catlin gravely inquired (*Thomas Hobbes*, 35) whether Hobbes was "tainted with moral imbecility." These critics seem to have forgotten the difference between peace and war. In *war*, said Hobbes, "force and fraud are the two cardinal virtues" (III, 115). There man, the wolf, was strong and low. But, in *peace*, man's ways were the ways of a God, not low but very high. I cannot see any reason to doubt that Hobbes was utterly sincere when he

III, 98): " Jus naturæ est, quod in lege et evangelio continetur, quo quisque jubetur alii facere, quod sibi vult fieri, et prohibetur alii inferre, quod sibi nolit fieri." Cf. *op. cit.* II, 178 *sq.* quoting from Paucapalea, a commentator on Gratian : " Naturale ius, quod in lege et in evangelio continetur, quo prohibetur quisque alii inferre, quod sibi nolit fieri, et jubetur alii facere quod sibi vult fieri, ab exordio rationalis creaturæ coepit, et inter omnia primatum obtinet ; nullo enim variatur tempore, sed immutabile permanet."

Hobbes's form of what he called the " old dictate " was " Quod tibi fieri non vis, alteri ne feceris " (IV, 107), and is to be found in Azo (q. Car., II, 47 n.), who did not, any more than Hobbes, distinguish the negative from the positive formula. The rule meant, according to Hobbes (III, 144), something quite positive, viz. putting oneself in another's place and so avoiding private partiality.

said (II, 62) that the whole *law*, although not the whole *doctrine* of Christ, was contained within his moral system. Certainly Hobbes's grounds were utilitarian; but if Hobbes should be condemned for that reason many theological and episcopal moralists should be condemned also.

In short, Hobbes accepted the traditional virtues, but professed to give a new deduction of them. " The way or means of peace," he said (III, 146, cf. II, 48), " which, as I have showed before, are justice, gratitude, modesty, equity, mercy, and the rest of the laws of nature, are good, that is to say, moral virtues, and their contrary vices evil. Now the science of virtue and vice is moral philosophy."

Indeed, in his own way, Hobbes agreed with the rationalists as well as with the Christians, for he said that the laws of nature were " immutable and eternal," whose opposites could never be made lawful (III, 145). Here, since the passions of men need not be eternal, there was the same sort of difficulty as in Hobbes's views regarding the " sempiternity " of true speech. But Hobbes maintained that voluntary law-breaking was " somewhat like to that which in the disputation of scholars is called absurdity " (III, 119). To break a promise, for example, was to treat the promise as if it were no promise.

Let us turn now to the best-known part of Hobbian ethics, his account of the foundations of contract and of justice.

Each man had to divest himself of his liberty, or of a part of it, for a " consideration " (III, 118, 297 ; II, 17 ; IV, 87) ; but, since the " right of nature " was a right to *everything*, a positive and sufficient privilege could be conferred (on the rulers) if those who divested themselves of their " rights " simply " stood out of the way " (III, 118). To avoid the state of war every man (who was to become a subject) had to renounce[1] some certain rights,

---

[1] Technically (III, 118) Hobbes distinguished between " renunciation " and " transfer." In the former a man " stood aside " from every one, in the latter from some particular person regarding some particular thing.

and, in substance, " to be contented with so much liberty against other men as he would allow other men against himself " (III, 118). The ultimate " consideration " was always " fear of some evil consequences " ; but any obligation, duly entered upon, really did " oblige " (*ibid.*).

Any such voluntary obligation had to be declared by " sufficient signs," even if it were ostensibly unilateral, as in the case of a gift made " to deliver the mind from the pain of compassion " (III, 121). A contract, however, was bi- or multi-lateral, being a mutual transferring or conveying of rights (III, 120 ; II, 20) ; and a contract became a pact or a covenant if there was a time-interval, during which one of the contracting parties had to trust the other (III, 121).

If a promise could not be fulfilled, only the " unfeigned endeavour of performing as much as is possible " was obligatory (III, 126) ; and certain covenants, being inherently void, could never be lawful. A man could not covenant to accuse himself (III, 128), or to yield his body to force. Even a condemned criminal had the " right " to resist the executioner (II, 25 ; III, 127). It was his neighbours who *stood by* and let him suffer. Again, some " natural rights " had to be retained, viz. those that were essential to life (rather widely interpreted), " as right to govern their own bodies ; enjoy air, water, motion, ways to go from place to place ; and all things else without which a man cannot live, or not live well " (III, 141, cf. 127, 270 ; II, 39 ; IV, 103)—a very elastic provision, and plainly absurd unless the man were *protected* on the highways and waterways.

Men could be freed from their covenants either by performance or by being forgiven (III, 126 ; II, 23) ; and one party was freed if the other broke the covenant. Indeed, every covenant was void " upon any reasonable suspicion " of bad faith (III, 124 ; II, 21). Hobbes also made a considerable concession to human infirmity when he said that " a certain high degree of fear " annulled obligation, because men were not " tied to impossibilities " (II, 25).   On the other hand, he stoutly asserted that a covenant " entered into by fear " was obligatory " in a condition of mere nature " (*e.g.* III, 126).   The civil law might override the obligation to pay brigands their ransom (II, 24).   Otherwise the ransom, being the genuine purchase of a life, had to be paid.

These general principles were closely connected with *iustice* in its narrower sense, viz. the *keeping* of covenants (III, 130).

There was, indeed, a wider sense of " justice," *i.e.* whatever was done " with right " (II, 32 *sq.* ;   46 n.), and it is to be feared that Hobbes equivocated sadly between the wider and the narrower senses, since he professed to deduce the *whole* of his ethics (II, vi) from the analysis of justice in the *narrower* sense, *i.e.* from the meaning of a man's *own* in the traditional definition (Ulpian's *Digest*, I, 10), " the constant and perpetual will to give each man his own."

In the narrower sense, the essential points were that the violation of a covenant had to be carefully distinguished from other forms of " damage " (II, 32 ; III, 136 ; IV, 96), " iniquity " (II, 33), " vice " (II, 101) and " mischief " (II, 32 n.) ;   and that a just act was in conformity with some law, natural or civil (II, 31 n.).   The clearest expression of Hobbes's principle that I have been able to find is the following (II, 185, and note) : " Contracts oblige us ; laws tie us fast, being obliged ;[1] the law holds the party obliged by the universal contract of yielding obedience. . . . More clearly, I say thus : that a man is obliged by his contracts, that is, that he ought to perform for his promise' sake ; but that the law ties him, being obliged, that is to say, it compels him to make good his

[1] The general idea was that *all* law, physical or moral, consisted in keeping things or men in their appointed place.   Cf. Suarez (L.L. I, i).

promise for fear of the punishment appointed by the law."

The general sense of this statement appears to be that there was an eternal moral obligation to keep promises, but that, when men had promised obedience to a government, they made themselves liable, in addition, to the punitive machinery of political power.[1] And so we come to a perplexing (but very fundamental) part of Hobbian theory.

As we have seen, Hobbes frequently held that moral laws might be anterior to civil laws. Indeed some of them *obliged* " in a state of nature." In other passages, however (and for the most part), he spoke, particularly regarding " justice," as if human morality were essentially political, not pre-political. " The laws of commonwealth are the ground and measure of all true morality " (VII, 75 *sq.*). Covenants had to be *compellable* (IV, 91). " Before the names of just and unjust can have place, there must be some coercive power to compel men equally to the performance of their covenants . . . and such power there is none before the creation of a commonwealth " (III, 131). " Before there was any government just and unjust *had no being* " (II, 151) ; or, briefly (B. 44), the sovereign's morality was summed up in " salus populi," the subjects' in *obedience*.

I cannot see how these views can be reconciled. But let us examine the matter.

(*a*) It might be said that although a duty was, by definition, an obligation, it might be unreasonable to undertake *any* obligation unless we knew it would be enforced. This interpretation, however, could not apply to what " obliged " in the state of mere nature.

(*b*) It might be argued that enforcement applied only to " justice " in Hobbes's narrower sense, and not to equity, mercy, or other laws of nature. If so, such statements as

[1] Cf. Hooker (E.P. I, 310 *sq.*).

(IV, 223) that what is against divine or natural law cannot be *jure* were censurable ; and Hobbes contradicted
himself in other ways. Thus, in an eloquent discussion
of the theme, " the fool hath said in his heart there is no
justice" (III, 32), he argued that the "specious reasoning "
that appeared to justify " successful wickedness " was
only specious because, in a state of war, confederacies
were necessary, and were impossible without mutual trust.
In that case, however, the contracting parties did *not* form
a commonwealth, and were *not* subject to a common
coercive power.

(c) Hobbes sometimes argued (*e.g.* II, 191) that while
the law of nature forbade, say, adultery, the civil law
declared what copulations were permitted. If so, he
should have inferred that the law of nature could never
tell us our duty in detail.

(d) It might be said that, on Hobbian principles,
covenants were " in the state of nature invalid " if there
was a " just suspicion " of probable non-performance
(II, 21) ; and that there was *always* a just suspicion unless
the covenant could be legally enforced. This argument
would be very sophistical ; but Hobbes, no doubt, was
capable of sophistry. In his principal explanation, however (*ibid.*), he maintained that a " just suspicion" in the
case of covenants implied " some new cause of fear,"
i.e. something absent from the minds of the contracting
parties when they made their covenants.

(e) In general, Hobbes was entitled to argue that a man
who was " modest and tractable " would be simply *soft*
if he allowed his predatory neighbours to take advantage
of his pacific disposition (*e.g.* III, 145), and so that the
laws of nature were necessary, but not sufficient, for the
peace of mankind. If so, many very un-Hobbian people
would agree with him, and would be arguing, not that
might was right, but that " right " (*i.e.* peaceable) action
had to be supported by might. I think this *was* sub-

stantially what Hobbes meant, but some of his applications of his principle were certainly peculiar, including his account of conscience.

" The force of the law of nature," Hobbes said, " is not *in foro externo* till there be security for men to obey it, but always *in foro interno*, wherein the action of obedience being unsafe, the will and readiness to perform is taken for the performance " (IV, 108, cf. III, 145 ; II, 46).

If this readiness to perform were an " unfeigned and constant endeavour " (III, 145) even the sectaries might have agreed ; and they would have accepted Hobbes's statement that if a man *thought* he was acting against the law, although in fact he was acting in accordance with it, he was unjust (*ibid.*). Such an endeavour, however, should have been an endeavour *to act*, whereas Hobbes said (*ibid.*) it was only a " desire they should take place," not always " the putting of them in act." " Conscience " was a *mere* disposition, and action was obligatory only if it was safe (II, 46).

This view was so clearly preposterous that even Hobbes did not always adhere to it. The sovereign, he said, had the duty " according to his conscience " to *further* the " benefit and good " of the subjects, and although Hobbes could argue consistently that civil laws were concerned with external obedience only, he could not use this argument about the laws of nature. Indeed, his account of " law " was confused, as may be seen by comparison of the statement, " All rules of life which men are in conscience bound to observe are laws" (III, 366), with the antithetic assertion, " a law obligeth no otherwise than by virtue of some covenant " (IV, 221).

Sometimes Hobbes argued (*e.g.* IV, 195) that force could not constrain the (private) conscience. His general doctrine, however, was that a private man should obey the *public* conscience, that is to say, the civil laws, unless the government expressly permitted him to follow his own

" settled judgment and opinion " (IV, 187). A man transferred his private right of judgment to his political superior,
and was seditious if he held that he ought, nevertheless, to
obey his private conscience (*ibid.*). If so, Hobbes should
have inferred that it was seditious to retain a private
conscience at all.

Hobbes had also a doctrine of " sin."

He usually regarded " sin " as voluntary disobedience
against the law (IV, 259 *sq.* ; V. 229, 234). If the civil
law was contrary to the moral, the sovereign sinned in
imposing the civil law, but the subject was blameless in
obeying it (II, 152). He also held, however, that " before
there was any government, just and unjust had no being,
their nature only being relative to some command ; and
every action in its own nature is indifferent ; that it becomes
just or unjust proceeds from the right of the magistrate "
(II, 151). Even in the narrower sense of " justice " this
argument was plainly misleading. Actions, in a pre-political
condition, might easily be hurtful, and therefore not
" indifferent," in any ordinary sense, although they could
not be legally " unjust."

More generally, Hobbes held that sin (II, 195 *sq.*) " in its
largest signification comprehends every deed, word, and
thought against right reason "—although a private man
(*e.g.* V, 193) had to presume that the laws of the land *were*
" right reason." Consequently, sin was what the city
decided to be " blameable with reason " (II, 196 *sq.*). It
was therefore different from depravity (*ibid.*), since a man
might be depraved and not break the civil laws, or might
sin " through human infirmity " without being depraved.

In the *Leviathan* (III, 277) Hobbes said that sin included
" contempt of the legislator " as well as transgression, and
he applied the conception to disposition as well as to
action. Against the Puritans he opined that the mere
imagination, say, of possessing another man's wife was
scarcely a sin, although it was " safer " to judge it so

(III, 278, cf. B. 26). A definite *intention* of the kind, however, was always a sin, although it was not a *crime* unless the intention were fulfilled. Thus " the civil law ceasing, *crimes* also cease " (III, 279), although offences against the *moral* law " can never cease to be sin " (*ibid.*).

I have mentioned Hobbes's addendum to his " laws of nature " ; but the principle of this addendum was of far greater importance than Hobbes seems to have noticed.

In the *De Cive* (II, 44) Hobbes enunciated as a twentieth law of nature the prohibition to destroy or weaken the rational faculty (*e.g.* by intemperance), and explained (II, 49) that he had enumerated those laws only that referred to peace although there were " other precepts of rational nature from which spring other virtues " (*e.g.* temperance and courage). Some of these other virtues, he noted, were obligatory *even in a state of war* (II, 45 n.), " for I cannot understand that drunkenness or cruelty—that is, revenge which respects not the future good—can advance towards peace or the preservation of any man." In the *Leviathan* (III, 144) he remarked, very curtly, that " drunkenness and all other parts of intemperance " were morally forbidden as " tending to the destruction of particular men," although such matters were not " pertinent enough to this place."

Clearly, on these principles, *all* a man's valuable powers, not merely those of his " reason," ought to be preserved and also developed. All the duties of self-culture and of public improvement should have been included, whether or not they had any special relevance to keeping the peace ; and Hobbes's ethical theory should have become a complete utilitarianism, probably of the broader, not exclusively hedonistic, type that is now currently styled " ideal utilitarianism." Very probably Hobbes would not have restricted his ethical theory to the problem of deliverance from civil tumult had the calamities of his own England weighed less heavily on his spirit.

(3) THE FREE-WILL CONTROVERSY

As I have pointed out, much that is most characteristic in Hobbes's ethics and psychology of action was most clearly put in his separate polemic concerning free-will, and the metaphysical as well as the ethical and the psychological aspects of this question formed an integral part of his philosophy. I propose, therefore, to consider this matter now, although part of it is a digression. As we shall see in Part III, the historical influence of Hobbes's treatment of this problem were very considerable ; and since Hobbes's views regarding the theme were highly important on their merits, they may even have a certain topical interest in these days when so many eminent physicists do not fear to tread the paths (or to beat the air ?) of indeterminism.

We have already noted the circumstances under which Hobbes's controversy with John Bramhall, Bishop of Derry, and later Archbishop of Armagh, achieved publicity, and now should remark that their dispute was one of the best of all philosophical duels,[1] and that, despite the asperity of some of their later exchanges, the disputants, on the whole, respected one another. " Though I honour T. H. for his person and for his learning," Bramhall said (V, 110), " yet I must confess ingenuously, I hate this doctrine from my heart " ; and Hobbes, although somewhat grudgingly, seems to have admitted that Bramhall had argued as well as " a learned school-divine " " depraved by doctrine " could do (V, To the Reader, and 113).

Although the combatants were not ill-matched, Hobbes was certainly the abler, and would have won on points had the contest been decided in that fashion. I do not think, however, that he convicted his opponent of

---

[1] Worthy to be compared with Locke's correspondence with Stillingfleet, Arnauld's with Malebranche, or Clarke's with Leibniz.

absurdity ; and there was much in Bramhall's argument
to which Hobbes showed either a " politic deafness "
(V, 229) or complete intellectual surdity. This I propose
to show.

Hobbes's fundamental contention was that a man was
free to *do* anything if he *could* do it when he had a mind
to do it (V, 38 *sq.*), but that the man's will or appetite to
perform the action, like any other event in nature, had
necessary causes (IV, 274 *sq.*). He interpreted this profound analysis, however, in terms of a very definite
philosophical theory, and the question is whether, as
Bramhall thought (V, 30), he gave himself " line enough "
to " trip up the heels of his whole cause."

" Necessary," said Hobbes (V, 35), " is that which is
impossible to be otherwise, or that which cannot possibly
otherwise come to pass," and he tried to prove that
whatever is, is necessary, on the ground that everything
must be precisely what it is (*e.g.* V, 423, 427).   Here,
however, like many contemporary British physicists, he
confused grossly between what is determinate (*i.e.* just
what it is) and what has been necessarily *determined*, by
antecedent causes, to become what it now is. It is greatly
to Bramhall's credit that he did eventually puncture the
fallacy. " ' I know that either it will rain to-morrow or
that it will not rain to-morrow,' " he said, " is a true
proposition ; but it is not true that I know it will rain
to-morrow, neither is it true that I know it will not rain
to-morrow ; wherefore the certain truth of the proposition
doth not prove that either of the members is determinately
true in present " (V, 414 *sq.*).   Therefore it was *not* senseless to say : " Either this or that will infallibly be, but
it is not yet determined whether this or that shall be."
(*ibid.*).

A proposition, of course, without being senseless may
very well be false. I am not saying that Bramhall proved
that there *was* contingency, but he *did* disprove Hobbes's

repeated assertion (*e.g.* V, 49, 378) that contingency could only mean that which had necessary but unknown causes. He also proved (V, 431) that God's foreknowledge did not prove determinism. (It would do so only if God foreknew because He inferred from antecedent conditions.)

What Bramhall was chiefly concerned to deny was that " all things be *extrinsically pre*determined *to one* " (V, 84), that is to say, that *each* of a freeman's acts was uniquely and completely determined by what had happened outside him ages before and by " the flux or concatenation of the second [*i.e.* natural] causes " (V, 33). Usually (*e.g.* V, 161) he confused between necessitation and compulsion—although not always (V, 249). For the most part, however, he denied, without great misunderstanding, precisely what Hobbes affirmed.

For Hobbes the question was about *motion*. All human action, even the " nimble local motion " of the Bishop's fingers (V, 188) was local motion, and was determined " physically, and extrinsically, and antecedently " (*ibid.*). Hobbes took his stand upon the mechanical philosophy, affirming that " all action is the effect of motion, and that there cannot be a motion in one part of the world but the same must also be communicated to all the rest of the world " (V, 305).

Hence he inferred that " the will is not free but subject to change by the operation of external causes " (V, 450), and that "all external causes depend necessarily upon the first eternal cause, God Almighty, who worketh in us both to will and to do, by the mediation of second causes" (*ibid.*). What Bramhall called " moral causes " would have to operate by a " moral," *i.e.* by a non-natural motion (V, 451). " A wooden top that is lashed by the boys, and runs about sometimes to one wall, sometimes to another, sometimes spinning, sometimes hitting men on the shins, if it were sensible of its own motion, would think it proceeded from its own will, unless it felt what lashed it " (V, 55, cf. 273). Such precisely was the state of man. Even in the making of a garment (V, 226) " the necessity begins from the first motion towards it ; though the tailor and the Bishop are equally insensible of it. If they ṣaw the whole order and conjunction of causes, they would say it were as necessary as any thing else can possibly be."

These contentions, if sound, followed from Hobbes's materialism rather than from his determinism. For determinism says nothing about the type of causes that operate. Indeed, there seems to have been a yawning chasm between Hobbes's political and ethical theory on the one hand, and these materialistic assertions on the other hand. In ethics all was based on selfishness and apparent personal good in defiance of the rest of the world. In these materialistic contentions the self was at the best a temporary aggregate, and the true causality was the reciprocity of motion throughout the entire universe. Hobbes emphasised extrinsic determination so much that he almost forgot that, as long as things like tops exist, they have a certain intrinsic potency regarding their own movements. Nothing on earth, Bramhall truly said (V, 374) caused its own *being*, but particular things, when in being, might be self-moving. And this seems *possible*.

When a man does what he wants to do, he may not usually raise the question why he wanted to do it ; but Hobbes, by holding that the reason was always *external*, interpreted his doctrine of necessity in such a way as largely to justify Bramhall's complaint that he made " a reasonable man no more than a tennis-ball, to be tossed to and fro by the rackets of the second causes " (V, 278), and Hobbes's reply—that a man might be a " great thing " like a " football "—was scarcely sufficient. Certainly, Bramhall (V, 270) should have distinguished between compulsion (co-action) and necessity (coarctation) ; but Hobbes's own argument went far towards excusing

his error. If all a man's actions, in every detail, were
necessitated by causes *outside* him, then his consent,
granting it to exist, might well be called " titular " and
" empty " (V, 239). Bramhall was quite wrong in saying
(*e.g.* V, 253) that, according to Hobbes, men were always
" compelled " to act against their wills and inclinations;
but Hobbes himself, although he appealed so confidently
to " the English and well-bred reader " (V, 262), defined
" compulsion " in a way that led to difficulty. " For my
part," he said (*ibid.*, cf. IV, 261), " I understand compulsion to be used of living creatures only, which are
moved only by their own animal motion, in such manner
as they would not be moved without the fear." This
statement admitted that animals *were* self-moving ; and
in Hobbes's extended use of " fear " (II, 6 n.) every precautionary measure would be " compulsory."

Bramhall (V, 84) distinguished four classes of action,
viz. " natural " action extrinsically caused (as a stone
thrown up), " natural " actions intrinsically caused (as a
stone falling down), " voluntary or spontaneous " acts
where there was appetition but neither deliberation nor
election, and " free " acts of will that were reasoned about,
and chosen. His complaint was that Hobbes reduced all
actions to the first.

That was false. Hobbes denied " stoical or violent
destiny " (V, 242), and made short work of the scholastic
pseudo-physics of the falling stone. By maintaining,
however, that all organic stimulation was external (V, 312)
he seemed to overlook the importance of the nervous
system itself. Again, in objecting to the term " spontaneity," he protested intelligibly against the notion that
a thing might act causelessly of its own accord (V, 93), yet
although Bramhall held that some " spontaneous " actions
were partly undetermined (V, 173), he believed that others
were " determined to one " (V, 66). Indeed, as Hobbes
sometimes perceived (V, 47 and 93), what Bramhall called

" spontaneity " Hobbes called " will " ; but they differed profoundly in their analysis of it.

Hobbes's " will " was the " last appetite," and Bramhall, admitting that the analysis was current—" in this and this only, I confess T. H. hath good seconds " (V, 72)— nevertheless decided against it. " The will," he said (*ibid.*), " is moved by the understanding, not as by an efficient having a causal influence into the effect, but only by proposing and representing the object." To say, as Hobbes did, that will was the " last feather," was to assume that each " feather " or the " horse load of feathers " (V, 110) had " a certain natural weight." In reality (V, 319 *sq.*), " the determination of the judgment is no part of the weight, but is the sentence of the trier. The understanding weigheth all things, objects, means, circumstances, convenience, inconvenience ; but itself is not weighed."

In these statements, no doubt, there was an overdose of metaphor, and Bramhall's account of human " faculties " was incredibly naïve. He answered Hobbes's statement that it was " absurdly said that to dance is an act allured or drawn by fair means out of the ability to dance " (V, 274), by the retort (V, 284), " it may be said aptly without any absurdity that the act of dancing is drawn out of the locomotive faculty helped by the acquired habit." Essentially, however, he was right when, anticipating M. Bergson, he denied that motives, before decision, need be assumed to have a constant weight (like feathers), or indeed to have any antecedent weight at all. Similarly, it seems clear that Hobbes, despite his protests (V, 365), did not discriminate sufficiently between a " sensitive appetite " and a " rational will." If animal and human deliberation, as he said (V, 95), did not differ in principle, the inference might have been that animals are more rational than men commonly suppose. If there was much more than an analogy (V, 195) between human rewards and the way in

which, according to Bramhall (V, 173), " setting-dogs, coy-
ducks, and parrots " were ruled " by their backs or their
bellies, by the rod or the morsel," Hobbes should have
been able to distinguish, by introspection, between a series
of pictures of rods or morsels and a synoptic review of
probable consequences with the purpose of deciding on
evidence.

In certain respects, therefore, Bramhall's analysis was
superior to Hobbes's, although I do not suggest that
Bramhall established his positive case. It does not seem
likely that " fortune " (V, 450) was a better foundation
of rational self-control than " fate," and Bramhall's
doctrine that the will was " the king of the little world of
himself " (V, 306) may have implied the absurdity that a
man could will to will (*e.g.* IV, 240). On the other hand, it
does seem clear that a man may *choose to deliberate* or to
postpone decision ; and, as I have said, Hobbes's egoistic
psychology did imply some sort of self-determination as
well as of self-seeking. I think, in short, that Hobbes's
defence of determinism was very sane, but that his attempt
to unite the egoistic determinism of his psychology with
his general materialism was much less successful.

There may, indeed, have been certain ethical " inconveniences " in determinism as such ; but Hobbes easily
showed that most of the " inconveniences " that Bramhall
alleged were mere misunderstandings. Determinism does
not imply that consultations are vain (V, 170), that
admonitions are without effect (V, 171), that praise and
dispraise are meaningless (V, 171 *sq.*), that " study, physic,
and the like " are inefficacious (V. 174), and that punishment must be "unjust and absurd " (V. 150). Counsel and
admonition might very well be the means that necessitated
a change in the person admonished (IV, 254 *sq.*). To praise
a thing was to call it good, and Bramhall himself admitted
that there might be " natural " goodness in determined
things, as when " the burning of the fire pleaseth me

when I am cold " (V. 171).   As for punishment, Hobbes,
" as having only humane ideas " (V, 177), believed in the
deterrent theory (V, 181) and in the right to destroy what
was *noxious* (V, 152).   More generally " it was a very
great praise, in my opinion, that Velleius Paterculus gives
Cato, where he says, he was good by nature, *and could not
be otherwise* " (V. 155).

On points of theology and Scriptural exegesis, Hobbes
was at least Bramhall's equal. He may have been wrong,
indeed, in saying that we worshipped God for His mere
power, and honoured Him with eulogistic epithets which
(for Hobbes) were strictly meaningless ; but Hobbes
conceded as much as was reasonable when he said that
God, although the creator of sin, was not its *author* or
warranter (V, 214 *sq.*) ; for Bramhall, who held that God
created all sinners, *foreknowing their actions*, was in an
untenable position. He had to hold that men were first
causes that nevertheless were *made*, and that God (V, 141)
was at least an accessory to their sins. To say with
Bramhall, that God " winked at " the times of ignorance
(V, 124), deserved Hobbes's comment that " God sees,
looks on, and does nothing, nor ever did any thing in the
business " (V, 140), if not something even more severe.
And Hobbes had Scripture and all experience on his side
when he pointed out (*e.g.* V, 237) that, whatever might be
true of " punishment," God *afflicted* just and unjust, and
brutes too.

VI

POLITICS AND RELIGION

(1) THE FOUNDATIONS OF DOMINION

WE have now to consider the celebrated political theory
that Hobbes constructed on the basis of his analysis of
human motives, combined with (as he thought) a clear-
headedness never attained before regarding the meaning
of the terms essential to political regiment and a deep
philosophical understanding of the realities of orderly
government. Religion was an appendage. Being the
chief cause of sedition, it had (he maintained) to be put
in its proper place ; that is, it was proved to be an affair
of law and of civil obedience.

Hobbes admitted that paternal and despotic dominion
arose " naturally " (*e.g.* II, 70 *sq.*) and were " submission
to natural force " (III, 159). It is clear, however, that
patriarchs, chieftains, and despots did not rule by *mere*
force, and consequently that their " natural dominion "
was more " artificial " than Hobbes commonly allowed.
But he gave most of his energies to the problem of *instituted*
dominion.

What had to be instituted was a power sufficient to
make external enemies tremble, and to prevent internal
enemies from hurting their neighbours ; and Hobbes
thought it was demonstrable that consent, contract, or
covenant (at least of a " tacit " sort) was of the essence
of the political device. Therefore he defined a civil society
as " a multitude of men, united as one person, by a common
power, for their common peace, defence, and benefit "

(IV, 122), it being understood that the union took place in some particular locality (II, 256 ; III, 210), and (III, 507) that the act of association into one body politic implied dissociation from others.

" Two or three men," Hobbes said, might establish a rudimentary city (II, 65; III, 154; IV, 119), and the optimum size (II, 65) depended on the probability of effective union. He believed, historically, that " little cities " (II, 84 n.) or families had preceded great ones. In the main, however, he thought of cities being founded in a large assembly (as when the Hebrews made Saul king), and his fundamental problem was the logical question how each citizen could be said to govern *although*, or *because*, he voluntarily submitted himself to some particular type of dominion.

He had therefore to distinguish between a mere multitude and a political "union" (IV, 121; II, 68), " public " (B. 113) or "people." "The people," he said (II, 158), " is somewhat that is *one*, having *one will*, and to whom *one action* may be attributed ; none of these can properly be said of a multitude. The *people* rules in all governments. For even in monarchies the *people*[1] commands ; for the *people* wills by the will of *one man* ; but the multitude are citizens, that is to say, subjects. In a democracy and aristocracy the citizens are the multitude, but the court is the *people*.[2] And in a monarchy the subjects are the multitude and (however it seem a paradox) the king is the *people*."

Since the multitude was a *mere* aggregate, it was not a contracting body ; for a contract implied a single " will " (II, 98). In a multitude, therefore, the only possible form of contract was between each several member and each

---

[1] Not the plebs, as Bellarmine had said of democracies (*De Rom. Pont.* I, 6).
[2] Cf. Occam (*Dial.* III, q. Gierke, *Gen.* 562 n.), " plures gerunt vicem unius et locum unius tenent," and Patrick of Siena (*De Inst. Reip.* I, 5 : q. *loc. cit.*), " multitudo universa potestatem habet collecta in unum, ubi de republica sit agendum, dimissi autem rem suam agunt."

of the others. This was the first step in political institution, and its formula was (III, 158) : " I authorize and give up my right of governing myself, to this man, or to this assembly of men, on this condition, that thou give up thy right to him, and authorize all his actions in like manner " (cf. II, 99).

Let us examine the implications of this procedure and of its formula :

(a) The multitude had to transform itself into a *people* by a covenant, each with each, that each would submit to dominion, and Hobbes, in his earlier writings, held that the multitude must begin by forming an assembly with intent to unite. Hence he inferred (IV, 139) that a democracy *must* precede any other type of city, since the first step of the multitude was necessarily to resolve itself into a sovereign demos deciding by a majority. Similarly, he said in *De Cive*, that " those who met together with intention to erect a city, were, almost in the very act of meeting, a democracy "[1] (II, 96).

(b) Hobbes held that the act of instituting a city must be a perpetual convention, and he argued the point, following Bodin (84) on very formal lines. If the first assembly dissolved, it must either have instituted a continuing government or else dissolve again into a mere multitude. Another assembly, in that case, would found a *new* city (*e.g.* II, 97). If the demos prorogued itself till a later appointed date, it would be the continuing sovereign body even if it gave a junta, a tyrant, or a consul temporary executive powers ; but, according to Hobbes, it gave up its power altogether if it prorogued itself *sine die*.

(c) Regarding minorities, Hobbes sometimes relied on the principle that *all* must bind themselves, at least tacitly (III, 162), to accept a majority decision ; but he also held, more logically, that any man who denied the city's will became thereby an outlaw (III, 163, cf. II, 74).

[1] Cf. Henry Marten's *Jus Populi* (1644).

(*d*) The nature of the institutive pact or covenant could be determined more precisely as follows :

(i) It was a pact or covenant of subjection. " Peace without subjection " was absurd (III, 155), because good-will without coercion was impotent (IV, 129). The procedure was " donation of right " (II, 91).

(ii) In Hobbes's earlier writings (IV, 88, 129 ; II, 68 *sq*.) the theory of " donation " was, that although rights could not be transferred, a subject, by abstaining from interference with the sovereign's " natural right " to *everything* (which the sovereign, like anybody else, always possessed) did all that could be required. What was really wanted, however, was that the subjects should " contribute their several forces for the defence of the whole " (IV, 130). The theory might perhaps have been saved by asserting that the sovereign appointed the citizens to be his agents, and so to help him actively, not merely passively. It is not surprising, however, that in the *Leviathan* this doctrine very nearly disappeared and was replaced by the theory of " artificial personality," less prominent, although not infrequent (*e.g.* II, 69), in the earlier works.

A " natural person " was any responsible adult (III, 150) ; and an " artificial " or " feigned " person was one (or many) who, by agreement, personated anyone (III, 147), the word *persona* literally meaning an actor's mask. Every natural person was the " author," owner, or lord of his actions (III, 148) ; and the *authority* of a representative was just the *authorship* or agency of the agent voluntarily transferred to the " artificial person " who personated him (III, 148).

Such was the " city " or " people," " every man giving their common representer authority from himself in particular, and owning all the actions the representer doth in case they give him authority without stint " (III, 151). Each member of the multitude conferred " all

his power and strength" upon his ruler or rulers, *i.e.*
upon those appointed "to bear their person. . . . in those
things which concern the common peace and safety"
(III, 157 *sq.*, cf. 212). Therefore the city really was *one*,
because each citizen gave his own *authorship* to this
authority, and acknowledged, indeed *did*, what his personator did.

Hence there was a second reason why the "people"
could not contract with any individual citizen or group
of citizens. If it did, it would be contracting with itself
or with a part of itself[1]—which was absurd (III, 161 *sqq.*,
cf. II, 153 *sq.*). No one would say that the people of
Rome made a contract with the Romans to hold the
sovereignty under such and such conditions (III, 162) ;
and, as we saw, the sovereign was always the "people."

Hobbes's "artificial person," therefore, was not the
persona ficta of Roman law. It was not a body permitted
for legal purposes to plead as if it were a natural person,
but the source and reality of all legal action.

It was not clear, however, how precisely Hobbes's
artificial person really was "one will." What happened
was that each citizen commissioned the "people" (*i.e.* the
government) to act for him. Even if the ruler were a single
man, he ruled in his representative capacity only ; and it
is not clear that a majority was literally *one will*. Perhaps,
however, much that Hobbes said is an implication of any
genuine self-government. All political authority must be
personal. Principles, laws, and traditions govern only in
a derived sense. And if some men govern other men, there
can be self-government only if governed as well as gover-
nors are the *authors* of the acts of government. We might
even have to speak with Lord Rosebery of " that nation for

---

[1] Cf. Bodin, p. 99. To-day in England " no engagement between the
Crown and any of its military or naval officers in respect of services,
present or past, can be enforced in a court of law." Judgment of Mr.
Justice Farwell, in *Kynaston* v. *Attorney-General*, as reported in *The
Times*, 1st December 1932.

which we legislate but which governs us."[1] The irony of
Hobbes's theory was that the subjects-to-be seemed to
will away, not their own subsequent agency only, but also
the subsequent agency of all future subjects.

(2) THE NATURE OF SOVEREIGNTY

" A king," said Selden in his *Table Talk*, " is a thing
men have made for their own sakes, for quietness' sake."
That was Hobbes's view in a phrase. " The right of all
sovereigns is derived originally from the consent of every
one of those that are to be governed" (III, 573, cf. III,
464). That was a law of nature (III, 577 *sqq.*, 579).
Yet, although the sovereignty was but a commission to
act (III, 151), granted by natural persons to their personator,
it became humanly indistinguishable from the most
arbitrary tyranny (*e.g.* III, 706) once it had been conferred.
The reason was that sovereignty, in its essence, was
perpetual, absolute, and indivisible.

Let us then examine these fundamental characteristics.

(*a*) *Perpetuity*.—We have already noticed Hobbes's
formal arguments on this point, and of course he had to
be formal since he was demonstrating principles, as in
" arithmetic and geometry," not practical skill, " as in
tennis play " (III, 195 *sq.*). Even formally, however, the
argument seems weak. Governments should be designed
for stability, and should not take unnecessary risks of
reverting to the " dissolute condition of masterless men "
(III, 170). Still, there would always be very strong motives
for convening another assembly with no greater irregu-
larity in its convocation than the first, and (human foresight being very ill-suited to perpetuity) such irregularities
might be less inconvenient (or even less disastrous) than
any other procedure. Again, by Hobbes's own admission,
a temporary dictatorship or consulship implied no

[1] Lord Crewe's *Life*, I, 203.

absurdity, but merely entailed that the government, in that case, was ultimately democratic. And why not ?

To most modern readers this claim of perpetuity seems absurd. How could any promise bind men, irrespective of what might transpire, not merely for all their future lives, but also for the lives of all their descendants ? Even if Hobbes was entitled to argue that " consent " was only a common direction of men's actions (II, 65), a " tacit coven-ant " of participation (III, 162), a presumed submission to government by accepting its protection (III, 705), how could such lazy acquiescence imply a perpetual promise ?

Presumed or " tacit " consent of this acquiescent order would apply to " status " as readily as to " contract " ; and neither of these need be perpetual. Certainly, when men had learned how to bind themselves by covenant, the formal institution of a government was an event of capital importance. Hobbes rightly laid stress upon pacts and covenants, just as his opponents laid stress upon Magna Charta. Such events should not be quietly sub-merged in the changing drift of social forces. Yet politics itself was ultimately a part of the social drift. It was not, as Hobbes (like his contemporaries), constantly implied, a vague term for describing what, when clearly thought out, implied the formal institution of a perpetual form of government.

(b) *Absolutism.*—Hobbes's general view was that " the right of sovereignty is such, as he or they that have it cannot, though they would, give away any part thereof and retain the " rest " (IV, 206). It was as great as was " imaginable "[1] (III, 195, 546 ; II, 80, 221) ; and civil liberty (as opposed to pre-political licence) lay " only in these things, which in regulating their actions, the sove-reign hath prætermitted "(III, 199).

[1] Cf. Bramhall's *Serpent Salve* (*Works*, III, 332) : " If we can purchase tranquillity, which we intend, with obedience and subjection, which we must undergo, we have no cause to complain of the bargain."

On the other hand, he held that no ruler could attempt to regulate *all* the actions of his subjects (III, 199), that the subject retained *certain* rights (*e.g.* III, 141), that a man had liberty to disobey if commanded to kill or maim himself, or to abstain from necessary food, air, or medicine (III, 204), and that he was not bound to kill his fellow or to undertake dangerous service unless his disobedience would, in principle, annul the sovereignty. (Thus men of " feminine courage " might procure substitutes in the militia.) Similarly, a condemned malefactor had not bound himself to submit to violence (III, 297). And, generally (II, 82), no one promised to do what he would rather die than do.

Here it must be objected to Hobbes that the malefactor, if not an outlaw, *had* commissioned or authorised the sovereign to undertake just those executive functions which, by an unexpected and most unpleasing inference, led to his own hanging.

More generally, Hobbes's views would be consistent only if, in the nature of things, certain powers could never be transferred to any ruler, so that absolutism meant simply that all the powers that could be transferred were in fact bestowed upon the ruler. This is what Hobbes said (III, 120 and 204). He further maintained, however, that no man could surrender any of his powers unless the surrender appeared to be to his advantage ; and it is clear that his determinism here made havoc of his absolutism. Every man, by the invincible constitution of his nature, *had* to seek his own greatest apparent good. Therefore, if law-breaking seemed to be to his advantage, he *had* to be a law-breaker. It was irrelevant if, entering into an irrevocable pact in the hope of personal benefit, he found, later on, that he had made a shocking miscalculation.

Again, Hobbes held that the artificial bonds of civil laws " in their own nature but weak, may nevertheless be made to hold, by the danger, though not by the difficulty, of

breaking them " (III, 198), and yet (III, 205) that all
men had " liberty to refuse " when obedience " frustrated
the end for which the sovereignty was ordained." From
the first statement, all that follows is that a government,
in the subjects' interest, must be strong enough to enforce
its laws and regulations.   From the second statement, it
would appear that Hobbes's theory contained a reservation
which, in principle although not in emphasis, brought him
very near to the author of the *Vindiciæ* and other opponents.   In principle, all government had an end, viz. the
security and prosperity of the subjects.   It could not really
be " absolute " in the sense that it could ignore its own *raison
d'être*.   And although Hobbes tried to make the government the judge of such matters, the ultimate question
was not what the government *thought*, but what it *was*.

Indeed, much of Hobbes's absolutism was little more
than technical.   Having the sword of justice, the sovereign
could not be proceeded against in his own courts (III,163)
—unless he waived his prerogative (III, 207).   Being
politically supreme, he could not be commanded by another
(*i.e.* by a legally superior) political power (III, 195 ; II, 88).
He was immune from legal punishment, for he was the
source of legal punishment (III, 163), and for the same
reason (*ibid.*) could not be (legally) unjust, although his
rule might be grievous (IV, 204) and iniquitous in the sight
of God.

Something, however, was substantial, for Hobbes
attempted to turn the premises of the parliamentary
party against the parliament.   Private men *could not* have
rights against the sovereign, for they were *subjects*.
According to Hobbes, the very idea of limiting or of con-
ditioning sovereignty was absurd.   When men had incorporated themselves into a commonwealth ruled by a
government, they really were incorporated (III, 160 *sqq*.) ;
and the body politic could not contract with, or condition,
itself.

It seems difficult to believe, however, that these abstract contentions really proved very much. Let us grant that the sovereign, if a monarch, could not, strictly speaking, contract with himself or with the citizens, and perhaps that if he made a " promise " to them he was, to speak precisely, only stating his intentions.[1] Nevertheless he had to *accept* the donation of sovereignty, and although his acceptance was not a legal contract on his part, there still might be *moral* conditions both for the givers and for the recipient. If the formula of donation had been " I renounce that portion of my natural liberty that is clearly a menace to security, on condition that you similarly renounce yours," what contradiction would be involved ? And where was the contradiction in the existence of an instituted government subject to a written constitution, as in Cromwell's Instrument of Government or in the United States to-day ? The whereabouts of indivisible sovereignty, in such instances, might indeed be obscure, for the interpreters might be held to be the ultimate rulers, and these, in the above instances, would be either private men or judges on the Bench ; but the formal property of being absolute (or without legal superior) would be retained.

In the concrete, Hobbes thought of " sovereignty " as the central government of England, France, or Holland in his own day, although he professed to deal, like Plato, with the " ideas " of things (III, 357 *sq.*), and admitted that the logical implications which he professed to discern were everywhere obscured by the prevalence of sedition (III, 195). He therefore, like Bodin, enumerated the " marks " of sovereignty, *i.e.* (III, 164 *sqq.*) all decisions regarding defence, all prohibition of sedition, the assignment (in ultimate analysis) of every form of private property, complete control over the judicature, peace and war, the

---

[1] Pope Innocent III denied the right of a king to diminish his regality even when he had sworn to do so (Figgis, G.G. 78).

militia, the appointment of magistrates, and the giving of titles. He thought, however, that the sovereign might transfer the control of the coinage and many other prerogatives without annulling his sovereignty (III, 167), the principle being, not absolutism in the abstract, but retention of " power to protect the subjects " (*ibid.*).

(*c*) *Indivisibility.*—Hobbes held that any attempt to limit sovereignty was an attempt to divide it (*e.g.* II, 96 n.), and that since sovereignty was necessarily indivisible in principle, any such view must be impossible. A " limited " or " mixed " monarchy, for example, would be a partnership of limiters and limited in the government, that is to say, *not* a monarchy.

Some of Hobbes's contemporaries thought that the *word* " sovereignty " begged questions of this order. " I know," said Coke,[1] speaking of the Petition of Right, " that prerogative is part of the law, but ' sovereign power ' is no parliamentary word. . . . Take heed what we yield unto. Magna Charta is such a fellow that he will have no ' sovereign.' "[2] In any case, a formal proof that a " limited " monarchy was not a *monarchy* would not prove that it was not a possible form of government.

In modern theory the most important question regarding the indivisibility of sovereignty is how far the unity of the community is connected with, or depends upon, the unity of its government. Hobbes, however, since he assumed (like his contemporaries) that the word " people " *meant* a body politically governed, did not really discuss this question at all. He simply offered the analysis that the unity of a *governed* people was constituted by the artificial person who bore the rights of the citizens. If,

[1] q. Tanner, *English Constitutional Conflicts of the Seventeenth Century*, p. 63.

[2] The word had probably a novel flavour in England, and Coke may have looked askance at it because it was a translation of Bodin's un-English view of law. Holland, however (*Jurisprudence*, 13th ed., p. 49), exaggerates the novelty of the term, and Hobbes's part in making it current.

however, in the modern way, we regarded a people as
primarily a community that *de facto* has invented certain
devices for living together, it seems plain that *any* significant sense in which such a " people " could be said to be
" one " would entail the formal property of " indivisibility."

Suppose, to choose modern instances, that there was a
professional army, largely autonomous, very willing to
fight against Germany, and not at all willing to coerce
Ulster. Suppose a Bench determined to follow its own
traditions, and very hostile to the " new despotism " of
bureaucracy. Suppose powerful Trade Unions exercising
extra-parliamentary influence, and Churches rather militant in asserting their duty to guide the community.
Suppose that the King-in-Parliament was often but a
nominal sovereign and in restricted ways. Why should
such a people fall ? Why should it not be *one* ? The
several authorities and powers might clash, and the result
might be disaster, but autocracy is not exempt from
disaster, and it would be to the interest of the authorities
in a " pluralistic " sovereignty to agree. If they agreed,
the community would, by that mere fact, be *one* ; and
the question to discuss would be primarily whether its
unity should strictly be called *political*. In short, these
problems of unity and plurality seem to be the same, in
this instance, as in any other where the " one " is contrasted with the " many." If many work together they
are, to that extent, *one* ; and the formal assertion of their
unity cannot determine how much autonomy each par-
ticipant has.

Hobbes never pretended that government had no
" inconveniences." Although, he said, the sovereign's
interest and the subjects' were the same (*e.g.* IV, 162),
the ruler had " continual care and trouble about the
business of other men " and incurred some " danger of
his person " (IV, 163). The subject had apparent griev-
ances (*ibid.*), partly because he was " tied to do according

to that will only which, once for all, he had long ago laid up," partly because he retained the confused idea that he owned private property in his own right (IV, 164). Hobbes's advice to his countrymen and to every one else was simply " that you will esteem it better to enjoy yourselves in the present state, though perhaps not the best, than by waging war endeavour to promote a reformation for other men in another age, yourselves in the meanwhile either killed or consumed with age " (II, xxi).

(3) PATERNAL AND DESPOTIC GOVERNMENT

Hobbes was fully prepared to admit that the " natural " dominion of procreation or conquest preceded instituted government. " It is very likely to be true," he said (V, 183), " that since the Creation there never was a time in which mankind was totally without society " ; and again, that "paternal government, instituted by God Himself in the Creation, was monarchical ; that other governments were compacted by the artifice of men out of the ashes of monarchy, after it had been ruined with seditions " (II, 129) ; " The beginning of all dominion amongst men was in families " (VI, 147).

It is also probable that he would have conceded that there was a good deal more in natural dominion than mere " power and natural force," for he admitted a similitude of wills and inclinations in such cases (III, 222). His point was that an instituted government arose from the consent of natural equals, whereas in the "little body politic " (IV, 149) composed of one lord and one servant the *inequality* of the parties was the dominating feature. Again, if a family grew into a patrimonial kingdom (IV, 158 *sq.*) there was submission of unequals, not a pact of voluntary subjection.

Regarding despotic government, Hobbes held that a man who surrendered at discretion (usually in war) might either be kept in fetters, or be, so to say, a prisoner on parole. In the former case he was a mere captive (II, 113) and might try to escape if he could. In the latter case he purchased a certain degree of liberty as well as mere life, by his promise to become his lord's property, and was bound by his promise unless manumitted (II, 110 *sqq.* ; IV, 150 *sqq.*). Hobbes maintained, however, that there was no difference between the " rights and consequences " of subjection to a despot and subjection in an instituted government (III, 190). The servant " by the covenant of obedience owned and authorized whatever the master shall do " (*ibid.*).[1]

Regarding paternal government, Hobbes was anxious to assert that the duties of children depended neither upon gratitude (*e.g.* II, 119) nor on the mere fact that they had been begotten (II, 115), but upon presumed consent. " The children, when they be grown up to strength . . . and to judgment . . . in that very act of receiving that protection, and not renouncing it openly, do oblige themselves to obey the laws of their protectors " (V, 180).

Such statements make a modern reader smile, but if he reflected that Hobbes's principal object was to get rid of superstitions about paternal right and reduce the rights and wrongs of family relationships to general social arrangements, the smile might dwindle.

More in detail Hobbes argued that " in the condition of mere nature " the dominion was maternal. The mother alone could " declare " the father (III, 187). At birth the infant was in her power (*e.g.* II, 117), and she nourished and trained it at least as much as the father (*e.g.* IV, 155 *sq.*). If she abandoned the infant, anyone who picked it up and fed it acquired the dominion (II, 117).

It was different in a " state of society." If a man and a woman made a covenant " for copulation only," they had to decide about the offspring " by covenants particular "

---

[1] The master, however, did not " bear the person " of the servant.

(IV, 156), as the Amazons had done. If they contracted " for cohabitation and society of all things," one of them had to govern (IV, 157; II, 118), and legal matrimony (except (III, 188) in the case of a queen and her consort) usually implied that the husband ruled. This arrangement, however, was only conventional.

When a political government was strictly paternal in form and essence, *patria potestas* prevailed (IV, 157). The children had to be enfranchised (II, 119) if they were not to be in complete subjection ; and Hobbes suggested that the parents enfranchised them in order to be honoured or, at least, thanked (*ibid.*). In another place (IV, 158) he said they were enfranchised " by the natural indulgence of the parents."

(4) DEMOCRACY, ARISTOCRACY, AND MONARCHY

Hobbes held that comparisons between these forms of government were largely academic, partly (II, xxii) because they yielded only probable, not demonstrably true, conclusions, partly because, in any state, " the present government ought always to be preferred, maintained and accounted best " (III, 548), since *it* was " the dominion of reason, peace, security, riches, decency, society, elegancy, sciences and benevolence " as opposed to " a dominion of passions, war, fear, poverty, slovenliness, solitude, barbarism, ignorance, cruelty " (II, 127).

On Hobbian principles, monarchy, aristocracy, and democracy exhausted the possible forms of government. He had no patience with " mixarchy " (B. 116) or with a view like Bellarmine's—that monarchy, ideally the best, should be mixed with other forms by fallen man (*De Rom. Pont*, I, 1). If we asked what person or persons bore the artificial personality of sovereignty, the answer had to be either all, or some, or none (II, 93).

In the comparison democracy showed up rather badly.

" A democracy, in effect, is no more than an aristocracy of
orators, interrupted sometimes with the temporary monarchy of one orator " (IV, 141, cf. B. 3). It was a trial of
wits, full of faction and enmities, the rule of eloquence
" whose property is not to inform but to allure " (II, 138).
Again, a sovereign assembly could hardly attend continuously to the public business (IV, 141). Therefore, oratory
apart, it tended towards committee rule, that is, to
approach oligarchy ; and oligarchy (II, 142) was usually
inferior to monarchy.

A monarch, Hobbes said, had only the inconstancy of
human nature (III, 174) ; assemblies, great or small, had
additional inconstancies. A monarch could not envy
himself. He could always attend to business (II, 101)
except when he slept. What he spent on favourites was
less than an assembly spent on bribes (III, 175). His
wealth and interest must coincide with the wealth and
interest of his realm (*e.g.* III, 174). By admitting, however,
that if a " tyrant " did not rule " by right " (II, 95, 153) he
was simply an enemy who should be slain, Hobbes almost
joined forces with the monarchomachs ;[1] and his statement
that a monarch might " in his wrath and sensuality
slaughter his innocent subjects, and those who never
offended against the laws " and so be responsible for " a
very great grievance " (II, 132), was scarcely palliated by
the explanation that the grievance in question was not
peculiar to monarchy.

Hobbes sometimes admitted that since a monarch might
abdicate at pleasure or convey his sovereignty to another
prince (IV, 147 *sq.*), the subjects might have other griev-
ances ; and his attempts (IV, 159 *sqq.* ; III, 183 *sqq.*) to
deal with the tangled question of hereditary succession
were, at the best, but adroit. Indeed, his admission
(III, 260) that the *verification* of a monarch's title " dependeth on the knowledge of the public registers, public

[1] Cf. B. 51 on the length to which tyrants should not go.

counsels, public ministers and public seals" scarcely
warranted the conclusion (*ibid.*) that since authorisation
was different from verification, ignorance of the true
sovereign did not excuse rebellious acts. A better working
principle (III, 706) was that where there was submission
to a conqueror or other ruler of doubtful antecedents
" approbation of all their actions past " had to be included
in the submission. Otherwise there was " scarce a commonwealth in the world whose beginnings can in conscience
be justified."

(5) THE DUTIES AND THE ART OF SOVEREIGNTY

" I am," said Hobbes (VI, 13), " one of the common
people, and one of that almost infinite number of men
for whose welfare Kings and other sovereigns were by
God ordained ; for God made Kings for the people, and
not people for Kings " (VI, 13). The citizens had the duty
of obedience. " It is not the right of the sovereign, though
granted to him by every man's express consent, that can
enable him to do his office : it is the obedience of the
subject which must do that " (B. 144). The sovereign,
however, had the *moral* duty of ensuring his subject's
welfare.

In other words, absolutism need not separate ethics from
politics. The sovereign, according to Hobbes, was subject
to moral law as much " as any the meanest of his people "
(III, 332). He was answerable before God for the public
conscience (*e.g.* IV, 214), and sovereigns (*ibid.*) were
bound to " procure to the uttermost of their endeavour
the good of the people."

The simplest division of the sovereign's duties (IV, 214)
was into (*a*) population, (*b*) commodity of living, (*c*) internal
peace, (*d*) defence.

(*a*) The sovereign (*ibid.*) knew that the subjects should
increase and multiply, and therefore should regulate the

relations of the sexes and forbid dysgenic practices such as unnatural vice. In the *Leviathan* Hobbes further argued that any able-bodied superfluity of men should be " transplanted into countries not sufficiently inhabited " (III, 335), although without exterminating or completely dispossessing the natives ; and that " when all the world is overcharged with inhabitants, then the last remedy of all is war ; which provideth for every man, by victory or death."

(*b*) " Security " included " benefit and good " (IV, 214), " happiness " or " delectation " (II, 167 *sq.*), and " the contentments of life " (III, 322), *i.e.* in essentials, " liberty," and wealth.

Lawful " liberty " was permission to do as a man listed in so far as the " artificial chains " of the civil laws were unnecessary (III, 198) ; and Hobbes, the absolutist, had the traditional English love of liberty. He abhorred over-government. The sovereign should lay no " traps for money " (III, 336), enjoin no " prohibition without necessity " (IV, 215, cf. II, 179). " A law that is not needful, having not the true end of a law, is not good " (III, 335).

Wealth sprang from labour, from thrift, and from the bounties of earth and water (II, 177). It had also to be protected. Each citizen, as in the Book of Nehemiah, had to " build with one hand, and hold the sword in the other " (III, 333), or else hire mercenaries. The sovereign ought to promote and defend opulence by encouraging the teaching of mathematics, navigation, and mechanics (II, 177), by prohibiting inordinate expense (II, 178), and by regulating trade (IV, 215). Excess of private wealth was dangerous, " because all things obey money " (II, 176). The able-bodied should be forced to work (III, 334). Yet Hobbes's sovereign, in Baconian phrase, had " the countenance of one that pitied men " ; for Hobbes held that there should be public charity, not capricious private alms for the infirm.

(c) To maintain internal peace was to uproot sedition, and Hobbes seldom tired of inveighing against dogmatic and ancient philosophers, ghostly fathers, Scots Presbyterians and all sectaries. He even tried to show that the decalogue was an anti-seditious manifesto (III, 327). I do not think there is warrant, however, for Sir James Mackintosh's statement (Diss. in Encyc. Brit., 7th ed.) that " a Hobbist is the only consistent persecutor."

Positively, Hobbes emphasised the sovereign's duty to provide proper instruction regarding the nature of government as well as in the useful arts. (He did not suppose (III, 199) that *all* education was necessarily the State's business.) Here the universities and the " schools of law " (for Hobbes (II, 172) had the courage to begin at the top) had, he said, been very deficient. University teachers had been Pope's men, not King's men, " till towards the latter end of Henry VIII " (III, 331 *sq.*). It was obvious, therefore, that the *Leviathan* should become a university textbook (III, 332).

For the better avoidance of sedition, the sovereign should settle property in a perspicuous way, appoint equitable judges,[1] etc. Regarding taxation, Hobbes argued that a tax on sales was the fairest since a man should not be penalised for frugality (IV, 216 *sq.* ; III, 334), and he professed to deduce this conclusion from simple equity (II, 174). There should also be equality of burdens, since men were angered more by the inequality than by the amount of the burden (II, 173).

[1] The principle was Justinian's (Codex, I, 14, 12) : " The emperor alone is the founder and interpreter of the laws." Even Bracton had held (II, 16, 3, q. Car. III, 70) " eius sit interpretari cuius est concedere " and inferred that private persons could not dispute the right. Hobbes, I think, did not contemplate the theory of the modern U.S.S.R. (Krylenko's " Court and Justice," etc., q. *The Times*, 12th April 1933) : " Every judge must keep himself well informed on questions of state policy and remember that his judicial decisions in particular cases are intended to promote just the prevailing policy of the ruling class and nothing else." It might be argued, of course, that he should have contemplated it (or adopted it).

(*d*) External defence was discussed most fully in the *De Cive*. It implied being warned, and being forearmed (II, 169). For the former purpose " discoverers " and spies were necessary ; for the latter a strong militia,[1] fortresses, power to billet soldiers, adequate treasure not subject to untimely depletion. Every wise sovereign knew " how difficult a matter it is to wring suddenly out of close-fisted men so vast a proportion of moneys " (II, 170). To be sure the militia " sometimes augments but more frequently lessens the subject's stock " (II, 176). But it was necessary.

Hobbes duly noted (III, 341) that excessive popularity in a commander was a danger to his sovereign.

(6) THE DELEGATION AND ADMINISTRATION OF SOVEREIGNTY

(*a*) *Subordinate Bodies*.—Hobbes strongly objected to factions, but admitted " systems " (or subordinate bodies) within the body politic. If lawful, these were the muscles of the greater body. If unlawful, " wens, biles and apostems " (III, 225).

There might be organised but unlawful " private bodies " (III, 222), such as corporations of beggars, thieves, and gipsies. On the whole, however, " private bodies " should be of little account, excepting the family, which, being prior to all government, retained whatever in its early status had not been expressly withdrawn by government (III, 222).

Municipal or colonial governments, chartered companies of merchants, and other subordinate " bodies politic . . . made by authority from the sovereign power " (III, 210) seemed more important to Hobbes, and he was so anxious to show that these bodies should not exceed their legal powers that (unlike Bodin, *e.g.* p. 365) he neglected the

[1] " By God, not for an hour," said Charles, when Pembroke in 1642 advised him to transfer the militia to Parliament (q. Tanner, p. 233).

critical question of their vitality and initiative. Thus many of his results were peculiar. If, he said, an assembly exceeded its legal powers, only the persons who voted for the illegality were liable in damages (III, 213). This argument applied to colonial assemblies and also (III, 217) to "a town, an university, or a college, or a church." Again, merchant companies, being established for "the particular gain of every adventurer" (III, 219), could not legally bind all their members to majority action or to the commitments which any particular adventurer made in their name.

(b) *Delegated Command.*—These "systems" or "corporations" were governments in little, the muscles of the greater body. *Officers* of the commonwealth were *organs* of that body, to whom it had delegated executive powers. Such were viceroys, judges, hangmen, schoolmasters, and professors, so far as the latter taught civil duty (III, 228), ("I never said that princes can make doctrines true or false" (IV, 329), "but I say every sovereign prince has a right to prohibit the public teaching of them, whether true or false"). On the other hand, spies and the king's private emissaries had no *public* office (III, 231) ; and the king's advisers *qua* advisers were regarded as private persons.

Hobbes thought that viceroys were like nerves and tendons (III, 227), teachers and judges like the voice, policemen like hands, spies like eyes, receivers of petitions like ears.

(c) *Supplies.*—All natural resources belonged to the sovereign. There was *private* property only when *public* authority gave to anyone the sole use of a thing (*e.g.* II, 188 *sq.*) ; and the lawyerly notion of property independent of government or the socialistic notion of a primitive community of goods was simply absurd.[1] Land and sea were

[1] It was disputed by the Roman jurists whether, in a pre-political condition, goods were *res nullius* or a *communio rerum*. Marcianus, on the *Digest* (I, 8, 2, q. Car. I, 143), took a balanced position : " Quædam naturali jure communia sunt omnium, quædam universitatis, pleraque omnium." Gratian (q. Car. II, 137) held that sinful appetite was the

the foundations of wealth, and Hobbes, who assumed (III, 234 ; VI, 21) that all English titles to property were derived from William the Conqueror, seems to have interpreted the feudal system in an ultra-legal and rather unhistorical way (*e.g.* VI, 154 ; III, 235 *sq.*).

Men should exchange what produce they could spare. Therefore the commonwealth had to regulate buying, selling, hiring, etc. (III, 237). This implied " portable nutriment " or currency. Gold and silver, being highly esteemed everywhere, could not have their value appreciably altered by any particular commonwealth. The rest of the currency depended for its value on its " stamp," and " being unable to endure change of air, hath its effect at home only " (III, 239).

Few commonwealths were self-sufficing, and most exchanged their purchasable superfluities in foreign trade. Shipping had to be reckoned among such services (III, 233) ; but strict regulation was necessary lest a subject " drawn for gain " should strengthen the enemy abroad, or, at home, make a profit on noxious goods (III, 237). .

A commonwealth might procreate by establishing plantations or colonies. Once established, such colonies might either be emancipated or remain colonies " depending wholly on their licence or letters " (III, 240).

The crown lands and the general question of the sovereign's public and private wealth led Hobbes into labyrinths. He sometimes admitted that the " infirmity " of sovereigns had led them to levy taxes additional to their patrimonial revenue (III, 236). At other times he took refuge behind the lath-and-plaster defence of declaring that the sovereign was " understood " to be acting for the common good (III, 235).

origin of private property. Azo, in one passage (q. Car. II, 45) said that property pertained to the *ius gentium* or *ius civile*, but not to the *ius naturale*. Aquinas (S.T. 29, 66 a 2 ; q. Gierke, *Gen.* 613 n.) affirmed : " proprietas possessionum non est contra ius naturale sed iuri naturali superadditur per adinventionem rationis humanæ."

(d) *Advice.*—A monarch, Hobbes conceded, would be wise if he did " his business by the help of many and prudent counsellors " (III, 249) ; and he should reward them suitably (III, 241). He should hear them apart, however (III, 247), and should not expect efficient advice from a parliament where the firebrands ignited by contagion, " especially when they blow one another with orations " (III, 248). In a simile that began well enough but ended ludicrously (III, 249), Hobbes said that the best tennis player had able seconds, the next best had no seconds at all, while a parliamentary monarch was " carried to the ball . . . in a wheel-barrow or other frame " (III, 249).

(e) *Civil Laws.*—Hobbes's intention was to be an analytical jurist and " not to show what is law here and there ; but what is law " (III, 251). One of his clearest definitions was (VI, 26) : " A law is the command of him or them that have the sovereign power, given to those that be his or their subjects, declaring publicly and plainly what every one of them may do, and what they must forbear to do." The sovereign declared trumps, and morality consisted in " not renouncing " ; but there was always the proviso (VI, 122) " that in matter of government, when nothing else is turned up, clubs are trumps."

Regarding statute law Hobbes quoted several passages from Bracton (VI, 31)—who spoke, however, with a divided voice—in order to show that Sir Edward Coke's *Institutes* wrongly endeavoured to diminish the king's authority[1] (VI, 62). He believed, indeed, that written or statute law *was* the civil law in all essentials. Thus canon law was law in England " by the great seal of England " (VI, 123). The word " written " included any clear declaration, such as being " put into verse " (III, 259) among rude, illiterate people.

---

[1] Hobbes occasionally admitted the legitimacy of the phrase : " the king *in* Parliament " (III, 255 ; VI, 34).

The common law should not be regarded as a distinct species of law ; and Hobbes had the greatest possible objection to the basing of law upon custom and precedent. " I deny that custom of its own nature can amount to the authority of law " (VI, 62, cf. II, 195 ; III, 264). " Equity " of natural law and " written " civil law were all the true law there was. The doctrine of precedents carried back far enough would base the law upon the antiquated ideas of *ignorant* judges (VI, 86).

In order to support this view, he had often to fall back upon the mere legal presumption (which he knew well enough (*e.g.* VI, 25, 37) to be frequently false) that the sovereign's acts were "to be supposed always consonant to equity and reason " (III, 259, cf. 267), and his view that " justice fulfils the law and equity interprets the law " (VI, 68) had its own difficulties. He strongly objected, however, to Coke's definition of equity as " an artificial perfection of reason, gotten by long study, observation and experience " (III, 256). The perfection alleged, he thought (VI, 45), was the perfection of lawyers' purses. The king's authority, not any special "legal reason," *was* the " public reason " that stood for, and was, the law (VI, 5).

Since laws had to be interpreted, however, he admitted that lawyers might have the function of grammarians ; and there had to be judges who should be upright, impartial, and faithful to the law how great soever the " incommodity " of such fidelity might be in any particular decision (III, 268).

(*f*) *Disobedience.*—Ignorance of the law excused only where the law had not been sufficiently declared (III, 280). Neither laws nor their penalties should be retrospective, and a customary penalty should not be exceeded any more than a statutory one (III, 281). Unspecified penalties (*ibid.*) might, however, be imposed. A man was totally excused (III, 287 *sqq.*) if he *could not know* the law, if he were captured, if he were threatened with certain and immediate death, if he were deprived of the necessities of life or of self-defence.

In these waters Hobbes's theory did not always sail on an even keel. It was a sin to *obey* the sovereign if the command contradicted the sovereignty (II, 289), the " king's reason notwithstanding." The sovereign's example (*e.g.* regarding duelling) might be contrary to his laws ; and then " it be our duty to do, not what they do but what they say " (III, 293). If the sovereign broke a tradition of clemency he was " unreasonable " and " had his part in the offence " (III, 291) ; for he had given " hopes of impunity."

(*g*) *Punishment.*—In his definition of (political) punishment (III, 297) Hobbes asserted : (1) that punishment was an evil, which was (2) inflicted by public authority; (3) upon an offender; (4) with the object of inducing greater *general* obedience to the laws.

Taking (1) for granted, Hobbes inferred from (2) that private revenge, informal social ostracism, and the stripes of usurpers and their minions were not *punishments* but simply hostile acts, that the natural sequels of actions (such as sickness) were not punishments either, and that " harm " in excess of the legal penalty was mere cruelty.

Regarding (3), while some of his statements may not have been fastidiously accurate, I suggest that he saw the essential point that so many writers miss, viz. that punishment is *by definition* penal (being inflicted on account of a past offence), but that it cannot be *justified* by its definition.

" Punishment," he said (III, 304), " is only for transgression of the law, *and therefore there can be no punishment of the innocent* "[1]—a profoundly simple consideration that makes nonsense of one of the usual objections to a utili-

---

[1] Unfortunately (*e.g.* II, 207) Hobbes himself sometimes spoke in this way.

tarian or deterrent theory of punishment, *i.e.* that such theories might justify *unjust* " punishments." Although Hobbes did not examine the point sufficiently, there would have been no difficulty, on his principles, in admitting that an evil (*e.g.* incarceration for quarantine) might be inflicted, non-punitively but quite justly, upon persons who had done no wrong.

(4) A clear-headed utilitarian theory of this matter has to maintain that a government should never inflict an evil except for an over-balancing social benefit, and that the infliction of evil *for an offence* comes under this general principle. That, in substance, was Hobbes's view. " All evil," he said (III, 298 *sq.*), " which is inflicted without intention, or possibility of disposing the delinquent, or, by his example, other men, to obey the laws is not punishment ; but an act of hostility ; because without such an end, no hurt done is contained under that name." It was a law of nature, of God, and of Christ " that in revenges, that is, retributions of evil for evil, men look not at the greatness of the evil past, but the greatness of the good to follow " (III, 140).

Certainly it might be argued that punishment, being for a past offence, or, as Hobbes admitted, " vindicative "[1] (II, 188), *had* to look at the evil past ; and, again, that penalties having been *promised*, the government had to keep its word. Hobbes was prepared to admit (II, 166) that governments had the right to exact all penalties, although they need not exercise the right, and that, when sin was no longer possible after the Day of Judgment, the original penalties (if reasonable at the time they were specified) might legitimately continue to be exacted (*e.g.* II, 55 *sq.*). In the main, however, his position was that pardon and mercy were laws of nature (*e.g.* III, 139)—that is to say, moral *duties*, not sentimental anomalies ultimately unjust, although superficially pleasing. To refuse pardon

[1] " Vindicativa *sive* poenaria " (L. II, 317).

to a man who had " given caution of the future time "
was, he said, " sign of an aversion to peace " (III, 139).
Alternatively, if retribution were the wages or price of
crime, lawbreakers who *paid* or were willing to pay
were not criminal at all. For they purchased a licence.
Punishment implied a *greater* evil than " the benefit or
contentment that naturally followeth the crime committed " (III, 299).

If Hobbes's consistency in this matter were challenged,
I conceive he could have said that he was technically
consistent, since a commonwealth was not bound to keep
promises to itself or to its citizens, and so could legitimately
disregard its ancient threats. He could also have said
that, technicalities apart, the law does not engage itself
to exact a penalty, but only to refrain from exceeding
such and such a penalty. Clemency, therefore, implied
no inconsistency. So far as I can see, the probability of
future benefit to the community is the sole justification,
and a sufficient justification, for exacting the penalty, for
limiting it, and for waiving it when it may safely be waived.

(7) THE DEATH OF SOVEREIGNTY

Despite his insistence that the very idea of sovereignty
implied perpetuity, Hobbes allowed that sovereignty
ceased when it became impotent to enforce security. The
decision on this matter, it would seem, was left to the
common sense of the subjects, not to the " king's reason "
or to any legal presumptions about it. Again, no reason
was given why a sovereignty strong enough to keep the
peace, but incapable of promoting the arts of peace
or the benefits of civilisation, should not similarly be
disowned.

Be that as it may, Hobbes's view was that sovereignty,
in any given region, might die a violent death from foreign
conquest (IV, 200) and might also perish from internal

weakness and disease. The fullest account of this matter was given in the *Leviathan*.

Although " nothing," said Hobbes (III, 308), " can be immortal which mortals make," there was no reason why a commonwealth properly instituted and carefully tended should perish from *internal* weakness so long as men endured. Actual commonwealths, however, could, and did, succumb to diseases which should either have been prevented at their institution or adequately doctored afterwards.

The first type might be compared to " defectuous pro-creation " (III, 309), and commonly occurred because a new-made king snatched at power without receiving enough of it, in the illusory hope that he might later acquire the power he really needed. Henry II or William Rufus were instances (*ibid.*). For Becket had the Pope, and the barons had the French, to back them in keeping the King of England to his word ; that is to say, to contra-dict the sovereignty by dividing and limiting it. Similarly, the ill-constituted governments of the ancients never recovered from their misbegotten start.

The second type included all the dangerous forms of sedition, viz. (III, 316) a private conscience, pretence of inspiration, the nonsense of pre-political private property, the vain notion of constitutional limitations of sovereignty, and tyrannophobia ; but Hobbes also discussed certain other maladies (III, 319 *sqq.*). A monarch, shivering with impecuniosity, then feverishly demanding huge subsidies, suffered from political ague. There was pleurisy in the commonwealth if a few private men had a stranglehold on the public treasure, and witchcraft if a man like Julius Cæsar became altogether too popular. Arrogant corpora-tions were like worms in the entrails of a natural man, and too much talk about politics was " like the little worms which physicians call ascarides " (III, 321). Am-bitious monarchs were as wounds, wens, lethargy, and consumption

We have seen what some of the royalists thought about the application of these principles to England after 1647, and need only remark here that Hobbes concluded (III, 703) that when the crown was subdued (without acknowledging its subjugation) Englishmen resident in England had to make their peace with the usurper, either expressly, or by prudent wordless acquiescence ; and that even the royalist soldiers, who had entered into quite special obligations, might, like other military men, surrender at discretion when the king's forces could not keep the field any longer (III, 704).

(8) THEISM, RELIGION, AND THE CHURCH

For Hobbes (B. 90), " religion in itself admits no controversy. It is a law of the kingdom and ought not to be disputed." But he argued about it a great deal.

He asserted that men could infer God's *existence* by reason (IV, 59 ; II, 198 n. ; III, 383), and consequently that at least one theistic belief was not due to fear (III, 95 *sq.*). The man who " could plunge himself profoundly in the pursuit of causes, shall at last come to this, that there must be, as even the heathen philosophers confessed, one first mover ; that is, a first and an eternal cause of all things ; which is that which men mean by the name of God ; and all this without thought of their fortune " (*ibid.*). Atheists therefore were fools (II, 199 n.), and " constant and resolved atheists " probably did not exist (IV, 294), although inadvertence might easily lead even the godly into " atheism by consequence " (IV, 384).

In this limited sense Hobbes may have been a genuine theist, although he remarked provocatively that these theistic proofs might be as difficult as an Archimedean squaring of the circle (II, 198 n.), and that questions about the magnitude and beginning of the world had best be left to the lawful interpreters of religion[1] (I, 412). He also saw that his demonstration of theism permitted the existence of *many*[2] first causes (I, 411), and of a first movent who might be eternally moved (I, 412) and " concreated with body " (I, 416).

Hobbes also held that belief in God's providence was a " natural dictate of right reason " (III, 345), and the denial of it " a wretched apprehension of God " (II, 214). Since he held, however, that " God had no ends " (III, 350), he might have had difficulty in defending these statements.

On the other hand, he maintained vehemently that we did not, and could not, know God's nature and attributes. All our ideas were finite, and (therefore ?) must be *of* the finite (II, 215). We could not significantly ascribe to God place, or bounds, or want, or sense, or knowledge, or understanding (*ibid.*), or design (V, 14) ; and the schoolmen's " eternal *now* " was as absurd as an " infinite *here* " (*e.g.* III, 677). Such attributes as we ascribed (meaninglessly ?) to God properly expressed not His nature but *our* reverence. They should either be negative " as infinite, eternal, incomprehensible," or superlatives " as most high, most great," or indefinite " as good, just, holy, creator " (III, 352 ; II, 216).

In practice, however (*e.g.* II, 51 *sq.*), Hobbes admitted that there was an analogical apprehension, not so very " wretched," of *some* of the divine characteristics ; but it must be confessed that his grounds for worshipping deity were profoundly inadequate. " Power irresistible," he said, " justifies all actions, really and properly, in whomsoever it be found ; less power does not ; and because such power is in God only, He must needs be just in all His actions, and we, that, not comprehending His counsels,

---

[1] There seems to be a definite contrast between this very reserved attitude and the confident theism of II, 182 *sqq.* and III, 92 *sqq.*

[2] A point discussed by the " heathen philosopher " Aristotle, *Physics*, VIII, ch. 7.

call him to the bar, commit injustice in it " (V, 116). On such grounds a manly reverence could not be distinguished from the merest lickspittle servility.

Many of Hobbes's arguments depended not on God's *natural* word (of reason) but upon His revealed and prophetic word (III, 345 ; II, 205).

Here the only intelligible question was why these things, which could not be *known*, were believed ; and the answer was that accredited teachers should be responsible for " the ordinary course of believing " (III, 589). Hobbes set himself, therefore, to elucidate the accredited story, only occasionally remembering (*e.g.* III, 386 *sq.*, 444, 711 ; IV, 366) that he himself, as a private person, was scarcely authorised to do so. Indeed, he candidly admitted (II, 307 n.) that he did not know what he would say to Churchmen who seemed to deny " the most evident testimonies of Holy Writ." Few men have searched the Scriptures with more diligence than Hobbes ; and I do not think he was appreciably less candid than his opponents.

Bacon, like many others (Essay III) had seen the great advantages " if the points fundamental, and of substance, in religion, were truly discerned and distinguished from points not merely of faith, but of opinion, order, or good intention." Hobbes maintained that the only article of the Christian faith necessary to salvation was the belief that Jesus is the Christ (III, 590). We should not believe " an angel from Heaven, nor the Church neither " (II, 310) if they taught the contrary ; and anyone who believed in this article could " receive no harm by the excommunication of men " whether the sovereign were Christian or heathen (III, 507). On the other hand, this apparently simple belief was sometimes said to contain very elaborate implications—for instance, that Christ was the son of an Omnipotent Creator, and would judge the world at the General Resurrection (III, 595 *sq.*). It was a " contraction " of the Apostles' Creed (II, 307 n.).

Therefore Hobbes, circuitously, was able to protest that he was " an enemy bitter enough against atheists " (II, 198 n.).

The evidence that Jesus was the Christ depended on the fulfilment of prophecy and therefore upon the accuracy of the Old Testament record. God had spoken to Abraham and to Moses (III, 416 *sq.*) in a dream ; but this only proved that some man " dreamed that God spake to him " (III, 361). The pretender to a revelation, " being a man, may err, and, which is more, may lie " (III, 362). Again, Hobbes had no sympathy with an inspiration " blown into a man . . . as a man filleth a bladder " (III, 394), or " like a bag-pipe " (IV, 448). Moreover, there had been abundance of false prophets—" four hundred false impostors but only one Micaiah " (III, 424). Miracles " had now ceased " (III, 365) ; and it was necessary to be certain that the Scripture records were canonical.

In the matter of what was canonical, Hobbes's sovereign decided the question for him (III, 367). To be sure, the Pentateuch, from internal evidence, could not have been written verbatim by Moses (III, 376), and other Old Testament books showed signs of later redaction. Hobbes allowed, however, in essentials that " the Old and New Testament, as we have them now, are the true registers of those things which were done and said by the prophets and apostles " (*ibid.*). But what *was* true prophecy ?

A prophet was God's spokesman, who might (but need not) be also God's " predictor " (III, 412). There had, however, been distracted and incoherent prophets (as at Delphi) ; and the test was the conformity of the prophet's message to the established religion, together with the miracles that proved his standing (III, 362). (So far as I can see, Hobbes attempted to prove the validity of the double test by demonstrating the separate invalidity of its constituent parts.)

" The testimony that men can render of divine calling

can be no other than the operation of miracles, or true prophecy which is also a miracle, or extraordinary felicity " (III, 107). Yet there had been plenty of unaccredited diviners like the witch of Endor (III, 414). In such cases it might be presumed that " all the miracle consisteth in this that the enchanter has deceived a man ; which is no miracle, but a very easy matter to do " (III, 434) ; and although, in the seventeenth century, there was nothing " that a man endued but with a mediocrity of reason would think supernatural " (III, 436), Scripture miracles doubtless had occurred ; that is to say, had been signs from God, strange in themselves, and due to non-natural causes (III, 428). True, the novelty might wear off and natural causes be suspected (III, 429). But not always. Again, true miracles were " done to procure credit " for a prophet " in the elect only " (III, 431). If the satire was marked, the conclusion was firm.

Hobbes proceeded to use the Scripture " with due submission " in his " necessary " task of attacking " the outworks of the enemy, from whence they impugn the civil power " (III, vi).

In a formal sense, he accepted the doctrine of the divine right of kings, " for as much as God overrules all rulers by nature, that is, by the dictates of natural reason " (II, xix) ; but he soon quitted formalities.

First there had been the Old Covenant with Abraham, the sign of which was circumcision (II, 22). In it, Abraham had the plenary power of a paternal despot ; his seed were *tied* to his commands (II, 230) ; and, since there were no written laws, Abraham was *obliged* to " the laws of nature, rational worship and circumcision " only (*ibid.*). At Sinai, however, a government was *instituted*, and the written decalogue superseded (while including) the unwritten laws of nature (II, 233 ; III, 465).

In short, a *sacerdotal kingdom*, hereditary to Aaron (III, 465), was founded in which the high priest had all sovereign authority, temporal and spiritual; and this sacerdotal kingdom continued to be the lawful authority (although there was a confused period after the death of Joshua) until the election of Saul, after which " whereas before, all authority, both in religion and policy was in the high priest ; so now it was all in the king " (III, 470). The high priest renounced his magisterial and accepted merely ministerial authority. Solomon blessed the people, dedicated the temple and " thrust out Abiathar from being priest before the Lord " (III, 471). Hezekiah, it is true, was regrettably subservient to the prophets ; but the king, strictly speaking, was the official " prophet," unless indeed " Huldah the prophetess had the supreme authority in matter of religion ; which, I think, is not the opinion of any doctor " (III, 474). After the Captivity, the Jews became so much corrupted by the " customs and demonology of the Greeks " that " nothing can be gathered from their confusion " (III, 475).

Hobbes even said (although he later (IV, 315 *sqq.*) admitted some " error ") that Moses and the high priests were the first person of the Trinity (III, 486) ; for the " persons " of the Trinity were God's representative *personæ* upon earth—hence being easily distinguished from the divine substance—and were chronologically successive. Let us pass, however, to the second person, *i.e.* to " the office of our blessed Saviour " (III, 475) in His *human* nature (III, 481).

Christ as Redeemer offered Himself as a sacrifice for human sins, the price not being equivalent, but sufficient in God's mercy " because there was no more required " (III, 476) ; and baptism was a " pact " made by the faithful to signify that the ransom had been paid (III, 477). Christ was a teacher and a preacher—nothing more seditious—during the time of the regeneration, and He was careful not to interfere with the government of the Jews and of the Romans (III, 480). His kingdom would begin at the Second Coming, and not before. Accordingly, before the Day of Judgment, no precedent could be drawn from Christ's teaching or preaching for any spiritual or ecclesiastical kingdom having dominion over temporal principalities and powers. And so Hobbes's argument passed triumphantly to the era of the Holy Ghost, *i.e.* to the rest of the time of regeneration between Christ's ascension and His second coming.

During the earlier part of this period the civil sovereign had always been an infidel ; and the circumstance materially affected men's prospects of enduring benefit. It was a " hard case " (IV, 188) if an infidel sovereign demanded a type of obedience that forfeited the possibility of life eternal, and the Christian had to be content, without resistance, to lay down his present life, " neither is any man so mad, as not to yield obedience rather to them that can remit and retain their sins, than to the powerfullest kings " (II, 284, 299). Such unfortunates " ought to expect their reward in heaven, and not complain of their lawful sovereign ; much less make war upon him " (III, 601). On the other hand, Hobbes tried very hard to prove that this desperate plight did not occur very often.

One of the things he said was that it was very important to consider " what is meant in Holy Scripture by life eternal and torment eternal " (III, 437). Adam, he maintained, was created with a naturally incorruptible body (III, 438), which he made corruptible by his sin, and he and the children that inherited his mortality would remain dead until the Resurrection, when an incorruptible or (in that sense) spiritual body might be restored (III, 578). The inference was (III, 439) that *this earth* was the place of everlasting life ; and Hobbes found no Scriptural or other reasonable ground for believing that heaven was the empyrean. The " kingdom of heaven " was simply the realm of Him who had His throne in heaven (III, 441) ; and it appeared from Isaiah's teaching (ch. 33) that

Jerusalem and Mount Zion were the abode of the elect after the Judgment (III, 452 *sqq.*).

Similarly, " the place of the damned after the resurrection is not determined, neither in the Old nor New Testament by any note of situation " (III, 445). Before the Resurrection it was either a man's grave[1]—for the " bottomless " pit could not be of infinite depth according to a sound cosmography—or under water where the " giants " or demigods were, or the lake of pitch where Sodom was destroyed by conflagration, or the Valley of the Children of Hinnon near Jerusalem (*i.e.* Tophet or Gehenna) where the corpses of certain malefactors were incinerated along with other garbage from the city (III, 447). Otherwise all references to fire and brimstone must be regarded as metaphorical (III, 446). Both Christ and Moses regarded the devil and all demons as names for earthly tormentors of the Church. Gnashing of teeth was only chagrin at the loss of eternal felicity (III, 449) ; and " we do not read that to any of the reprobate is promised an eternal life " (III, 450). On the contrary, at the Resurrection, a sinner was literally condemned to a " second death " (III, 450 *sq.*), " after which he shall die no more," because he would not live any more.

Hobbes's principal argument, however, was to the general effect that the early Christians, under infidel monarchs, need not have been *very* seditious. He admitted (III, 485) that a certain " power ecclesiastical " belonged to the apostles and to their successors, since they ordained by laying on of hands. In essence, however, they were a pastorate, and their office did not include coercive power (III, 491). The Paraclete assisted them as schoolmasters, not as commanders ; and even the " power of the keys " referred to the Day of Judgment (III, 499). Those who were " called " to bear witness and convert the infidel, it was true, might also be called to suffer martyrdom (and

[1] Hobbes (III, 623) piously quoted *Ecclesiastes* iii. 19.

therefore, one would suppose, would be perfidious (III, 656) if they were *not* seditious) ; but other Christians might very well follow the example of Naaman the Syrian ; and Hobbes (III, 586 *sqq.*) went as near as he could to saying that submission to the civil laws was the prime duty of a Christian even under an infidel sovereign. The " infidel king," he petulantly remarked (III, 602), would be very " unreasonable " if he discerned sedition in a claim to dominion that had to await the Resurrection. In the early Church the election of the pastors (III, 525) and all judgments concerning excommunication belonged to the local ecclesia (III, 501). The pastor was simply the chairman of the congregation, convoking it (III, 528) and pronouncing its sentence.

Since Hobbes also maintained that as soon as the sovereign became a Christian he straightway assumed the pastoral office—since otherwise he would dirempt himself of a necessary part of his sovereign power (III, 538)—and gave subordinate pastors an office strictly comparable to a magistracy, it is scarcely possible that he was satisfied with these attempts to prove that the early Church was not seditious.

In appearance, Hobbes's task became much simpler when (and where) the sovereign became a Christian. " He which heareth his sovereign, being a Christian, heareth Christ"[1] (III, 564) ; and the Church was " the same thing with a Christian people " (III, 569). " The universal Church was indeed one mystical body " (II, 279) ; and the Church of Rome had at one time been as wide as the City of Rome ; " but after that the civil empire was divided into parts, the single cities thence arising were so many Churches "[2] (*ibid.*).

---

[1] When, in a collect, Charles II was described as "our most religious king," Bishop Burnet admitted (*History*, I, 183) that it was "not easy to make it go well down, however much the Latin might import 'the sacredness of the king's person ' " (q. Tanner, p. 226).

[2] *i.e.* : " cuius regio, eius religio," as in the Peace of Augsburg.

In short, when it was granted that there was only one
body politic to which a man could belong, it followed that
" both State and Church are the same men "[1] (III, 546),
and " a man, though but dull of apprehension, may collect
that in a Christian city, that is to say, in a city whose
sovereignty belongs to a Christian prince or council, all
power, as well spiritual as secular, is united under Christ,
and therefore it is to be obeyed in all things " (II, 298).
Kings were " not so merely laic[2] as not to have sacerdotal
jurisdiction " (IV, 199, cf. B. 14). The monarch could
exercise all apostolic functions, including baptism and
ordination (III, 541 *sqq*.), although, if he chose, he could
delegate such functions to a Pope or to anyone else
(III, 546). " The fact of St. Ambrose in excommunicating
Theodosius the Emperor, if it were true he did so, were
a capital crime " (III, 583). In brief, " temporal and
spiritual authority are but two words brought into the
world to make men see double and mistake their lawful
sovereign " (III, 460) ; and " Papists, Lutherans, Cal-
vinists, Arminians, &c." should note the fact.

A considerable part of Hobbes's very long chapter on
" power ecclesiastical," which occupied one-seventh
of the entire *Leviathan* (III, 485–584), was a polemic
against Cardinal Bellarmine, whose *De Potestate summi
Pontificis in rebus temporalibus* (1610) was the most
skilful reply of the age to the posthumous book of
William Barclay.

In disputing Bellarmine's first four books, Hobbes
indulged in a battle of texts, a species of warfare in which

[1] Hooker (E.P. III, Pt. I, 412) had argued regarding Church and
commonwealth that although " no person appertaining to the one can
be denied to be also of the other," yet they were two corporations " in
substance perpetually severed," although they might have the same
head ; and again (*loc. cit.* 474), " Kings are Christ's as saints ; and kings
are Christ's as kings." The general mediæval idea was that of one
body having temporal and spiritual functions. According to Marsilio
(q. G.A. 228) the Church was " pars et officium civitatis."
[2] Rufinus, a canonist (q. Car. II, 149) said the Emperor was " non
omnino laicus." Cf. Hooker (III, Pt. I, 524) : " not wholly of the laity."

he would never have been silenced had his case been very much worse. His polemic against Bellarmine's fifth book, however, introduced other artillery.

Bellarmine argued that the Pope had temporal power *indirectly* over all other princes. Hobbes, of course, disputed the claim and its very practical implications (III, 574), such as the absolving of the subjects of an excommunicated king, " in the deposing of Chilperic, King of France, in the translation of the Roman Empire to Charlemagne, in the oppression of John, King of England, in transferring the kingdom of Navarre, and of late years in the league against Henry the Third of France, and in many more occurrences."

According to Hobbes, if Bellarmine meant that temporal government was a means to spiritual felicity, as saddles are means to riding, he was not entitled to argue that " every saddler is bound to obey every rider " (III, 575), whereas if he meant that clergy and laity formed one commonwealth under the Pope, the truth was that there were many commonwealths, such as France, Spain, and Venice, each of which was *one* and therefore civil. Alternatively, there was no spiritual commonwealth " amongst men that are yet in the flesh," and if there were one or more, the Pope, as a sovereign " in the state of nature," might be attacked like any other sovereign (III, 577 *sq.*). Again, a civil sovereign *could not* be heretical (since a heresy was only an obstinate *private* opinion) ; and an infidel sovereign, although it would be a mistake to elect one, ought to be obeyed. It was absurd to claim temporal power on the ground that the Pope was the sole judge of heresy or of infidelity (III, 579 *sqq.*). Indeed (B. 21) " there was never such another cheat in the world."

Hobbes made light of the texts regarding the two swords (sacerdotal and civil) and of the two luminaries (III, 620)—where the moon was supposed to signify the king and the sun the Pope. He admitted, however, that Beza's argument (III, 617 *sqq.*) to the effect that the kingdom of God, according to the Scriptures, began at the resurrection *of Christ* was more difficult to answer than any of Bellarmine's.

(9) SUPERSTITION

It is pretty clear, I think, that Hobbes thought that all supernaturalism was superstition. His famous and very imprudent statement : " Fear of power invisible feigned by the mind, or imagined from tales publicly allowed, religion ; not allowed, superstition " (III, 45), was scarcely saved by the addendum, " and when the power imagined is truly such as we imagine, true religion " (*ibid.*), or by the explanation (III, 105) that " an opinion of a deity and powers invisible or supernatural, can never be so abolished out of human nature, but that new religions may again be made to spring out of them, by the culture of such men, as for such purpose are in reputation."

Hobbes, like the Roman poet, rejoiced not only in the discovery of the causes of things, but also in the silencing of unworthy fears and of the murmurs of greedy Acheron. He came very near to proclaiming his complete emancipation, especially in the last and longest book of the *Leviathan*, " Of the Kingdom of Darkness," where he piled learning upon irony, and irony upon invective, in a savage and magnificently incisive peroration.

Here his governing assumption was that superstition was *dangerous* only when priest or presbyter fathered it. The kingdom of darkness was a confederacy of *these* deceivers (III, 604) who had added the errors of Greek demonology and the vanity of Aristotelity to their own politically subversive enchantments. The papacy, as the older, the wilier, and the stronger, had to bear the brunt of the charge ; but Hobbes attacked others, under another name, or remaining nameless, as all the world might see (*e.g.* III, 109).

Christendom, said Hobbes, was "yet in the dark" (III, 604). The enemy had abused Scripture, accepted a heathen mythology, mixed it with vain philosophy, and mingled the two latter with "feigned or uncertain history" (III, 605). The Scriptures could not sustain the claim that the Pope was the vicar of God, that the laity should pay tribute to the clergy, that consecration was "conjuration or enchantment," that conjured salt or conjured water prevented little children from becoming demoniacs (III, 613), that there was a purgatory, or a hellish eternity of suffering, or any virtue in prayers for the dead. The doctrine of incorporeal spirits was a relic of Gentilism, never properly authenticated in the Scriptures (III, 641)— although "probable and pious reasons" (III, 643) had to be found for certain of Christ's expressions. In effect, the supernaturalists converted the spectres or idols of a man's own imagination—for *fancy* was the stuff of dead men's ghosts, and fairies, and other matter of old wives' tales— into the absurdities of demonology. Hence all idolatry and the scandalous powers of priests "that can make God" (III, 675).

Hence also the unholy alliance between papacy (or prelacy) and the vain philosophy of Aristotle. "The writings of School-divines are nothing else, for the most part, but insignificant trains of strange and barbarous words" (III, 686), employed to suppress true philosophy and the human sciences "by such men as neither by lawful authority, nor sufficient study, are competent judges of the truth" (III, 687). Fatuities regarding "essence" were used to frighten men away from civic obedience by empty names, "as men fright birds from the corn with an empty doublet, a hat, and a crooked stick" (III, 674). Again, "case-divinity" was almost as bad as "school-divinity."

All was for the worldly profit of the clergy (III, 688 *sqq.*). The Pope took his title of Pontifex Maximus from old Rome (III, 661). " The first that ever was canonized at Rome was Romulus " (III, 660). The *fulmen excommunicationis* was really Jupiter's thunderbolt (III, 509). The madonnas and bambini in Catholic churches were Venus and Cupid over again (III, 660). *Aqua lustralis* had become holy water, *bacchanalia* had become wakes, the procession of Priapus was renewed in English may-poles (III, 663). The new wine of Christianity had been enclosed in the " old empty bottles of Gentilism " (III, 663), and the papacy " is no other than the ghost of the deceased *Roman Empire*, sitting crowned upon the grave thereof " (III, 698).

The Pope used the ghost of the old Roman language (*ibid.*), and ecclesiastics mimicked fairyland.[1]

" The ecclesiastics are spiritual men and ghostly fathers. The fairies are spirits and ghosts. Fairies and ghosts inhabit darkness, solitudes and graves. The ecclesiastics walk in obscurity of doctrine, in monasteries, churches and church-yards. . . . The fairies are not to be seized on, and brought to answer for the hurt they do. So also the ecclesiastics vanish away from the tribunals of civil justice. . . . The fairies marry not, but there be amongst them incubi that have copulation with flesh and blood. The priests also marry not. . . . What kind of money is current in the kingdom of fairies is not recorded in the story. But the ecclesiastics in their receipts accept of the same money that we do ; though when they are to make any payment, it is in canonizations, indulgencies and masses " (III, 698 *sq.*).

The Roman priests had demanded such excessive credulity that it was not " a very difficult matter for

[1] Cf. James I, *Apologie* (ed. McIlwain, p. 109) : " The Pope must be content in that style to succeed according to the law and institution of Numa Pompilius, and not to St. Peter, who never heard nor dreamed of such an office."

Henry VIII by his exorcism, nor for Queen Elizabeth by
hers, to cast them out " (III, 700). *But* " it is not the
Roman clergy only that pretends the kingdom of God to
be of this world, and thereby to have a power therein,
distinct from that of the civil state " (*ibid.*).

PART III
INFLUENCE

VII

PRELIMINARIES CONCERNING HOBBES'S INFLUENCE

(I) RETROSPECT AND PROSPECT

A GREAT philosopher is one who has the courage to attack the greatest themes, and the tenacity to sustain his point of view.

Therefore Hobbes was very great indeed ; for, as I have said, he was the boldest intellectual circumnavigator of the earlier half of the century of genius, and our admiration for the man is increased by the circumstance that he had to equip himself, relatively late in life, with the new technique of mathematical and physical thought. Hobbes was middle-aged when he came to see, in all its fullness, how the new science called for a new philosophy. Had he been younger and better trained he might well have blenched at the magnitude of the new (yet imperative) theme. Instead, he set himself to unlearn what was old and dead, and to become a leader in all that was living and new.

We have therefore to ask whether, in essentials, he thought himself out of the old world into the new (not necessarily because the old was bad, but because, most emphatically, he thought it was). We have also to ask whether his philosophy attained the unity that he planned.

Regarding the first of these questions, I have tried to indicate that a simple " yes " or " no " is impossible. Hobbes's excursions into geometry, although more unfortunate in their fate than in their conception, did not suggest that he was a reliable guide into the new ways of thinking. His physical theories, again, although, as we shall see, they earned Leibniz's admiration, were largely those of a scholastic mechanist ; and physics was the weakest department of scholasticism.

Such relative failures, even if the second of them had greatness in it, might not have mattered very much in some philosophies, but they mattered enormously in a philosophy which professed to be the first that was erected clear-headedly upon the true understanding of physical motion.

Criticisms of this order should not be directed against the other parts of Hobbes's philosophy, *i.e.* against his psychology or his ethico-political theory. Many of Hobbes's psychological observations, it is true, were borrowed from classical sources ; but Hobbes, who had a genius both for introspective observation and for divining the motives of other men, might rummage where he chose and still retain his obvious originality. Moreover, nothing in the new science had antiquated these treasures of insight. Again, in matters political, I have tried to argue that Hobbian novelties, however startling they might be, were nevertheless the moves of a master-player who knew and kept to the mediæval rules ; but I did not make the suggestion in criticism of Hobbes, since my opinion (for what it is worth) is that the mediæval political thinkers were the best in European history.

One's estimate of the unity of Hobbes's philosophy, however, involves rather different considerations.

Clearly, Hobbes possessed a flair for philosophical architecture, and an eye for the grand metaphysical lines, that have seldom been equalled. His designs, however, were, in parts, very incomplete. A ground-plan of bodies in motion ; vague sketches concerning biology ; the plans for an entire storey devoted to sensation with an optical vestibule frequently drawn in detail ; very sketchy designs regarding the anatomy and physiology that should have connected the sensory storey with its materialistic foundations ; very full plans for a higher storey of introspective psychology rather arbitrarily connected with the former by the theory that conceptions might do all the work of logic, although, in their essence, they were only decaying sense ; at the top an elaborate political philosophy with a character all its own and planned in terms of a psychology of self-interest that could hardly be reconciled with the monistic determinism of the ground-plan of the edifice. Such (to speak with misleading brevity) was Hobbism. Had it really the unity that the architect claimed for it ?

I have argued that Hobbes's employment of introspective methods and of a certain type of phenomenalism did not necessarily contradict his materialism, and indeed that he attempted to cement something more than a merely official union in this connection by developing his determinism into a doctrine of *extrinsic* determination and by insisting that human motives were literally motions within the organism.   Nevertheless, by his own admission, his psychology and his phenomenalism could be understood and elaborated independently of his materialism.   Similarly, his ethico-political theory, while partially based upon psychology, was also based upon a new and quite special set of definitions.

Except for the lacunæ in biology and in cerebral physiology, it is likely enough that Hobbes attempted all that was reasonable in the way of philosophical unity.   Indeed, it may be contended that *every* philosophy is forced to add fresh principles, derived largely from special experience, to its primary foundations, and cannot derive all its consequences directly from its primary principles.   Philosophy has to construct a building, not to erect a monolith, and it should be accounted successful if the building stands, even if brick has to be erected upon granite and wood upon the brick.

If so, Hobbes, at the worst, deserved censure for being too sanguine a materialist. Nevertheless, his theory, as it stands, was subdivided into three great compartments, its materialism, its phenomenalism, and its ethico-political doctrine. One or other of these compartments, seldom all of them together, influenced his contemporaries and succeeding philosophers, if, indeed, their interest was not further limited to narrower themes, such as his determinism, his theory of the functions of speech, his anticipation of " associationism," his " selfish " psychology, his legalistic morality, or his autocratic absolutism.

Consequently, in attempting to trace his influence, I have to follow this threefold division into materialism, phenomenalism, ethics and politics ; and I hope to present a verifiable although (as I fear) a rather intricate narrative. If the reader is disposed to complain that he is offered too much to keep in his head, I can only say that I am sorry about it, but that Hobbes was responsible. It was Hobbes who developed so many departments of philosophy, each of them big enough for a very big man, to so high a pitch of accuracy; and Hobbes, too, who was responsible for so many special developments that kept men thinking. I may also plead that my plan has at least one considerable advantage. It is reasonable to be interested not so much in the whole of Hobbism, as in some one of its departments, say its ethics and politics ; and readers who have this specialised interest may readily select what they chiefly want without incommoding themselves with the rest.

I have to warn such readers, however, and others too, that the remainder of the present chapter will deal with smaller points or with smaller people than its successors. But I shall be as brief as I can.

(2) MINOR COMMENTATORS, PRINCIPALLY
CONTEMPORARY

To some small extent Hobbes's notoriety found its way into general literature, and Leslie Stephen (St. 68) collected some instances, the most interesting of which was in Farquhar's *The Constant Couple* (1700), where Vizard, the villain, read Hobbes privily, and the *Practice of Piety* in public. Farquhar, however, had a touch of pedantry in his composition and expected to raise a laugh by making one of his heroes swear " by the universe." Indeed, considering how much Hobbes was read, it is surprising that Stephen did not find more instances of the kind.[1]

In the same place Stephen said that the " only concrete instance " of Hobbian principles working practical moral disaster was the suicide of Charles Blount the Deist. This Blount had been censured by T. Browne, D.D. (1683) for translating Hobbes and Spinoza together ; but, in fact, Hobbes was held responsible for at least one other suicide (a very un-Hobbian act). When Cardonnel, a Fellow of Merton, hanged himself in 1681, Prideaux wrote to Ellis (Camden Soc., p. 116) : " I understand there was something of more deep concern than the affront he received from the Warden. . . . It seems he had lived with the Earle of Devonshire as præceptor to his grandson, where, having been poisoned by Hobbs, on his return hither, blasphemy and atheism was his most frequent talke ; of the guilt of which being at last sensible, this, 'tis supposed, præcipitated him into despair." It may also be noted that the edifying end of the notorious John, Earl of Rochester, as narrated in the funeral sermon preached by his chaplain, Robert Parsons (which ran into several editions) included the confession that " that absurd and foolish philosophy which

[1] Among later writers, Hazlitt and B. Disraeli in *Vivian Grey* may be mentioned.

the world so much admired, propagated by the late Mr. Hobbs and others, had undone him, and many more of the best parts of the nation."

In this general sense Hobbes was regarded as an apostle of licentiousness, a reproach that endured,[1] and was even made in a very unphilosophical passage in Hume's *History* (ch. 72), where Hume said that "Hobbes's politics were fitted only to promote tyranny, and his ethics to encourage licentiousness." For the most part, however, these attacks upon Hobbes would now be vulgarly described as a clergyman's ramp,[2] although many of the

---

[1] Illustrations are J. Vesey (Bishop of Limerick), *Life of Bramhall* (1677): "Mr. Hobbs, a very natural philosopher, whose doctrines have had so great a share in the debauchery of this generation that a good Christian can hardly hear his name without saying of his prayers"; McMahon's essay on "The Depravity of Human Nature" (1774), where Hobbes was included (approvingly) along with La Bruyère, Helvétius, and others as exponents of original sin; Warburton (*Tracts*, published 1789), "the jolly philosopher of Malmesbury . . . intoxicated with his new-brewed hypothesis of human baseness."

[2] Two unliterary but sincere "elegies" on Hobbes, published in 1679 and in 1680 respectively, have some interest in this connection. The second of these broadsheets was vigorously anti-clerical, and argued that,

"So great a wit perhaps the world ne'er bore,"

and that

"All Christendom does fairly yield
England for greatest wit has gained the field,"

on the ground that

"The peevish Memphian priests appear to be
Dull Scots compared to our brave Malmesbury."

The other showed genuine affection :

"Is he then dead at last, whom vain report
So often had feign'd mortal in meer sport ?
Whom we on earth so long alive might see
We thought he here had immortality,
As he, like what he wrote, could not expire ;
Whom all that did not love, did yet admire,"

although its theme was the qualified praise :

"If he mistakes, 'tis still with so much wit,
He errs more pleasingly than others hit."

placed or aspiring bishops must have believed, honestly if erroneously, that speculative "atheism" had a good deal to do with the licentiousness of the age. In any case, there was point in the lines of a contemporary satire (q. A.G. XVII, 308, and ascribed to the author of *Hudibras*):

> " Lo !   Those who wear the holy robes
> That rail so much at Father Hobbs
> Because he has exposed of late
> The nakedness of Church and State ;
> Yet tho' they do his books condemn
> They love to buy and read the same."

Among these writers, the Catholics, despite Hobbes's vehemence against them, were, in England, comparatively restrained.   Thomas White was Hobbes's friend, who agreed with him in many things ; and P. Scot (*A Treatise of the Schism of England.*   London, 1650) " modestly accosted" Mr. Hobbes, deploring his misconceptions of the Catholic position, but regarding him as otherwise (p. 222) " singularly deserving in moral and socratical philosophy." Again, the Presbyterians had a delicate doctrine of Church and State to defend, although the great Richard Baxter was convinced (*Holy Commonwealth* (1659), p. 225) that Hobbes's " way of absolute impious monarchy" was utterly objectionable, if only because " the irreligious author pretendeth not to any such thing as the securing a succession of the Christian religion without which a righteous government is not to be expected."   Even the better critics in the Church of England, however, were apt to use very uncharitable language, and the inferior among them were ludicrously violent.   " To adorn the memory of such a man as T. H.," one of them asked, " what is it but to provide that the corpse of one that died of the plague may lie in state, that people coming to behold it may contract the infection."[1]

----

[1] *Animadversions* on Hobbes, published anonymously 1694, along with certain letters to Henry More.

One of the earliest in the field was Alexander Ross, Aberdonian and schoolmaster at Southampton, who, in 1653, wrote his *Leviathan drawn out with a Hook*. He used the most varied tackle, and in the end accused Hobbes of being a Cerinthian, a Mahometan, an Anthropomorphist, a Manichæan, a Tertullianist, an Andæan, an Arian, a Sabellian, a Montanist, probably a Priscillianist, a Sadducee, an Arabian, a Luciferian, an Originist, a Tacian, a Jew, and a Socinian. In 1654, R. Vilvain, a pleasant-tempered old gentleman, censured Hobbes, " sans sordid envy " (253), in his *Theoremata Theologica*. In 1657 Bishop Lucy[1] (" Pike " or " Christophilus ") defended the schoolmen against " this Mr. Hobbs," and George Lawson, Rector of More in Salop, produced his " Examination of the Political Part of the *Leviathan*," which traversed Hobbianism in detail, and, admitting that Hobbes in the earlier books of the *Leviathan* had " some use of his reason," thought him a lunatic with occasional lucid intervals when he came to " Christian politics " (156). T. Pierce, Rector of Brington, in 1658, produced a " Self-condemnation " of " Mr. Calvin, Mr. Zuinglius . . . Doctor Twisse, and Master Hobbs."

The celebrated Joseph Glanvil, in his *Scepsis Scientifica* (1661) and in his *Philosophia Pia* (1671) referred very obliquely to Hobbes as a " somatist " and a " sadducee," although the chief object of the former book (*Pref.*) was to give the lie to " the mechanical hypothesis (to which a person that is not very fond of religion is a great pre-

---

[1] Among his early critics, Hobbes said that he ignored " Dr. Ward, Mr. Baxter, Pike, and others " (IV, 435), and he indicated (IV, 237) that he was almost flattered by the animadversions of the learned Mr. Ross. We have already seen how he answered Ward (*i.e.* Vindex), Wallis, Bramhall, Boyle, and some others. Of a foreign critic, Moranus, a Flanders Jesuit (*Animadversiones*. Brussels, 1655) Hobbes said (VII, 338 *sq.*) that a visit to England should have improved that author's " common and childish learning," and that his attack upon " That civil and renowned old man, Dr. Harvey," showed that he was inconsiderable.

tender)." Bishop Laney's " A Letter about Liberty and
Necessity" (1676) contained a historically interesting criticism (88 *sq.*) of Hobbes's " excellent new engine " of
Nosce teipsum, and called it by its later name, " Reflection."[1] Samuel Parker, Bishop of Oxford, while accepting
much of the political theory of the *Leviathan* in his " Discourse of Ecclesiaticall Politie "[2] (1670), showed his
superiority by remarking that " the plebeians and mechanicks have philosophised themselves into principles of
impiety and read their Lectures of Atheism in the
streets and the highways " (q. D.N.B.). John Eachard's
dialogues between Philautus and Timothy (" Mr. Hobbes's
State of Nature Considered " (1672)) had several editions,
and was commended by Stephen (St. 68), who liked its
classification of Hobbists into those of pit, box, and
gallery.[3] John Shafto's " The Great Law of Nature or
Self-preservation Examined " (1673) tried to prove in an
un-Hobbian way that self-love and conscience were
coincident, but said little of note. J. Templer's *Idea
Theologiæ Leviathanis* (1673) contained an amazing intro-
ductory Latin ode by the Rev. C. Robotham of Norfolk,
in which the Trinity, the Angels, all Nature, Councils,
Synods, and Martyrs united in praising Templer's victory
over the horrid monster with its terrible dogmatic jaws.[4]

---

[1] Reid's term (*Works,* p. 201) for what was later called the " philosophy
of mind," *i.e.* a wary and self-examining epistemology.   In a general
way this method may be said to have been *the* method of British
philosophy from Locke to the Mills, although there were mutual accusations of infidelity to the method.   It was the method of Hobbes's
" Nosce teipsum," or, as Hobbes said regarding free-will (IV, 275):
" there can no other proof be offered but every man's own experience,
by reflection on himself."

[2] See also his *Disputationes de Deo* (1678), p. 88.

[3] The piece was sprightly, but not, I think, valuable.

[4] I have not seen the anti-Hobbian work of Philip Tandy (about
free will, 1656).   In 1679 W. Howell, Rector of Fittleworth, answered
Hobbes's " affronts " in *The Spirit of Prophecy.*   In 1683 J. Dowel,
Vicar of Melton Mowbray, in *The Leviathan Heretical,* tried to prove
that Hobbes *was* a heretic, and started the rumour about Cromwell's
offer of a secretaryship.   In the same year an anonymous author, in
Miracles no Violations of the Laws of Nature, answered " a late trans-

Among the lawyers, Roger Coke, a grandson of the great Chief Justice, argued ably that the prerogatives of monarchy could not be derived from the people, and in his *Justice Vindicated* and other works, published in or shortly after the year of the Restoration, argued against White, Hobbes, and Grotius, finding Hobbes clear (but clearly wrong) and Grotius confused. Again, John Whitehall, of the Inner Temple, produced a mediocre book, *The Leviathan found out*, in 1679, showing special animus against the *Behemoth*, repudiating Hobbes's theory of property (p. 53), and endeavouring to fill some minor gaps that Clarendon had left. Historically speaking, however, the most significant event of this sort was the reaction of Sir Matthew Hale, Lord Chief Justice, to Hobbes's legal theory.

It is an ironical comment upon the sneers of Clarendon (*Survey*, 56) and others regarding Hobbes's " extraordinary and notorious ignorance " of the laws of England that

lation " of Hobbes and Spinoza. J. A. Lowde, a Yorkshire rector and formerly Fellow of Clare (1694), attacked Hobbes (and also Locke) in an honest, careful, and reasonably temperate piece of work. C. Gildon, Gent., in *The Deist's Manual* (1705) [the preface addressed to the Archbishop of Canterbury], wondered that Hobbes's books "were not sunk yet," but hopefully supposed that the learned clergy had made the " would-be-wits " and " debochees " ashamed of " so baffled an instructor." B. Hampton of the Middle Temple attempted to refute Hobbes's (but principally Dr. W. Coward's) denial of " immortal substance," in *The Existence of the Human Soul after Death* (1711). Bentley, in 1713, *Remarks upon . . . Free Thinking*, waxed sarcastic about substituting the *Leviathan* for the Bible (p. 223, ed. 1792), replying to Collins, the Deist and friend of Locke, who, in the same year (*A Discourse of Free Thinking*) had likened Hobbes to Socrates, Plato, and Tillotson, calling him (p. 170), " a great instance of learning, virtue, and free-thinking." A. Smith, in 1718, vindicated anti-Hobbism against an alleged revival by Dr. Broughton. Alex. Innes, D.D., a disreputable opponent of Mandeville's, denounced Machiavel, Hobbes, Spinoza, and Bayle in his *Enquiry into the Original of Moral Virtue* (1728). V. Perronet, in 1740, inquired into " Mr. Hobbes's Opinions " about " Spiritual Beings " ; and the " *Ophiomaches* " *or Deism revealed* (2nd ed., 1751) included Hobbes among the deists examined in its four dialogues. Catherine Macaulay's *Loose Remarks . . . in a Letter to Signor Paoli* (1767) gave an oddly close examination of the *De Cive*. An imaginary conversation with Hobbes appeared in a popular work, *Visits from the Shades* (1st ed., 1704).

Sir W. S. Holdsworth to-day speaks as if Hobbes's *Dialogues of the Common Law* marked a turning-point in British legal history (*A History of English Law*, V, 500), since (*ibid.*) they " resulted in the first comprehensive and reasoned criticism of these laws " by Matthew Hale, " one of the greatest lawyers of his time, and the only historian of English law who can be put on a level with Maitland."

These encomia were made upon Hale's *History of the Common Law*, but Hale's account of Hobbes was given in a tract, " Reflections . . . on Mr. Hobbes, his *Dialogues* . . ." which existed only in manuscript (Harl. 711) until recently published by Holdsworth as Appendix III to his fifth volume. (It is not unlikely, however, that the tract was circulated in manuscript ; and Hale's attempts to discriminate between Hobbes and Selden were matter of common knowledge.)

The tract was in two parts, of which the first made the point that no single man's " reason " could apply the law adequately, and so that a trained lawyer, careful of precedents and established rules, "will be much better fitted for right judgment therein than he that hath no other stock to trade upon than the bare exercise of his faculty of reason or that hath only taken the pains to read over the titles of the statutes or indexes or repertories of some law books " (505). (The point was fair, but it may be doubted whether the " consonance and consistence of the law to itself " (506) became very evident by these means.)

The second part " Of Sovereign Power," as Holdsworth admits (VI, 206), was fundamentally irrelevant when regarded as a criticism of Hobbes, since it assumed that Hobbes's " sovereign " was necessarily the British monarch, and proceeded to explain how the government of Britain had been historically " mixed " and in what proportions. Its history was better than Hobbes's—although it may not have mattered very much what William the Conqueror *professed* when he claimed to succeed Edward after Harold's usurpation. Again, Hale's historical defence of private property was no answer to Hobbes's analytical assertion that the very meaning of *meum* and *tuum* depended on political regiment.

The contemporary English works on Hobbes, very near the first class but definitely falling short of it, were those by Clarendon, Sharrock, and Tenison.

Clarendon's *Brief View and Survey* (2nd imp., 1676) was finished at Montpelier in 1670 (p. 4) when the author was in exile and very bitter. Its real object, it would seem (p. 311), was to complain of Hobbes's " undeserved sanctuary " ; that is to say, of Charles's favour towards Arlington and other supporters of Hobbes. Apart from personalities barbed with the appearance of candour and respect, the book was a fairly elaborate critical commentary on the *Leviathan*, chapter by chapter, becoming much fuller when Hobbes's political and ecclesiastical theory was reached, complaining that Hobbian absolutism excelled that of the Great Turk (p. 42), that Hobbes's theory of the contract[1] was but a levelling fancy (p. 71), and that Hobbes invariably made the sense of Scripture " as difficult as he was able to do " (p. 203).

The *De Finibus et Officiis* of Robert Sharrock, later Archdeacon of Winchester (1673), has received much less attention from later writers than Cumberland's rather similar treatise that preceded it by a year, and the author's attempts to submerge his opponents—that is to say, Epicurus and Carneades among the ancients, Selden, Pufendorf, Spinoza, and Hobbes (but principally Hobbes) among the moderns—in the placid and profound stream of his learning was not very likely, perhaps, to have lasting influence. He had, however, a scholar's sensitive con-

---

[1] Sir William Temple, in his " Essay upon the Original and Nature of Government " (1672), gave some acute historical reasons for holding that the governmental authority of unequals preceded the institution of government by equals.

science, and when he encountered the difficult question whether Hobbes really did deny the " laws of nature " in their traditional sense, scrupulously examined the evidence (pp. 124 *sq.* of 2nd ed.), confessed to a doubt (which, however, he later forgot) and said, very truly, that Spinoza outdid Hobbes (p. 126). Sharrock's genuine if intermittent impartiality may be seen in his admission that Hobbian utilitarianism, although different in principle from the true theory, need not differ appreciably regarding practice (p. 171, cf. p. 177).

Some of the same qualities, although in a less eminent degree, were shown by Thomas Tenison (later Archbishop) in " The Creed of Mr. Hobbes examined in a feigned conference between him and a Student of Divinity" (1670). True, the student was very rude. " As is the manner of divers who have an itch for writing, you claw yourself " (p. 162). On the other hand, although victorious as a matter of course, the student saved himself from the grosser kind of unfairness by faithfully giving his references in his accusations of plagiarism from Descartes[1] (p. 5) or from Aristotle (p. 79) and in all other matters. Again, he made some shrewd comments, as when he said (p. 82) of the Hobbian theory of sense-impressions, " Might we not strongly argue that a looking-glass saw and a lute heard ? "

Hobbes had great influence on the Continent, as we shall see with reference to some famous names.

Oddly enough, however, Blackbourne and Aubrey were able to cite only a few oversea supporters of Hobbes, and Blackbourne (L. I, lxxix) said Hobbes had only one completely faithful convert,[2] the author of the (*Epistolica*

---

[1] Gilbert Clark was a whole-heartedly Cartesian critic of Hobbes and others in *Tractatus de Restitutione* (1662) and *De Plenitudine Mundi* (1680).

[2] Among partial supporters, Blackbourne cited Sorbière and R. Rapin (" Réflexions," Paris, 1676). Aubrey (I, 374) added Becman (*Meditationes Politicæ*, Frankfort, 1679) and C. Zeigler (*De Juribus*, etc., Wittenberg, 1681). In Pope-Blount's *Censura Celebrorum Authorum* (Geneva, 1694), Boëcler, a Grotian, was said to have counted Hobbes

Dissertatio de Principiis Justi et Decori (Amsterdam, 1651)).
The writer was Lambertino Velthuysen, apparently a
Cartesian in metaphysics (H. More, *Ench. Met.*, 363), who
professed to defend the *De Cive* with all his heart, although
his t᠍ᴗme, in fact, was general and ethical rather than
political.

Yet there were others ; and in France, according to
M. Lacour-Gayet (A.G. XII, 202 *sqq.*) Du Verdus in his
translation (one of several) of the *De Cive* (1660) told the
young Louis XIV, in his Preface, that the only two
demonstrative sciences were Euclid's *Elements* and
Hobbes's *Elements of Politics*. He begged the monarch to
make the *De Cive* an obligatory part of French education.
Again, in 1685, Merlat (a refugee theological professor
from Lausanne), and, in 1687, the anonymous author of
Essais de morale et de politique, were avowed Hobbists in
their politics, while Desbans, in 1715, was obviously a
plagiarist from the same source.

In Germany and in the Netherlands, however, Hobbes's
detractors[1] were much more numerous than his supporters,
the theologians for obvious reasons, the jurists because
they followed Grotius. Some idea of Hobbes's influence

a great intellect who had gone astray by neglecting the classics ; and
Pope-Blount himself, who translated Cowley's ode into Latin, admired
Hobbes highly (p. 1083). Other compilations of this type, *e.g.* the
Theatrum Virorum Clarorum (Nürnberg, 1688) or Hagen's *Memoriæ
Philosophorum* (Frankfort, 1710), give ample evidence of Hobbes's fame,
although not of his popularity.

[1] Some opponents mentioned by Blackbourne were G. Coquius (in a
series of *Vindiciæ*, Utrecht, 1661-8) ; Rachelius and J. A. Osiander
(*Tractatus*, etc., Tübingen, 1660) ; also J. F. Le Grand (Paris, 1657) ;
Mansfelt (against Spinoza, Utrecht, 1674) ; and Roberval (on mathe-
matics). Aubrey added the name of S. Siremesius against Hobbes's
" pythanology " in *Praxiologica apodictica* (Frankfort, 1677). C.
Kortholt (with whom Lange (*Gesch. d. Mat.*, I, 318), conjoined Genthe's
Compendium) followed Rachelius in a feeble work, *De Tribus Im-
postoribus Magnis* (Cologne, 1680), the impostors being Herbert of
Cherbury, Hobbes, and Spinoza. G. Galeatius complained of Hobbes's
" Cyclopean license " (q. Pope-Blount's *Censura*, which also mentioned
Eisenhart, Voëtius, and Maresius). In 1681 (at The Hague) Adrian
Houtuyn Jct. carefully tabulated sixty-four Hobbian errors in political
theory.

may be gathered from the recent publications ("Classics of International Law") of the Carnegie Endowment for International Peace. As early as 1650 Zouche mentioned the *De Cive*, and Textor in 1680 referred somewhat more fully to Hobbes. The celebrated S. Rachelius (*Dissertationes*. Kiel, 1676) was scurrilously anti-Hobbian, and greatly delighted with Robotham's extraordinary ode.

According to M. Lyon (*La Philosophie de Hobbes*, 218 n.), Adam Rechenberg (*Thomæ Hobbesii, Εὕρημα*. Leipzig, 1694) was the most effective opponent of Hobbes's " synthetic atheism." Among the jurists, Conringius, who in his *Letters* (published 1708) called Hobbes " bold, dictatorial, and foolish," and therefore delighted good Churchmen in England (Worthington's *Diary*, I, 328), seems to have been one of the most notable of Hobbes's early opponents.

VIII

MATERIALISM AND PHENOMENALISM

(1) MATERIALISM

IT was not to be expected that the pious, or even those who wanted to be reputed pious, would accept the new mechanical philosophy ; and we may begin by considering the attitude of the Cambridge Platonists in this matter, particularly Henry More and Ralph Cudworth.

Henry More emancipated himself, as he believed, from the Calvinism of his upbringing, and from the menacing insecurity of scepticism, by a study of Platonism, and lived, ever after, in an atmosphere of mysticism that still seems radiant. Despite his theosophy and credulity, he was a philosopher of real eminence, as the tone of Descartes' correspondence with him sufficiently attested.

He was amused at Hobbes's vanity. "Hobbes takes himself to be the lob of philosophers," he wrote (*Conway Letters*, 307), and he believed, at any rate at one time (*The Immortality of the Soul* (1662), p. 13), that Descartes, not Hobbes, was "the profoundest master of mechanicks" of the age (p. 197). In the same work he criticised Hobbes's question-begging denial of the existence of spirit (40), although he thought Hobbes had put an untenable case as well as it could be put (37), and rejected Hobbes's theory of sensation (62 and 91), his necessitarianism (70 *sq.*), and the nominalism with which he "befooled his followers" (69).

Had the matter rested there, we might be astonished at the statement in R. Ward's *Life of More* (1710), that Hobbes had "been heard to say that if his own philosophy was not true, he knew of none that he should sooner like than More's of Cambridge" (p. 80). I think, however, that More's later *Enchiridion Metaphysicum* (1671) explains the puzzle. In his later work, More's Platonism had become pretty thoroughly de-Cartesianised, since it attacked Descartes' mechanical philosophy relentlessly, and although "Hobbius noster" came in for some incidental criticism, especially regarding his untenable views about gravity (114 *sqq*.), it was clear that More believed that the serious metaphysical alternative was between Hobbian corporealism (which More rejected) and his own theory that spirit was a new dimension of " essential spissitude " (384).

Like Hobbes, More scorned the ideas of the "nullibists" (*i.e.* that mind was *nowhere*), and also of the " holen-merians," who believed in the " mad jingle " (*Imm.*, 43), " totum in toto ac totum in qualibet parte." " All sub-stance must have its three spatial dimensions " (E.M. 383) ; but physical matter was only a stupid and broken congeries of mere physical monads (*ibid.*). The spiritual dimension was needed even for mechanical purposes, to say nothing of the implications of sensation, thought, and (it must be added) a reverent necromancy.

Ralph Cudworth, Master of Clare, and subsequently of Christ's College, was commonly supposed, before he published, to be *the* opponent of Hobbes,[1] and, according to his biographer,[2] wrote several thousand folio pages, mostly unpublished, against that author. When *The True Intellectual System* (1678, imprim. 1671), the only philosophical work Cudworth published in his lifetime, appeared, Hobbes, through some affectation, was mentioned, not by name, but as " a modern atheistic pretender to wit," " a late pretender to politics," etc. He was quoted freely, however, although some of the quotations were paraphrases

---

[1] Worthington's *Diary*, II, ii, 293.
[2] Birch. Prefaced to Harrison's edition (1845) of *The Intellectual System*. I quote hereafter from this edition.

and others were disingenuously curtailed (*e.g.* II, 521, 562).

Cudworth's original design (at I, xxxiii *sqq.*) had been to attack Fatalism of three species, and so to defend theism, " natural " morality, and the liberty to sin and be punished. He involved himself, however, in a general discussion of atheism, principally " Democritic," and there he remained. Since he was a book-glutton, his work was monstrously obese. The pious were afraid he had put the case for atheism too well ;[1] and he conceded that the *natural philosophy* of atomism was " unquestionably true " (at I, xxxix). On the other hand, he seldom made the mistake of being fair to Hobbes. For example, it did not follow that if sense were the original of all knowledge, atheism must be inferred (II, 510), that the absence of a positive idea of infinity formally denied God's omnipotence (II, 531), or that if religion were " not philosophy but law " it must be " a mere political scarecrow " (II, 557).

Cudworth's substantial criticism was that life and cogitation could not arise from local motion or " the mere fridging up and down of the parts of an extended substance " (III, 395), but most of his 600,000 words were devoted to proving choice pieces of pseudo-history—as that the ancients had always been monotheists (*e.g.* I, 62), believers in immaterial spirits (*e.g.* I, 74), except the few that had been " depraved and adulterated " by Leucippus and Democritus (I, 92), and had always agreed with Galileo about the status of secondary qualities (I, 58)—or in narrating the lore of Orphism, Mithraism, and Hermism. Many pious readers must have been pleased with the hint that Descartes was " a hypocritical theist or personated and disguised atheist " (II, 533, cf. I, 217, 275) ; but Hobbists need not have been greatly perturbed even when they were certified to be suffering from " hylomania " and from " pneumatophobia " (I, 200).

[1] As Shaftesbury and Dryden duly noted ; see I, xvi *sq.*

The times, however, became increasingly unpropitious to materialism in the strictest sense ; that is to say, towards materialism as distinguished from sensory phenomenalism. Continental Cartesianism, say, in Malebranche, could never be called materialism by anyone even moderately candid. Spinoza, it is true, was often named along with Hobbes in common obloquy ; and Spinoza was not a *Christian* theist. He was scarcely, however, a materialist, for although he held that " God or Nature " was extended, he made the attribute of " thought " at least equally important. When Cartesian theories gave way to Locke's, materialism, in any strict sense, was, at any rate nominally, out of fashion. Certain relics of materialism may be found in Locke ; but Locke usually repudiated physiological explanations (*e.g. Essay*, Introd. 2) and in the main opposed his phenomenalism to any materialism whatsoever.

When he discussed the mechanical theory, Locke took the view that plants, even " sensitive " ones, were only mechanisms (*Essay*, II, ix, 11), that mechanism might explain all the actions of birds that tended towards their self-preservation (II, x, 10), but that a singing bird's imitation of notes could not be so explained (*ibid.*), and, in short, that *perceiving* could not be the action of bare insensible matter (IV, x, 10). Thinking of Cudworth,[1] Locke said that the materialism of " some of the old philosophers " was an unexamined prejudice (IV, xii, 4). Thinking (I submit) of Hobbes, he said that although " thinking being may also be material," " men devoted to matter " had no business to " argue all to be matter " (IV, x, 13). True, Locke's assertion that *bodies might think* (IV, iii, 6), and his preference for the term " cogitative " to the term " immaterial " (IV, x, 9), gave offence in many quarters ; but Locke always affirmed that, if bodies thought, cogitation was " superadded " to matter,

---

[1] Whom he had praised in *Thoughts on Education*, § 193.

and in no intelligible sense derived from or explained by it.

No doubt Collins the deist, by arguing that consciousness was a " fleeting transferrible mode " *of the brain* (Clarke's *Third Defence*, pp. 64 *sq*.), came very near to developing Locke's thought materialistically, and a certain quasi-materialism may perhaps be discerned in Hume.[1] None of these authors, however, any more than Condillac or Helvétius, was, properly speaking, a materialist, and theirs was the fashion of thought that prevailed.

Apart from political theory, speculative Hobbism waned at home and overseas. The article in Bayle's *Dictionary*, while describing Hobbes as one of the greatest minds of his century, was tepid in tone, and Hume, in the middle of the century, spoke the mind of most when he said in his *History* (ch. 72) : " In our time he is much neglected ; a lively instance how precarious all reputations founded on reasoning and philosophy." Priestley, a generation later, was decidedly exceptional. His " Christian material-ism," although an adaptation of Newton and Boscovich, was broadly Hobbian, and supplemented Hobbes's references to the materialism of Athanasius and Tertullian, with an elaborate proof that most of the Fathers were materialists (*Disquisitions*, pp. 204 *sqq*.). Of " Mr. Hobbes," Priestley said (*Free Discussion* (with Price, 1778), xxv) that he appeared, " so far as I can judge from such of his writings as have fallen in my way, to have been no atheist, but a sincere Christian and a conscientious good man."

On the Continent, however, there was a distinct revival of interest in Hobbes when the Enlightenment moved towards materialistic atheism. It is true that La Mettrie, the first to show this tendency explicitly in his *L'Homme Machine* (about 1750), expressly denied (q. Lange, *Gesch. d. Mat.* I, 422) that he owed anything to Hobbes. On the other hand, Diderot's article on Hobbes in the *Encyclopédie*

[1] e.g. *Treatise* (Selby-Bigge), p. 211, from which I shall quote henceforth.

(1765) showed family pride ; and there was genuine enthusiasm in Diderot's appendix to the article (see ed. 1792), for he said : " How diffuse and slack Locke seems to me, and how thin and insignificant La Bruyère and La Rochefoucauld in comparison with this Thomas Hobbes." Again, the Baron d'Holbach, the celebrated author of the *Système de la nature*, translated Hobbes's *Human Nature* into French in 1772. On the whole, however, Hobbes's materialism was not an active force in the eighteenth century, and if he was, as Lange said (I, 294), " the most logical of modern materialists,"[1] neither Daltonian atomism nor physiological materialism went to school with him in the nineteenth century. He was not the instructor of Büchner, Moleschott, or Vogt. In the twentieth century, Royce (*Spirit of Modern Philosophy*, pp. 30 and 58) was one of the few considerable writers who praised Hobbes very highly in this regard. Hobbes was, Royce said, " a speculative materialist, and, as I fancy, the most well-knit and highly-organized thinker in the whole history of English philosophy."

In natural science where, in comparison with the philosophy of nature, the retiring age of ideas is very early, Hobbes had a much shorter run. In his favourite subject of optics, for example, his influence was negligible, and the histories of Optics, including Priestley's, did not mention him,[2] although Berkeley (*Theory of Vision*, § 75) mentioned some papers of Molyneux's[3] in which Hobbes's optical theories were considered along with others. Condillac did not refer to Hobbes in his history of natural science (*Logique*, posthumously published 1781), although

---

[1] Cf. Höffding, *Hist. of Modern Philosophy* (trans.), I, 264 and 271.

[2] Except very inadequately in the bibliography.

[3] Molyneux translated Descartes' *Meditations* together with Hobbes's objections (but not the others). Hobbes, he said (113 *sq.*), was " a man famously known to the world abroad but especially to his own the English nation, and therefore 'tis likely that what comes from him may be more acceptable to his countrymen than what proceeds from a stranger" (ed. 1680).

when he came to political theory he gave a whole page
to Hobbes's penetrating, if prejudiced, genius.

Modern writers on physics may find a parallel between
Hobbes's fluidity theory and the work of Christian
Huygens, but Huygens himself regarded Hobbes as a
tiresome old circle-squarer : " What shall I tell you now
about Mr. Hobbes's book ? He is so absurd that he
becomes amusing, and I don't know whether I should try
to silence him by condemning his paralogisms " (*Corr.*,
Aug. 1662, q. Brockdorff, 159) ; and Huygens' corre-
spondent, Moray, sympathised with him (in November)
about Hobbes's " unconquerable impertinence."

There was, however, one very notable exception. In a
letter to Oldenburg (Nov. 1670, Huygens' *Corr.*, q.
Brockdorff, 160 *sq.*), Leibniz, recounting the history of
his thoughts regarding the cohesion of bodies and its
relation to dynamical " conatus," showed how profoundly
he had been influenced by Hobbes. Accepting Hobbes's
contention that the " conatus " was the *beginning* of
motion, he inferred that it must initiate a real union,
that is to say, involve the penetration of terminal points,
although not of bodies. Earlier in the same year he wrote
to Hobbes himself, and, after some lawyerly criticism of
Hobbes's political theory, went into these same matters
of conatus, union, and cohesion.[1] In the course of the
letter he said that Hobbes had made " a most profound
scrutiny into the principles of all matters," and, at the end
of it, that he knew " no writer on philosophy who was more
exact, clearer, or more elegant, not excepting Descartes
himself with his godlike genius."

This was no empty compliment. In his *Mathematical
Writings* (Gerhart, VI), Leibniz's references to Hobbes were
numerous (34, 54, 71, 72, 75, 78, 79, 83). He was amazed,
indeed, that an intellect so penetrating should dispute
the foundations of geometry (71), but otherwise would say

[1] The best text is given by Tönnies in *Phil. Monatshefte*, xxiii.

nothing to the detriment of a man " whose depth he rated so high." Later, it is true, he referred without much respect to Hobbes's materialism and nominalism (*De Ipsa Natura* and *Second Letter to Clarke*), and said in 1686 or later (*Opuscules*, ed. Couturat, p. 178) that there was " a mixture in Hobbes of a marvellously penetrative mind with strange futility," and that Hobbes " had not profited sufficiently from mathematics to keep himself from para-logisms." In the *Theodicée*, however, while not agreeing entirely with Hobbes about free-will, Leibniz treated Hobbes's arguments with greater deference than the exordium (2nd ed., p. 1. Amsterdam, 1712), " he usually produces something good and ingenious," would suggest.

It is surely probable that a man whom Leibniz thought " deep " really *was* deep, and that depth in natural philosophy, acquired so late in life, was indisputable evidence of authentic genius. Again, if Hobbes's attacks on the algebrists antiquated him almost before the ink on his pages was dry, it is something that the man who did so much to discover the technique required for dealing mathematically with continuous motion should have paid such close attention to the philosopher of Malmesbury.

(2) PHENOMENALISM

The first question that has to be asked in this section is whether Hobbes influenced Locke and, through or after him, Berkeley and Hume.[1]

Locke was accused of plagiarising from Hobbes by

[1] I should like, however, to quote a passage from the Petty-Southwell *Correspondence* in order to show how near one of Hobbes's friends came to the type of phenomenalism we associate with Cambridge to-day.

Sir William Petty, in obviously Hobbian vein, maintained that " Ratiocination is nothing but Adition or Substraction of *Sensata* " (p. 295), and the comment in the *Correspondence* was : " As to your advice of collecting a world of *sensata*, I do admire It, and doe begg of you, dear cousin, to send me 20 good ones. . . . These are the same, I suppose, which Sir William calls varyety of matter, *data*, *Phenomina*, and his *Media Probationis*."

certain contemporaries, by some continental historians,[1] by Hazlitt, and by Whewell ;[2] and Fox Bourne (*Life of Locke*, II, 89) said that Locke, in his early days, had been " a diligent and wise student of Hobbes " and had " learnt quite ᴀꜱ much from " Hobbes as from Descartes.

Locke was scornful of the contemporary accusations. It was disingenuous of Stillingfleet, he said (*Second Reply, Works*, 10th ed., IV, 471) to link his name with Hobbes's and Spinoza's, and he was " not so well read in Hobbes or Spinoza as to be able to say " (*op. cit.* 477). In his *Second Vindication of the Reasonableness of Christianity* (*op. cit.* VII, 420) he said he had borrowed his view of the substance of Christianity not from the *Leviathan* but from the Gospels, and had not troubled to examine the charge of plagiarism.

Hence G. H. Lewes inferred (*loc. cit.*) that " Locke never read Hobbes," and others have said the same thing recently.[3] Clearly, however, no such conclusion follows.

Fox Bourne's evidence (at II, 98, and I, 153), as Mr. Gibson has shown, was vague, although Mr. Gibson's counter-argument (*Locke's Theory of Knowledge*, p. 235) was mistaken in arguing (*a*) that Hobbes always regarded " imagination " as excluding sensation, and (*b*) that he did not admit the revival as well as the decay of sense in memory.

It is altogether unlikely that Hobbes ever influenced Locke in the way Descartes did. When he was an undergraduate at Christ Church (1652–5) Wallis and Ward were getting ready to pounce. Later, Locke's sympathies were with the Royal Society, and the men he admired were Boyle, Sydenham, Huygens, and Newton (*Essay*, Epistle to the Reader). When he was in France with the Shaftesbury family, he studied the Cartesians, translating Nicole

---

[1] See *Lange*, I, 328.

[2] See G. H. Lewes, *Biographical History of Philosophy*, Series II, Epoch iii, ch. 3.

[3] *Camb. Mod. Hist.* VI, 812 ; the *Observer*, 28th August 1932.

and (later) "examining" Malebranche. After his return to England, his friendship with Lady Masham (Cudworth's daughter) and other members of the Cudworth family made him increasingly anti-Hobbist. On the other hand, it is difficult to believe that he had not read the book of the day, the *Leviathan*, when he was an undergraduate; and since Cudworth and Boyle, to mention no others, had spent so much labour in refuting Hobbes, Locke must have known, pretty exactly, what Hobbes's main theories were.

The solitary passage in the *Essay* in which Hobbists were named (I, ii, 5) concerned ethics and politics. Regarding phenomenalism, I shall note a few passages in which Hobbian influence seems apparent.

(*a*) The view that wit assembles and judgment separates (II, xi, 2) was Hobbian (III, 56), and I think that Locke's account of belief, assent, and knowledge owed a good deal to Hobbes.

(*b*) Locke's demand that "substance" should be described in plain English ("under-propping"), together with his fable of the "poor Indian philosopher" (II, xiii, 19), may be compared with various passages in Hobbes, especially (IV, 427) : "Stands under what ? Will you say *under accidents* ? "

(*c*) The illustration of dancing as a pseudo-faculty (II, xxi, 17) was Hobbes's (V, 274).

(*d*) As Mr. Gibson has shown (*op. cit.*, p. 249), it is probable that an early paper of Locke's regarding space was greatly influenced by Hobbes (I, 92).

(*e*) As Leibniz noted (*Nouveaux Essais* on Locke, IV, v), the nominalism of Locke's third book was, in the main, markedly Hobbian.

I think, therefore, that Hobbes was more than a mere "precursor" of Locke ; but I do not think he had much influence upon Berkeley, whose references to Hobbes in his published works were, nearly always, a mere inclusion in some list of notorious atheists (*e.g.* Fraser's ed., II, 383, and III, 293).

Berkeley may have begun with a livelier interest. In his *Commonplace Book*[1] he said (811) that the " opinion that existence was distinct from perception " was " of horrible consequence " and " the foundation of Hobbs's doctrine." In other memoranda he tried to approach his own doctrine that spirit was *will* and not idea by criticism of Hobbes and Locke concerning the " will." Two other items were of even greater interest, viz. items 849 and 846. The first of these ran : " *Mem.* When I treat of mathematiques to enquire into the controversy 'twixt Hobbes and Wallis." The second quoted a Latin passage (L. IV, 522) in which Hobbes adjured Wallis to " receive in his mind by vehement cogitation the images of things themselves and not of symbols or sounds." While Berkeley's attacks upon contemporary mathematics were directed chiefly against Newtonian " fluxions," it seems probable that his views about indivisible points, infinity, and the dependence of arithmetic on geometry were influenced by Hobbes ;[2] and item 846 suggests the possibility that a materialist might become a Berkeleyan if he remembered that " ideas of sense " were *realities* (cf. *Princ.*, §§ 18 and 87).

In *De Motu*, § 55, Hobbes was indicated (I, 92), and Hobbes seems to have been " Cimon " in Berkeley's *Alciphron* (at II, 54). In that dialogue, however, the younger " men of fashion " were the really dangerous villains, particularly Collins (" Diagoras ") and Shaftesbury. Again, although Berkeley's account of abstract ideas borrowed one Hobbian solution (*i.e.* " considering " instead of " abstracting "), Berkeley was less of a nominalist than Hobbes, Locke, or Hume.

While Hume the middle-aged historian (as we saw)

---

[1] The numbers as in Dr. Johnston's edition.
[2] Cf. the sixty-seven questions in *The Analyst*, especially, I think, the second and the forty-fifth.

regarded Hobbes as an extinct dogmatic volcano, Hume
the ardent young philosopher was of a different mind ;
but he looked upon Hobbes (I think) rather as an author
to be consulted than as an illuminator of the " new scene
of thought which transported him beyond measure " and
made him, "with an ardour natural to young men, throw
up every other pleasure or business to apply entirely to it "
(Letter to a physician).   The " new scene " was the
experimental (or Newtonian) method applied to impressions and ideas of sense.   It was Locke, and after
him Berkeley, Hutcheson, and others (*Treatise*, Selby-
Bigge's ed., xxi n.) who lighted the lamp whose flame
Hume hoped to make clearer, purer, and, in the end, more
useful.

Frequently, however, Hume consulted Hobbes when
he wanted a clear technical definition of a metaphysical
term.   Thus his " degrees of quality " (*op. cit.*, 18), his
final definition of cause (172), his account of the "sole
cause " (174), and of concomitant variations (174) were
either markedly or exclusively Hobbian ; and Hobbes (80)
was criticised by name for attempting to demonstrate
causality *a priori*.   The technical term, " matter of fact,"
may have been borrowed from Hobbes (*e.g.* V, 390), and
(as we saw) Hume's new theory of causality might be
described, with some precision, as a proof that the
" prudence " Hobbes had so brilliantly described (III, 97)
was all that scientists as well as the vulgar were entitled
to mean by " causing."   Again, although Hume's examination of abstract ideas professed, in the main, to be an
appreciative commentary upon Berkeley (17), there is
evidence that Hume read this part of Berkeley with
nominalistic Hobbian spectacles.

Hume's philosophy relied very much on the association
of ideas to which Hobbes's " trains of imagination "
afforded an obvious parallel except in name.   The historical
question of Hobbes's influence upon the celebrated

theory of associationism, however, has to be treated circumspectly.

J. S. Mill, the greatest of the later associationists (*Dissertations and Discussions*, III, 98), said that " the foundation of the *a posteriori* psychology was laid by Hobbes (to be followed by the masterly developments of Locke and Hartley)," and went on to explain its vogue in France and in England up to James Mill, who opened up " the deepest vein of the Lockian philosophy . . . to still greater depths."

Hobbes's influence upon Locke in this matter, however, must remain doubtful, despite the phrase, " trains of motion in the animal spirits " (II, xxxiii, 6). For Locke introduced his chapter upon association into the *fourth* edition of the *Essay* as an afterthought, and seems first to have become interested in the question in 1695 (Fraser's ed., I, 527). When he did discuss association he treated it as " a sort of madness " and not as the fundamental law of the human mind.

This narrow Lockian interpretation was quickly extended, but I do not think Hobbes played any important part in the eighteenth-century development of the theory. Even Hume seems to have been thinking rather of certain hints at the end of Newton's *Principia* and of some of the queries in Newton's *Optics* than of Hobbes, and Hartley, in his *Observations on Man* (1748), without (I think) any thought of Hobbes, developed his theory firstly from these suggestions in Newton, secondly from Locke, thirdly from Gay's *Dissertation* prefixed to Law's translation of King's *Origin of Evil* (1731). It was Hartley's influence that dominated in England up to the time of James Mill ; and in France there were several indigenous opinions that could readily be assimilated with Locke's. For example, Condillac used the term " liaison " for the association of ideas, and Malebranche had done much the same (*e.g. Recherche*, II, Pt. III, 1). Hobbes's theory of association probably had some influence on Spinoza (*Ethics*, II, xiii *sqq.* and xl). Again, Destutt de Tracy, one of the chief of the French ideologues, translated Hobbes's *Logic* about 1805 ; but, in the main, Hobbes was only a forerunner of this phase of historical development.

In the nineteenth century, however, Thomas Brown (*Philosophy of the Human Mind*, Lects. XI and XXVII) showed by relevant quotations that Hobbes had been a pioneer in the " philosophy of mind," and added the interesting judgment that Hobbes's greatness lay, not in ethics or politics, but in his " analytical investigations of the nature of the phenomena of thought." James Mill, again, was a devoted admirer, and in his acid *Fragment on Mackintosh*, said of Hobbes that " the character of modern speculation was to a great degree determined by his writings " (p. 20), principally on account of "the power with which he traced the phenomena of the human mind to their general laws " (p. 26). James Mill saw the importance of the maxim " Nosce teipsum " in Hobbes's theory (p. 29).

J. S. Mill said of Hobbes (*Edin. Rev.* (1841) p. 242) that he was " a great thinker and a great writer for his time, but inferior to Locke, not only in sober judgment, but even in profundity and original genius,"[1] and this relatively adverse judgment may have arrested the revived interest in Hobbes's psychology, although Horne Tooke in his *Diversions of Purley* attempted to resuscitate Hobbes's nominalism. Nevertheless, James Mill's clear obligations to Hobbes in his *Analysis* made Hobbes a living if in-

---

[1] Writing to Comte (*Lettres Inédites*, p. 78), Mill spoke of his affinity with " the school of Hobbes and Locke " and their type of positivism (*i.e.* in this connection, phenomenalism). Comte, in reply (p. 85), said : " I think like you about the school of Locke, or rather of Hobbes, improved among ourselves by Condillac and Tracy."

Thanks to Mr. Stocks I am able here to add that the reader should also consult J. S. Mill's Preface to his father's *Analysis*, p. x, and (concerning J. S. Mill's early study of Hobbes's *Computatio*) *Autobiography*, p. 15. In his *Logic* (I, v, § 2) Mill said that Hobbes was " one of the clearest and most consecutive thinkers whom this country or the world has produced."

direct influence upon the later associationist movement. To-day, I suppose, Hobbes is not much studied in this part of him. But he ought to be ; for his psychological observations were almost always candid and acute as well as brilliant ; and it does not seem possible that time can stale them.[1]

[1] Some indication of the extent of Hobbes's influence upon German philosophy in the eighteenth century may be obtained by comparing the number of references to him with the references to other English authors, in G. Zart's excellent monograph upon that general theme (Berlin, 1881). Judged by this standard, Hobbes's influence was excelled only by Locke's and Hume's, and was approximately equal to Bacon's and Shaftesbury's.

The references may be classified, roughly, as follows :

On materialism, Wolff, Rüdiger, Feder, Tiedemann (an empiricist who, quite late in the century, favoured a modified materialism largely based upon Hobbes). On general metaphysical questions, Hollman (an opponent), Belfinger (a populariser of Wolff about the middle of the century, who paid considerable attention to Hobbes), Knutzen (an opponent), Mendelssohn (late in the century, but very much interested). On phenomenalism and the psychology of cognition, Tschirnhaus (sense-theory), Thomasius, F. A. Müller (nominalism), Daries (Baconian, but interested in Hobbes's introspective method), Platner (belleslettristic; on general ideas), Maasz (who maintained that Hobbes's associationism was inconsistent with his materialism). On moral psychology, Thomasius, Reimarus (man's sociality), Platner (following Shaftesbury), Jacobi (largely in agreement with Hobbes's view of the passions). On free will, Eberhard, Feder, and many others. On ethical method (mathematical), Hamann. On political theory, among others, Thomasius, Budde, Gundling, Arnold, Tschirnhaus, Platner. Of these Gundling was the most appreciative and not the least important. His first book on the subject (Halle, 1709) was entitled " Dissertatio de statu naturali Hobbesii."

IX

INFLUENCE IN ETHICS AND POLITICS

(1) ETHICS

IF Hobbes's influence in metaphysics, like his own decaying sense, was obscured by later luminaries and revived only fitfully, the survival-value of his ideas about ethics and politics was incontestable. "Even at the present moment," Dugald Stewart wrote in 1824 (*Diss., Encyc. Brit.*), "scarcely does there appear a new publication on Ethics or Jurisprudence where a refutation of Hobbism is not to be found."

In ethics, Hobbes's opponents chose one or other of two lines of argument. Either they contended, rationalistically, that rectitude was eternally superior to human desires and social devices, or they maintained, psychologically and inductively, that human nature, so far from being incorrigibly self-interested, was generous and public-spirited in an obvious, unforced sense. We shall therefore examine both these schools of criticism and, after that, follow the development towards utilitarianism.

(a) *The Rationalists*

The group called the Cambridge Platonists supplied the earlier antagonists of the first kind, although (perhaps excepting Cudworth) their intentions were constructive rather than polemical. John Smith, the best loved of them, "left Hobbes alone,"[1] and so in effect did Whichcote.[2]

---

[1] Inge, *The Platonic Tradition*, p. 59.   [2] *Op. cit.*, p. 48.

Again, I cannot think that Henry More's *Enchiridion Ethicum* was primarily a refutation of Hobbism. Its sparse references to Hobbes referred the reader back to More's *Immortality*.

More strongly deprecated " the more refined exercises of a sort of theological Hobbianism " (Ward's *Life*, p. 14), but it is not at all clear that he was entitled to do so. Ethics, he held, was the art of attaining beatitude. This beatitude was the *delight* appropriate to a rational " boniform faculty " ; and a sweetly superior suspicion of selfishness pervaded his theory. Indeed, he said emphatically (25), that the only intelligible sense of " good " was good to *oneself*.

Cudworth's *Eternal and Immutable Morality* (published 1731, long after the author's death) took Hobbes to task pretty early (ed. Harrison, III, 528), and called him a " philosophaster " towards the end (640 and 643). The fragment, however, was directed against modern " theologers " (529), and, indeed, against Descartes (536) rather than against Hobbes.

The book stopped short with the metaphysical foundations of what might have become an ethical argument, this metaphysical contention being (531) that " things are white by whiteness and black by blackness," and therefore that *nothing* could be merely " thetical " or arbitrary, but that everything was determined by its intellectual nature. It is doubtful, however, whether this argument should have disturbed a Hobbist, since, if moral laws were enactments, they would still be what they were (*i.e.* enactments). Cudworth's strength, if he had strength, came from his argument that " morality, ethics, politics and laws " " belonged to mind and intellect " (643), and that everything sensory, " brutescent," mutable, or conventional was only a sort of half-being.

Indeed, even in ethics, Cudworth's *Intellectual System* was his principal criticism of Hobbes. The vigorous concluding pages of that work trounced the " artificial

justice-makers, city-makers and authority-makers " (499)
to some effect, exposed several inconsistencies in Hobbes
(e.g. 513), and elaborated the inherent difficulties in trying
" by art to consociate into bodies politic those whom
nature had dissociated from one another " (503).

Richard Cumberland, later Bishop of Peterborough,
whom Pepys (18th March 1667) admired so much that
" if he would accept of my sister's person, I should give
£100 more with him " than to a wealthier suitor, was also a
Cambridge man, but, I think, rather a Cambridge Zenonian
or Ciceronian than a Cambridge Platonist. His book,
De Legibus Naturæ (1672. Imprim. 1671. Englished in
a summary by Tyrrell the historian, 1692. Translated
J. Maxwell, 1727) was constructive in the main ; but about
a fifth of it was criticism of Hobbes. Hobbes, he maintained, held with some inconsistencies that moral could
be reduced to civil obligation, that there was nothing
objective about goodness, and that human nature was
utterly selfish and predatory. Cumberland set about to
expose these pernicious errors by the use of mere natural
reason ; and he deserved his bishopric.

It was a fallacy, he said, to speak of the " right " of
nature when nature was lawless, and right had been
defined as what was lawfully permitted (49). If the
legislator were the sole judge of the goodness of laws, he
might judge laws to be good that in fact were noxious
(165) ; if he were always presumed to be good it would
be impossible to distinguish between good and bad rulers
in different communities (405). Too many bellicose pre-
cautions were a cause of insecurity (311). Force and legal
sanctions could not give the safety that Hobbes desired
(354). A comparison of the Latin with the English texts
of the *Leviathan* (e.g. III, 206, compared with L. III, 167)
showed Hobbes's astonishing vacillation on important
points of theory.

For the most part, Cumberland was deductive and

metaphysical rather than inductive in his method ; and although his " geometrical method " (about which he was rather apologetic except when he digressed into geometry itself) amounted to little more (*e.g.* 63) than the statement that the good of the whole was greater than the good of the parts, he asserted firmly and with some impressiveness that human action, in the last analysis, was directed towards the common good of all beings—but principally of rational beings—that the proper felicity of each was contained in the common good (p. 2), and that the " laws of nature " were " propositions of immutable verity that direct voluntary actions towards the election of good, and the avoidance of evil, and bring about an obligation to external acts " (p. 1). The detail of this general injunction to benevolence, however, was a little vague, and the sting of Hobbianism was rather easily drawn by such comfortable assertions as that, in the " system of all rationals " (260) " all men, even if they are not subject to the same human government, are nevertheless members of the very ample City of God " (303).

Let us turn to the work of Samuel Pufendorf, whose reputation stood firm for a century or more—Vinogradoff[1] said that Napoleon's Code Civil was " in a sense its greatest triumph "—and was a major influence in European University education.

In the year 1658, Pufendorf, then a young tutor in the family of the Swedish ambassador at Copenhagen, was interned owing to the sudden outbreak of war between Sweden and Denmark, and in his captivity attempted a systematic reconciliation between the principles of Grotius (lately deceased) and of Hobbes, the result being his *Elements of Universal Jurisprudence* (1660). He continued to be equally Hobbian in his greatest book, *De Jure Naturæ et Gentium* (1672 and 1673) as well as in the short compendium, *De Officio hominis et civis* (1682). The result

[1] *Outlines of Historical Jurisprudence*, I, 113 *sq.*

was an edifice whose structural defects were not very obvious to the eye, which did not creak under timid criticism, and, after Hobbes had been amended and reproved for his naughtier sallies, seemed as respectable as Cicero. Indeed, Locke recommended the book (*Of Education*, § 186) along with Cicero for the sedulous study of " a virtuous and well-behaved young man."

The *De Jure Naturæ* contained excellent and unbiased criticisms[1] of Hobbes's " right of nature " (I, vi, 10) and of his " mushroom " simile (II, ii, 7). It also endeavoured to maintain that egoism was not inconsistent with, and did not always prevail over, " humanity " (II, iii, 16 *sqq.*). In the main, however, it accepted the " selfish theory," although with certain " restrictions and mitigations " (VII, i). " Man naturally loves himself more than company " (VII, i, 2). " Man first embraced civil society, not as led to it by the bias of nature, but as driven by fear of greater evils " (*ibid.* 4). Self-protection was " the true and leading cause why the fathers of families would consent to resign up their natural liberty, and to form a commonwealth." Again, Pufendorf accepted the Hobbian theory of punishment (VII, vi, 12, and VIII, iii, 7), although " with some grains of allowance."

On the other hand, Pufendorf, rising far above his usual pedestrian tone, defended the equality of men on grounds utterly different from Hobbes's, and anticipated the " rights of man " and Kant's famous formula that humanity should never be treated merely as a means. The true meaning of equality, he argued (III, ii), was *equality of right*, based on the fact that a man can never be a mere thing (III, ii, 1) ; or, as he said in *De Officio*

---

[1] I quote from the English translation of 1729. Pufendorf rejected the " idle niceties " of Hobbes's determinism (I, iv, 2), and professed to follow a different sort of geometrical method, adapted from his own master, Weigel, professor at Jena, who had written an *Ethical Arithmetic*. Indeed Pufendorf in his first book (Eng. trans., p. 182) attempted to geometrise ethics according to the similitude of a solid sphere.

(I, vii), " Man is an animal not only bent upon self-preservation, but also an animal in whom a sensitive self-esteem has been implanted. . . . Even the word *man* is thought to contain a certain dignity, so that the last and most effective argument in repelling the insolent contempt of others is this : ' I am certainly not a dog, but a man as well as you.' Every man, therefore, should esteem and treat every other as naturally his equal, that is, as a man even as he is."

Before returning to British ethics, it seems necessary, because of Spinoza's greatness as a moralist, to examine his indebtedness to Hobbes.

In many general respects, their common "mathematical" method, their faith in demonstrative reason, their determinism, their insistence that the springs of human action should be studied in the detached way appropriate to science and very unusual in the pulpit, Spinoza and Hobbes resembled one another closely. On the other hand, Spinoza's enraptured rationalism and the sublimity of his acquiescence in a Nature that was also Deity, made his pages so unlike those of Hobbes that the same intellectual hemisphere could scarcely contain the two.

In the first phase of his argument respecting good and evil (especially *Ethics*, I, App.), Spinoza attempted to show that good and evil, as currently interpreted, were illusions. Each man supposed himself an *imperium in imperio*. The truth was that men were appetite-ridden ; that good was the result, not the cause, of appetite ; that men thought themselves free because they were ignorant of natural causes ; and that there could be no contingency in nature.

Hobbes had said most of these things, although he held that there *were* final causes, which were efficient psychological causes ; and this was the substance of the second phase of Spinoza's account of the matter. A thing's individual essence, Spinoza said, was its self-assertion or

" conatus " to continue, a psycho-physical *cupiditas* that on the bodily side was called " appetite," and on the mental side " will." This *cupiditas* was *power*, and pleasure was the feeling of transition to greater power. The relativity of good and evil followed : (*a*) because our estimates were comparative and relative to our moods (IV, Pref.) ; (*b*) because good *was* different to different constitutions. " The wars of bees, the jealousy of doves, etc., things which we detest in man, are nevertheless things for which we consider animals more perfect " (Letter xix).

It does not require much penetration to discern Hobbes's influence on this theory. The governing term " conatus " was Hobbes's, and so was the reference to " power." Again, both theories had similar obscurities, for example the gulf between the strivings of men and the unity of physical determinism, as well as the uncritical equation between pleasure and strength. It is sufficient to quote Spinoza's celebrated statement that " we do not endeavour after, will, seek or desire a thing, because we judge it to be good, but, on the contrary, call anything good because we endeavour after, will, seek and desire it " (III, ix, Schol.), to show how sedulously, from this point of view, Spinoza dotted the i's of Hobbes's moral psychology.

So far as I know, the last of the great ethical rationalists in England to pay elaborate attention to Hobbes's views[1] was Dr. Samuel Clarke in his Boyle Lectures on Natural Religion, given in 1705.

On their positive side these lectures attempted a combination of Cudworth's Platonic essences with Cumberland's rational benevolence, and the author, boldly abandoning the high and safe ground of generality, defined certain axioms of ethical " fitness," and enunciated with exactitude his fundamental " rules of righteousness," viz. Equity, Love, and Theism. His prolonged criticism of

---

[1] Wollaston, Balguy, and other later writers of the school dealt with different opponents.

Hobbes, however, said little that was new. Like other lecturers by invitation, he had to achieve a prescribed length, and, being himself suspected of heterodoxy, wished to show that he could demolish the infidel before a sympathetic audience as well as any other divine.

His criticisms were principally : (a) that since the dangers and miseries of Hobbes's alleged " state of nature " *were* evils, good and evil could not be wholly arbitrary ; (b) that if civil laws *were* beneficial, the benefits would be objective ; (c) that if civil obedience were based upon the sanctity of contract, promise-keeping must be an independent " law of nature " ; (d) that each man's " right " to *everything* in Hobbes's " state of nature " made all such "rights" contradictory in principle ; (e) that Hobbes confused sanction with duty in his account of civil obligation; (f) that his " state of nature " was depraved, not natural ; (g) that God's irresistible power would authorise devil-worship if deity were diabolical.[1]

Locke's ethical theory made a bridge between rationalism and the psychological treatment of the subject, his account of moral law having affinity to the former and his account of the nature of good to the latter.

Every moral law, even the Golden Rule itself, he said (I, ii, 4), required a demonstrative reason. This part of the subject, therefore, was equated with mathematics (*e.g.* I, ii, 1). Indeed (IV, iv, 10) it was a question of God's definitions, together with the fact that He had " by an inseparable connexion joined virtue and public happiness together " (I, ii, 6). The three relevant types of law were (II, xxviii, 13) : " the law of God ; the law of politic societies ; the law of fashion or private censure." Agreement with these (*ibid.* 14) determined " moral rectitude," and the sort of proposition said to be demonstrated was (IV, iii, 18) that " where there is no property there is no

---

[1] A criticism subject to the trifling objection that God was not the devil, and that, if all evil were weakness in the end, He could not be.

injustice." Locke further explained that since moral definitions were "mixed modes," *i.e.* arbitrarily contrived, the terms of the deduction were of the mind's own fashioning, and therefore within its control (*e.g.* IV, iii, 11). The " law of God " was said to imply the existence of " laws of nature " antecedent to civil society (Ep. to the Reader), and Hobbists (IV, xii, 4) as well as " Archelaus " (II, ii, 5) were censured—but not very severely.

Psychologically, however, Locke held that there was nothing *innate* in these affairs except the " inclinations of the appetite to good " (I, ii, 3). It was through " perception of delight " that we stirred our bodies or employed our minds (II, vii, 3). Good *meant* either pleasure or the cause of pleasure (*e.g.* II, xxi, 63). It was therefore relative to personal " relish " (*ibid.* 56), and (*ibid.*) philosophers who discussed the *summum bonum* " might have as reasonably disputed whether the best relish were to be found in apples, plums or nuts." Similarly, Locke was as much of an egoist as Hobbes. The proper object of any man's desire had to be " a necessary part of *his* happiness " (*ibid.* 44).

(b) The " Generous " Psychologists—and Some Others

Shaftesbury, Locke's pupil and the first of the great psychological opponents of the " selfish theory," usually referred to Hobbes indirectly. In *The Moralists*, however, he said that the state of nature (which, as he supposed, implied that a man was " stripped of all his natural affections " and " separate from all his kind . . . like some solitary insect in his shell ") involved the same sort of absurdity as if an organic body were imagined to arise from the chance conjunction of an eye here and a tail there. In reality, men " can no more by their good will abstain from society than they can possibly preserve themselves without it." And nations *grew*. Therefore

" those transformers of human nature " spoke appropriate language when they talked of " dragons, leviathans and I know not what devouring creatures." Even the statement " man is to man a wolf " was absurd ; for wolves " howl to one another to keep company."[1]

On the whole, if he was rather superficially acquainted with Hobbes's " extraordinary theory " (at II, 80), Shaftesbury, nevertheless, gave an effective account of man's sociableness. " If eating and drinking be natural, herding is so too " (I, 110). A man would not be *whole* if he were not sociable as well as self-regarding (II, 110 *sq.*). Even prostitutes knew how important it was that their customers " should believe there are reciprocal satisfactions " (II, 128). Shaftesbury opposed the " kind-system " to the " self-system " (II, 78), although, when he " took things pretty deep " (II, 8), he made a spectacular dive from the comparative firmness of friendship for one's kind to the dangerous metaphysics of a grandiose " system " of all nature.

There was an oscillation of the pendulum when Mandeville attacked Shaftesbury, but association with Mandeville's name could not mend Hobbes's damaged reputation. Mandeville, it is true, had probably no deliberate intention of encouraging licentiousness, but he would have sold his soul for an aphorism, and he certainly repudiated the reality of disinterested philanthropy in any of its forms. Indeed, he developed this theme more skilfully than Hobbes. He himself, he said, was a great lover of company, but only because he liked it (*Fable of the Bees*, Kaye's ed., I, 337). Compassion, and the impulse to rescue a child from danger, were perfectly genuine (I, 255 *sq.*), but their motive was always to gratify or to ease ourselves. In short, he took Hobbes's cue, according to Aubrey's story (A. I, 352). Once Hobbes, " with eies of pity and compassion "

---

[1] *Characteristicks*, 3rd ed., 1723, II, 311 *sqq.* There was a personal reference to Hobbes at I, 88 *sqq.*

gave an alms of sixpence to a poor old man in the Strand,
and a divine (Dr. Jasper Mayne[1]) who stood by told him
that he would not have given the alms except for Christ's
command. Hobbes, however, had a ready reply. " I was
in pain to consider the miserable condition of the old
man," he said, " and now my alms, giving him some relief,
doth also ease me."

Mandeville's account of the origin of society also came
near to Hobbes's. Assuming (I, 344) that every man's
endeavour was necessarily " the business of self-preservation," Mandeville argued that a body politic implied a
" disciplined creature " (I, 347). At this point, however,
he parted company from Hobbes, for he held that the
reason for the development from savagery was primarily
economic. There was no other way of satisfying some
men's expansive and expensive desires, and the development was due not to a contract of hard-headed cravens
but to the cajolery of the powerful few. The moral virtues
were " the political offspring which flattery begot upon
pride " (I, 51), not the legitimate offspring of reason and
egoism. Men had to be cheated into industry (I, 358).
Even salesmanship would be impossible without cozening
stratagems, and these social processes were gradual, not,
like a contract, a sudden thing.

According to Bishop Butler, the abstract deductive
way and the psychological inductive way of treating
moral science led to the same conclusion. In the *Sermons*
he chose the latter method, and (Preface) regarded the
Epicureans, Hobbes and Rochefoucauld as his chief
opponents in matters of theory. We have therefore to
treat him primarily as an opponent of Hobbes's " selfish
theory " on psychological grounds.

Like Shaftesbury (but with rather tepid acknowledgment, since Shaftesbury was a deist), Butler tried to prove
that man was made for society as much as for private

---

[1] The Earl of Devonshire's chaplain.

good (Sermon I). He also tried to prove (Sermon III) that man was made to be governed by the authoritative principles of conscience and reflection, and said (*Dissertation on Virtue*) that Hobbes had inadvertently admitted the point when he distinguished between injury and mere harm.

In the eleventh sermon Butler stated certain elementary psychological truths more clearly (I think) than any philosopher since the Stoics. Self-love (*i.e.* the desire for maximum personal satisfaction), he said, could not create the satisfaction desired. It presupposed native propensions that satisfied when exercised in their due degree. Since these " propensions " " rested in the external things themselves," man's benevolent impulses must similarly " rest " in the objects of the benevolence. Again " disengagement" might be essential to happiness-getting. He who would be happy should not scheme overmuch for happiness lest " the contracted affection disappoint itself."

The former contention made prominent what Hobbes, like so many others, had left in obscurity, and Butler, in a long footnote to the first sermon effectively criticised Hobbes's statement that the " appearance of benevolence " could be reduced to a species of ambition. As he showed, we often rejoice when a third party helps one of our less fortunate friends ; we bestow favours unequally where ambition would be gratified equally ; and love of power would lead not only (as it does) to resentment and envy, but also (as Hobbes would not say) to mere cruelty.

It may be doubted, however, whether Butler's arguments devastated the subtler forms of egoism in Mandeville and (sometimes) in Hobbes. In terms of his argument it would follow that a man's " propension " for the bottle would be as " disinterested " as his benevolence, and it was not at all clear why a man should not stop his benevolence as soon as it ceased to please him. Indeed, Butler conceded the point when he said (Sermon XI) that " when we sit down in a cool hour, we can neither justify to ourselves this or any other pursuit, till we are convinced that it will be for our happiness, or at least not contrary to it." In the last analysis it could not be inferred from Butler's pages whether self-love, utilitarianism, God's commandment, or rational intuition justified moral action, despite his statement in the *Dissertation* that benevolence (*i.e.* the utilitarian pursuit of an " overbalance of happiness " to the public) was *not* the whole of virtue, since " treachery, violence and injustice " might sometimes have a utilitarian but never a moral justification.

Francis Hutcheson, another of the " generous " psychologists, numbered Shaftesbury among the immortals (*Inquiry*, Pref., 4th ed., 1738) and followed him closely. Hutcheson's fundamental thesis (*The Passions*, p. 213, 4th ed., 1756) was that Nature had made us virtuous in so far as she had made us benevolent, and that the moral sense, in approving virtue, approved and stimulated benevolence. Since Hutcheson maintained that rationalistic systems of ethics, such as Wollaston's, neglected the very foundations both of moral approval and of moral choice, he believed that the serious business for a moralist was to decide between an ethics based on benevolence and a pseudo-ethics based on self-love (*Pass.*, 213). He had no doubt (*ibid.*) that benevolent ethics accorded with human nature, and that egoistic pseudo-ethics travestied it.

Accordingly, although he argued chiefly against Mandeville, Hobbes was one of his most formidable opponents,[1] and he criticised the Hobbian theory of pity in detail (*Inq.*, Additional Note).

Hutcheson defended " disinterestedness " with special care, and pointed out that we did not condemn a buffet from the wind, although we did condemn a buffet from a

---

[1] When Hutcheson said that the old Epicureans, Hobbes and Rochefoucauld had been " followed by many better writers " (*Pass.*, 210), he meant, I think, that the " better writers " were *morally* better, *i.e.* were the " Christian moralists of this scheme " (*ibid.*).

neighbour (*Inq.*, 113) ; that we approved the heroes of distant ages, and *e.g.* the frugality of the Dutch, although we could not hope for personal benefit (*Inq.*, 117) ; that we condemned traitors even when we found them useful (*Inq.*, 127) ; that a dying man, even if he " feigned annihilation," provided for his children by will (*Inq.*, 148) —in short, that a straightforward interpretation of human actions gave the lie to egoism. There were, he admitted, subtler ways of arguing the egoists' case, but " men are conscious of no such intentions or acute reflections about those actions. Ingenious speculative men, in their straining to support a hypothesis, may entertain a thousand selfish motives which a kind, generous heart never dreamed of "—a contention very relevant to the accurate description of normal motives, but perhaps not so strong when the argument turned upon the justification of actions.

(c) *Utilitarianism*

A great part of Hutcheson's historical importance was due to his anticipation of the later utilitarian theory in England, and Hume, the next great name, was even more utilitarian than Hutcheson. Hume's ethics, however, was based very largely upon Hutchesonian approbation and election, for which reason Bentham and Helvétius censured him because he was not utilitarian enough. Hume developed Hutcheson's "moral sense" theory when he tried to answer the question *why* we approve ; but he was essentially utilitarian when he examined *what* we approved.

There was a general connection between Hume's utilitarianism and Hobbian ethics, especially when Hume argued that certain virtues, particularly justice, were *artificial*, and had public utility for their *sole* object (*e.g. Enquiry*, Selby-Bigge's ed., p. 183). The other part of the theory was a criticism of Hobbism, and was to the effect that the virtues were primarily social, that the natural virtues were generosity and benevolence, and that the artificial virtues were inventions designed to benefit society (*e.g. Essays*, ed. Green, I, 454 *sq.*).   We *approved* all virtues because we were able to extend our " confined generosity " by means of an extensive " sympathy " that might even generate the impartiality of a disinterested spectator (*e.g. Tr.*, 591).   It was enough if the " particle of the dove " in our frame could be trained to overcome " the elements of the wolf and serpent " (*Enq.*, 271).

" So far from thinking that men have no affection for anything beyond themselves," Hume said (*Tr.* 487), " I am of opinion that tho' it be rare to meet with one who loves any single person better than himself, yet 'tis as rare to meet with one in whom all the kind affections taken together do not overbalance all the selfish " ; and in the *Enquiry* (App. II) he gave a careful analysis of the question.   It was mere depravity, he said, to hold that benevolence was hypocrisy or friendship a cheat ; but Epicurus, Hobbes, and Locke, " who maintained the selfish system of morals, lived irreproachable lives " with complete consistency.   What they held (Hume said) was that genuine benevolence was ultimately " self-love twisted and moulded by a philosophical chymistry."   The evidence, however, was against them.   In all matters of introspection the presumption was that passions were as they seemed. Therefore benevolence *was* disinterested if it *seemed* disinterested,[1] and the analysis of the egoists was only " excusable," not correct.

Other passages in Hume (*e.g. Tr.*, 543) were not very easy to reconcile with this verdict.   In particular, Hume's theory of " justice " (which with him had to do principally with property) was intentionally Hobbian.   This virtue, according to Hume, " arose artificially though necessarily

---

[1] Cf. Adam Smith, *Moral Sentiments*, VI, iii, 2, where the censure of Hobbes was gentle.

from education and human conventions" (*Tr.*, 483). It was artificial because it *was* an artifice. It was natural because mankind was an " inventive species " (*Tr.*, 484).

Yet Hume transformed his Hobbism. *Political* government, he said, was usually founded contractually, but social life existed long before political pacts (*Tr.*, 540 *sq.*), and the pact would have no meaning unless the fundamental artificial virtues, viz. stability of possession, transference of goods by agreement, and promise-keeping, had been firmly and slowly developed with reference to " the necessities and interests of society " (*Tr.*, 519). These obligations had to become an *acquired* moral or social sense, for the most part unreflectively accepted, and *all* such obligations had the same source, including political allegiance itself. It was therefore sophistical to base sociableness upon political allegiance (*Tr.*, 549). In particular, ancestral promises should not be taken seriously. " It never was pleaded as an excuse for a rebel that the first act he performed, after he came to years of discretion, was to levy war against the sovereign " (*Tr.*, 548). Social necessities dominated the entire situation. What they had given they could take away—although they could not justify a rash rebellion.

Bentham, the founder of English utilitarianism, had a radically unhistorical outlook, and even said (q. Halévy's *Rad. Phil.*, I, App. iii) that " the inventor of the system of original contract, or at least the first man of great name whom it is customary to consider as the author of it, is Locke." It was Helvétius, Hume, and Beccaria who were the luminaries in Bentham's firmament. Hobbes, at the best, was a dark sun.

Nevertheless, if Hobbes anticipated without instructing Bentham, the anticipations themselves were sometimes striking. As M. Halévy has shown (*op. cit.*, I, 277 *sq.*), the idea of a calculus of pleasure based on the dimensions of intensity and duration may be found in Hobbes's

De Homine (L. II, 102) in the short paragraph entitled " bona comparata " ; and egoism, pleasure-pain determinism, the deductive method on a psychological basis, the transition from egoism to utilitarianism by the artificial identification of interests, and other such pieces of Hobbism were the very framework of Bentham's system. Hobbes was not the first to invent these notions, but it is doubtful if, without him, they would have flourished in Bentham's youth.

Here, except for an addendum, I propose to abandon the story of Hobbes's ethical influence. He was the precursor of utilitarianism, and the originator of the prolonged eighteenth-century debate about the nature of ethical motives. These problems are still with us, and we might do worse than return to Hobbes ; but we should probably be wiser if we regarded him, not as a living influence, but as a voice in the past whose clarity and incisiveness on a host of particular questions is a perpetual refreshment and a persistent incitement to the *un*thinking of many prejudices and to the *re*thinking of moral theory.

(d) Free-will and Determinism

It remains to say something about the free-will controversy.

In my opinion, Henry More was by far the most effective of Hobbes's contemporary critics on this question (*Immortality*, II, iii). He denied that self-determination, in the sense of intrinsic development, was a metaphysical impossibility, exposed the questions begged in Hobbes's deductions from the " sufficient cause," and showed himself a much better logician than Hobbes regarding what followed from the proposition : " it will either rain tomorrow or not." The historically interesting matter, however, is the way in which Hobbes's statement of the problem of free-will dominated subsequent discussion in Locke, Collins, Hartley,[1] Jonathan Edwards, and Priestley.

" So far as a man has power to think or not to think, to move or not to move, according to the preference or direction of his own mind," Locke began (II, xxi, 8), " so far is a man free." " Voluntary, then, is not opposed to necessary but to involuntary," and the question " whether man's will be free or no " was altogether " improper " because unintelligible (*ibid.*, 14), since the will was not an *agent* but only the ability of a *man*. Locke's illustration from the alleged " dancing faculty " (*ibid.* 17), as we saw, was Hobbes's ; and the same influence seems to have determined his further argument (*ibid.*, 23) that there would be an infinite regress if a man were free to will instead of being merely free to act " according as he shall choose or will." Indeed, in the first edition of the *Essay* (Fraser, I, 375), Locke said that " the will or preference is determined by *something without itself*."

Thereafter, it is true (and without much credit to his reputation), Locke diverged from Hobbes. The most pressing satisfaction or uneasiness, he said, was the " last judgment of good or evil " that determined the will (*ibid.*, 49). This analysis may have been an advance ; but having introduced the explanation to account for the fact that men did not *always* choose the greatest good, Locke, to explain how men *might* choose it, fell back upon an alleged power to suspend determination (*ibid.*, 57) ; and although decisions may certainly be postponed, it is clear that such postponement is as much an action as any other action. As Jonathan Edwards showed (*Freedom of Will*, II, vii, 2), Locke's solution was " the grossest nonsense," and would imply that " suspending " could suspend itself.

Edwards himself said (at IV, vi) : " I confess it happens

---

[1] For Collins's views see especially " Essay concerning the Use of Reason in Propositions " (1707), pp. 47 and 49. Hartley built on Locke.

I never read Mr. Hobbes " ; and that, in a divine and a Calvinist, was prudent.[1] He interpreted moral necessity, however (I, iv, 2), in a way that Hobbes might have accepted, and had no difficulty in showing that Dr. Whitby and other Arminians, while they pretended to repudiate Hobbes, actually defined liberty in Hobbes's way as " doing what we will."

Priestley had read Hobbes. In his *Philosophical Necessity* (1777) he wrote : " After the most diligent inquiry that I can make it appears to me that Mr. Hobbes was the first who understood and maintained the proper doctrine of philosophical necessity ; and I think it no small honour to this country . . . that he should have proposed it so clearly and have defended it so ably " (xxvi *sq.*). He was surprised that Locke, " who seems to have been so much indebted to Mr. Hobbes," should have bungled his later explanations (xxix) ; and he agreed with Hobbes that materialism and determinism went together (*Correspondence with Price*, Introd., v), and that " all self-determination, properly so called, was an impossibility " (*ibid.*, 129). By maintaining, however, that " in the most proper sense of the words it depends entirely upon [a man] *himself* whether he be virtuous or vicious " (*Necessity*, 153), Priestley, it may seem, kept at some little distance from Hobbes's *extrinsic* determinism.

(2) POLITICS

(a) Contemporary Matters

The great and immediate fame of the *De Cive* and of the *Leviathan* makes it tempting to speculate about the influence of Hobbes's political theory before and during

---

[1] As late as 1864, Dr. Whedon in *The Freedom of the Will*, regarded Hobbes and Edwards as the " leading advocates " of philosophical determinism.

the Protectorate ; and it is likely enough that Hobbian absolutism was useful to the " usurpers," if not even to Cromwell himself.

In 1647 there was reason for believing that " Cromwell only shot the bolts that were hammered in Ireton's forge " (q. Gooch, 135), and although Ireton's desire for a managed monarchy, the abolition of the Church's civil power, and for biennial parliaments was quite un-Hobbian, the doctrine of his *Heads of Proposal*, viz. the contract theory of instituted government, the entire dependence of property upon that institution, and the depravity of political mankind may have been directly influenced by the *De Cive*.

After Ireton, his son-in-law, was dead, Oliver himself may have learned from the *Leviathan* (for he was not unstudious, and we know that he read Harrington[1]). Indeed, the man who preferred to address the Scots Commissioners "in a long discourse according to the principles of Mariana and Buchanan" (Burnet's *Own Times*, i, 72), could not be accused of aversion to questions of general principle. Cromwell, it is true, was prepared to regard the dominion of the saints (if it could occur) as somehow superior to the interest of the nation (*e.g.* Speech VIII) ; but he was also convinced that in the " next-best " or " fleshly " order there were certain very fundamental principles ; and most of these principles, although not quite all, would have received Hobbes's approval. Against Parliament-men, Commonwealth-men, Brownists, Levellers, Fifth-Monarchy-men, and the sterner sort of Republicans, Cromwell protested (Speech XIII) that " he must be a pitiful man who thinks the People of God ever had the like liberty either *de facto* or *de jure* ; *de jure* from God I think they have had it from the beginning of the world to this day, and have it still—but asserted by a *jus humanum*, I say they never had it so as they have

---

[1] Whose *Oceana* he called " a little paper shot " (Toland's ed., p. xx).

it now." Even misrule was better than no rule (Speech XVII), and either a king or a protector had to do the ruling. " Some things are fundamentals. . . . The government by a single person and a parliament is a fundamental. It is the *esse*, it is constitutive. . . . That parliaments should not make themselves perpetual is a fundamental. Of what assurance is a *law* to prevent so great an evil, if it lie in the same legislature to *unlaw* it again ? " (Speech III).

Certainly, in Cromwell's position, the balancing devices of what Hobbes slighted as " mixarchy " were almost inevitable, just as it was inevitable that Cromwell should rule autocratically when the *Instrument of Government* did not succeed. Cromwell, I dare say, did not need to learn very much from the *theory* of absolutism ; but many of his opinions coincided with Hobbes's. Accepting liberty of conscience (except for papists), Cromwell nevertheless maintained (Speech III) that " the magistrate hath *his* supremacy ; he may settle religion, ' that is church-government,' according to his conscience." Similarly, Cromwell's sympathies were with the modernists in education—he wanted to have business taught, together with history, mathematics and cosmography (Letter 100), and to found a new northern university at Durham (Letter 169). Again, in 1653, he proposed to simplify the " tortuous ungodly jungle " of English law.

In the main, however, the practical experiments in government under the Protectorate turned men's thoughts away from abstract questions regarding the grounds of obedience to problems in the technique of government. Consequently, it was Harrington, not Hobbes, who caught the English ear in the later 'fifties of the century and stimulated the tongues of political casuists at the Rota Club in the New Palace Yard (A. I, 289). Certainly, Harrington was a political theorist as well as a constitution-monger ; but his theories depended principally upon an inductive survey of constitutions such as the Venetian, and upon the economic basis of political power.

Harrington began his treatise (*Oceana* : The Preliminaries) with an attack upon Hobbes. To pave the way for his elaborate written constitution, he argued, not very forcibly, that laws governed as well as men.[1] He denied that Hobbes could work the miracle of " making you a king by geometry" (Toland's ed., 587, cf. 70), and praised instead the " historical" methods of Machiavelli and of the ancients (41, cf. 52). In reality, he said, *riches* were power (249). When Hobbes talked about the militia he forgot that " an army is a beast that has a great belly " (41). Overbalance of power meant overbalance of property ; therefore a democracy should limit private estates. Again, he advocated rotation of governments, and conceived that he had consequently to deny the Hobbian doctrine of indivisible sovereignty (58).

It was generally supposed, however, that Hobbes and Harrington were complementary rather than antagonistic. Thus, Richard Baxter (Orme's *Life* in *Works*, I, 704), explaining why he wrote his *Holy Commonwealth* against Harrington—and, incidentally, why he put that author " in a Bethlehem rage "—said : " Every self-conceited fellow was ready to offer his model for a new form of government. Mr. Hobbes's *Leviathan* had pleased many. Mr. Thomas White, the great Papist, had written his *Politics* in English for the interest of the Protector to prove that subjects ought to submit and subject themselves to such a change." And the reason why Hobbes did not reply to the *Oceana* may have been that Harrington had paid him the highest of compliments. " It is true I have opposed the politics of Mr. Hobbs," he said (259), " . . . Nevertheless . . . I firmly believe that Mr. Hobbs is and will in all future ages be accounted, the best writer at this day in the world. And for his Treatise of Human Nature

---

[1] An Aristotelian question, *Politics*, II, ix, xi, and III, xv.

and of Liberty and Necessity, they are the greatest of new lights, and those which I have followed and shall follow."

Despite the complete restoration of the Church of England after 1660, it would be fair to say that the doctrine of the divine right of kings had tumbled with the first Charles's head, and that the absolutism of the royal prerogative rolled about with it.   On the other hand, the ghosts of these doctrines continued to walk, as may be seen especially in the revived interest in Filmer's theories on the part of the High Tory party.

During his lifetime (he died in 1653, and his *Patriarcha* was published posthumously in 1680) Filmer published a polemical tract, "Observations . . . upon Hobbes, Grotius, Milton, and Hunton" (1652), and proved himself an acute critic whatever his defects as a constructive thinker may have been.   Hobbes's mushroom men, he said in effect, were unnatural because they were naturally subject to some sort of *patria potestas* ; they were not necessarily in a state of war and they had no rights to give away.   " If . . . he had handled paternal government before that by institution, there would have been little liberty left in the subjects of the family to consent to institution of government " (The Preface).   " With no small content I read Mr. Hobs book, *De Cive*, and his *Leviathan*, about the rights of sovereignty, which no man, that I know, hath so amply and judiciously handled ; I consent with him about the right of *exercising* government, but I cannot agree to his means of *acquiring* it " (*ibid.*).

(b) Development of the Contract Theory

This doctrine of the contract was the reason why Hobbes's works were burned along with those of Bellarmine, Buchanan, and Philip Hunton in a great bonfire ignited by Gigur, the University Bedell at Oxford in 1683.[1]   Of

[1] Clark's *Life and Times of Wood*, iii, 63 *sq.*

these works, Hunton's manual, a short quarto of thirty-eight pages, had been published in 1643, but was reprinted in 1680, presumably as an antidote to Filmer. It was a moderate anti-royalist statement, emanating from Wadham College in Oxford, very lucidly subdivided ; and it maintained that monarchy was " originally " elective because based on consent (I, iii, 2), that British sovereignty was radically limited (II, i, 2), and that " the authority of this land is of a very mixed and compounded nature in the very root and constitution thereof " (II, ii, 3, § 1)—as the King's declaration at Newmarket (9th March 1641) had emphatically shown.

Another of Filmer's opponents was Algernon Sidney, whose *Discourses concerning Government* preceded his execution in 1683 by about two years. Its general tenor may be collected from the following excerpts : " All just magistratical power is from the people " (I, 20) ; [1] " A monarchy cannot be well regulated unless the powers of the monarch are limited by law " (II, 30) ; " I cannot reasonably expect to be defended from wrong unless I oblige myself to do none . . . but without prejudice to the society into which I enter I may and do retain to myself the liberty of doing what I please in all things relating peculiarly to myself, or in which I am to seek my own convenience " (III, 41). Sidney mentioned Hobbes occasionally, and usually without heat, although he deplored Hobbes's hostility to the classical writers (I, 16), and censured him for being the first to devise " a compendious way of justifying the most abominable perjuries " regarding the coronation oath of " the people " to itself (III, 17).

When James II fled, the Tories unwillingly declared, with their Whig opponents, " that King James II, having endeavoured to subvert the constitution of his kingdom by breaking the original contract between king and

---

[1] Of the first edition.

people ; and by the advice of Jesuits and other wicked persons having violated the fundamental laws ; and having withdrawn himself out of the kingdom ; has abdicated the government, and that the throne is thereby vacant." Thereafter the legitimists became rebels, and the contract theory, in its bilateral un-Hobbian form, became the accepted creed. But the High Tories still continued to use Filmer's arguments ; and Locke set to work to demolish Filmer.

Locke wrote with a practical design. He wanted " to establish the throne of our great restorer, our present King William" (*Of Government*, Pref.) and (*ibid.*), " to make good his title in the consent of the people." Therefore he attacked Filmer's doctrine of divinely appointed inequality, and the perpetual grant of sovereignty to Adam and his lineal heir ;[1] for these doctrines were the current pulpit-politics of the Tories (*ibid.*). Locke referred to Hobbists vaguely as " some men "; but he was well acquainted at least with what Filmer had said in detail about Hobbes.

According to Locke, " some men " had strangely con-fused the state of nature with a state of war (*Civil Govern-ment*, § 19) ; and Locke affirmed that pre-political man began in a sort of Golden Age (C.G. 111), where the acquisi-tive spirit had not begun to be mischievous, and God's decalogue was universally binding. Again, each man had by nature a certain " property " in his own life and limbs, and in the fruits of his labour upon the common land (C.G. 32 and 37).

A state of war, however, could very easily arise.[2] The greater part of men were unjust (C.G. 123) ; men were *quickly* driven into society because of the inconveniences of doing without it (C.G. 127). Indeed, while every man

---

[1] Locke wanted to know (*Government*, 104) who Adam's legitimate heir was.

[2] For Locke agreed, in the main, with Hooker. See his note C.G. 111.

had by nature the moral right to punish moral delin-
quencies, and to kill a would-be thief, although not to rob
him (C.G. 182), there would be chaos if an " umpire "
backed by sufficient force did not take the matter out of
private hands.

Pre-political society—*e.g.* conjugal (C.G. 78)—was emin-
ently natural, but it never implied the power of life and
death. Such power, however, belonged legitimately to a
political body as well as to a pre-political moral avenger,
provided that the political body were voluntarily instituted
by freemen who resigned their coercive power of punishment to a legislature and executive (C.G. 88). Hence
Locke inferred (C.G. 90) that " some men " were quite
wrong in believing in practical absolutism. Men might
reasonably submit to laws, but not to unlimited despotism.
Again, since the function of government was *salus populi*,
the institution of coercive political power was conditional
upon the performance of the function (C.G. 94).

The " common good " (C.G. 131) was held, rather
vaguely, to prescribe the implied conditions ; and the
doctrine of " tacit consent " (C.G. 119) was held to be
implied in *any* enjoyment of government privileges, even
(for visitors) in " a lodging only for a week " or " barely
travelling freely on the highway."

The original contract may perhaps have been more of a
historical reality on Locke's view than on Hobbes's
(C.G. 101 *sqq.*) ; and Locke came very near to absolutism
by asserting (C.G. 134) that the legislature was " sacred "
and " unalterable," and that it was " ridiculous to imagine
one can be tied ultimately to obey any power ,in the
society which is not supreme " (*ibid.*). Indeed, Locke's
theory was the statement (not the solution) of a puzzle.
It was " ridiculous to imagine " the absence of ultimate
supremacy in the government, but a gross absurdity to
suppose (C.G. 138) that men should " lose that, by entering
into society, which was the end for which they entered

into it." (As we saw, Hobbes, despite his protests, entangled himself (*e.g.* III, 203) in the same snare.)

Locke's form of the contract theory, however, continued to give general satisfaction in England for over half a century. Defoe, in his *Original Power . . . of the People of England*, found no difficulty in combining it with a doctrine of checks and balances, and Bolingbroke (*Dissertation on Parties*) took the view that the English Constitution, with its balance of powers, was " in the strictest sense a bargain, a conditional contract between the prince and the people, as it always has been and still is between the representative and collective bodies of the nation " (D.P. xiii), the bargain in question being the *original* contract of which the " Magna Charta of the Revolution Settlement " was only " the delicious and wholesome fruit " (xii).

In the middle of the century, however, Hume was much more critical, although he conceded a good deal to the contract theory (without discriminating very closely between Hobbes's form of it and Locke's). " The people," he said in his essay, " Of the Original Contract "[1] (1748), " if we trace government to its first origin in the woods and deserts, are the source of all power and jurisdiction, and voluntarily, for the sake of peace and order, abandoned their native liberty and received laws from their equal and companion." Their approximate equality in strength made any other theory untenable ; and their habitual acquiescence quite naturally resulted. Such natural origins, however, were impossible in the case of classical city-states or of modern nations, which depended " in plain terms " upon force. " Tacit " consent would apply to any servile state, and genuine voluntary acceptance occurred so seldom as to be negligible. Ultimately, the

---

[1] Enlarging the arguments of the *Treatise* (III, Pt. III, 10) and of some earlier essays, now usually numbered Essays iv, v, and vii in *Essays*, Pt. I.

necessities of social life determined *all* moral and political duty. It was therefore absurd to try to base the duty of allegiance upon the duty of promise-keeping.

(c) Continental Influence

Let us now consider the adventures and rebuffs of Hobbian political ideas on the Continent. And, first, Spinoza.

In the *Ethics* (IV, 35-37) Spinoza's account of the transition from the wolf to the god in man was obviously borrowed from Hobbes, but we shall here consider the fuller theory of Spinoza's two political treatises, the *Tractatus Theologico-Politicus* (1670), which appeared seven years before its author's death, and the unfinished *Tractatus Politicus*, published shortly after that event.

Of the former book Hobbes said to Aubrey (A. I, 357) that Spinoza " had cut thorough him a barre's length, for he durst not write so boldly." This statement presumably referred to Spinoza's " higher criticism," his contemptuous rejection of miracles, and the like. Hobbes was often thought to be the devil quoting Scripture, and he may himself have wondered whether his shoes were roomy enough to conceal a cloven hoof ; but, in argument, he was always a Rabbi of Malmesbury who treated the Scriptures as an authoritative document. Spinoza, on the other hand, had risen to the stratosphere whence he regarded every wind of rabbinical doctrine with complete detachment. Nevertheless, Hobbes's comment showed some generosity, for although Spinoza had taken so much from Hobbes (as any one might perceive), he gave the credit, not to Hobbes, but to St. Paul (201), and his solitary reference to Hobbes (276) was a remarkable and very captious piece of exegesis.[1]

For brevity's sake I shall deal principally with the

[1] The pages refer to the translation by Elwes.

Tractatus Politicus and indicate the chief respects in which the earlier part of the book[1] either agreed with or differed from Hobbes.

The resemblances leap to the eye. Existence was power (291). Everything in nature, man included, strove of necessity to continue its existence (293), and this was a man's natural right to all things, all men being enemies in that state (306) which, both in nature and in time was prior to religion (T.T.P. 210). Rationality, indeed, was strength (313), but the ultimate question always was wherein strength resided. " A constitution cannot remain unconquered unless it is defended both by reason and by common human passion ; otherwise, if it relied only on the help of reason, it is certainly weak and easily over-come " (383). The device of dominion arose from common consent (297) to be guided " as it were by one mind " (297) ; and Spinoza (*e.g.* 303) did not disown his earlier doctrine (T.T.P. 205) " that each individual hands over the whole of his power to the body politic."

The differences, however, even if not always intended, were frequently very great, and resulted in part from Spinoza's avowed Machiavellianism, including inferences Spinoza drew from the premiss (*e.g.* 309, 313) that questions of abstract right were one thing, questions of beneficent or even of feasible government quite another thing. There was also, however, a critical difference in theory. " With regard to politics," Spinoza wrote to Jelles (Letter 50), " the difference between Hobbes and me, that you ask about, is due to the fact that I always keep the natural

---

[1] In the later part of the book, Spinoza followed Harrington's example and took to constitution-building, an exercise in which he was not conspicuously proficient. Indeed, Spinoza was capable of a sort of stupid ferocity that makes us thankful he was not a philosopher-king, but only a philosopher who ground lenses. He maintained, for instance, that any patrician who publicly questioned any fundamental law (356) was " not only to be condemned to death and have his goods confiscated, but some sign of his punishment was to remain visible in public for an eternal memorial of the event."

right intact so that the supreme power in a state has no more right over a subject than corresponds to the power of its superiority over the subject." In short (whatever Spinoza may elsewhere have said), it was only a legal presumption that the State acquired a man's natural rights (302). " If we weigh the matter aright, the natural right of every man does not cease in the civil state " (*ibid.*). A man *must* act for what he takes to be his own interest ; and a commonwealth, in the end, only supplied a means for securing private interest that would be absent in a solitary condition of mankind.

This was (I think) the logical consequence of Hobbes's egoistic determinism ; but it made nonsense of the political theory. Every one *had* to do precisely what seemed to suit him. If he thought civil disobedience paid, he *had* to be disobedient ; and Spinoza did not perceive these utterly devastating consequences. Nevertheless he developed the doctrine far enough to elicit consequences (genuine or supposed) that sent Hobbes's indivisible sovereignty, and other favourite tenets, drifting rudderless in a sort of Miltonic limbo. A monarch, Spinoza said, was only a single man (317)—though he also said (339) that he was the entire civil law—and his " indivisible " sovereignty (326), as in an aristocracy also, ought to be safeguarded by a thicket of restrictions. Since Spinoza lived in the Dutch Republic, Hobbes need not have objected to the loyally democratical theory of the *Tractatus Theologico-Politicus*, and might have admitted it was impossible to coerce thought, and unwise, except for temporary reasons, to restrain freedom of speech ; but I do not think he could have accepted most of the arguments of the *Tractatus Politicus*.

Again, the naked Machiavellianism of Spinoza's account of international relations was not Hobbian. " Every commonwealth," said Spinoza, " has the right to break its contract with other commonwealths, whenever it

chooses, and cannot be said to act treacherously or per-
fidiously in breaking its word as soon as the motive of
hope or fear is removed " (307). That was not Hobbes's
view, although, if commonwealths were always in a state
of war, it very likely should have been. Again Spinoza,
in a quite un-Hobbian way, held that rulers were *not*
subject to divine law (T.T.P. 210).

On some of these matters Spinoza may have been more
consistent than Hobbes, but his praise of piety and of
charity seem to be intruders from another view of ethics,
and his various assertions to the effect that fear was a
weak and sympathetic co-operation a strong foundation
for civil government did not seem to march with his
fundamental contention that men were naturally enemies
and retained their " right of nature " in a political state.
Again, he made no attempt whatsoever to show why
different civil communities should not co-operate in the
service of humanity, or why it stood to reason that duty
could not be extra-territorial. Speaking generally of
Spinoza's ethics as well as of his politics, I think we might
say that Spinoza had a most subtle and penetrating appreciation of values (even if he overrated the intellectual ones),
but that he had no appreciation of duty at all. Hobbes
had a very strong sense of duty, although, except in the
case of monarchs, he frequently diverted it into civil
obedience.

As we saw, Hobbes's influence upon the Scandinavian
and Teutonic peoples was largely due to Pufendorf's work.[1]

[1] A list of Pufendorf's principal followers, including some fourteen
names, may be found in Gierke's *Althusius*, 102 n.

Many of Pufendorf's minor criticisms of Hobbes were both just and
acute. Thus, he remarked that every right implied the duty of others to
abstain, and therefore that non-resistance to government was a *consequence* of the Hobbian donation of right (II, *v*, 3 *sqq.*). He also showed
that Hobbes's reservations concerning punishment were delusory
(III, vii, 4, cf. VIII, iii, 1). Pufendorf's Grotian account of private
property (VIII, v, 1), however, was weakly argued, and his criticisms
of Hobbes regarding the relations between patriarchal and instituted
government were hesitating and captious (VI, iii, chiefly § 1 ; VII, i, 7,

Accordingly, we may here turn to what Pufendorf said about the contract theory (VII, ii, 9 *sq.* of *De Jure Naturæ*).

Hobbes's doctrine, he affirmed, showed too much nicety. The preliminary covenant of each with each was unnecessary,[1] and Hobbes's attempt to make the " people " mean the court was also over-subtle. Again (VII, vii, 9), while all or most of the citizens could not remain in perpetual assembly, there might easily be a " tacit " covenant to re-assemble when need arose.

The governing question was whether the prince contracted with his subjects, and, if so, under what implied conditions. Here, after a longish discussion of the historical situation when Hobbes composed his *Leviathan*, Pufendorf concluded that there had to be a mutual engagement of obedience of the one part and of protection of the other part. In detail, he said (VII, ii, 10) : " In covenants, where one of the parties is made subject to the other, the latter may, as he thinks fit, prescribe what shall be done by the former ; and hath likewise a power of forcing his compliance in case of refusal ; whereas the former party cannot, on any account, be said to hold the like reciprocal power over him. Wherefore a governor cannot be taxed with breach of covenant unless he either utterly abandon all care of the public, or take up the mind and carriage of an enemy towards his own people, or manifestly and of evil design recede from those rules of government the observation of which was by the subjects made the necessary condition of their obedience."

I do not propose to follow the influence of Hobbes in Germany before Kant's time further than I have already

and VIII, i, 5). He highly commended Hobbes's account of the duties of sovereignty (VII, ix, 9), and gave a very Hobbian account of the ways in which subjection ceased (VIII, xi).

[1] He himself, however, wanted *two* covenants and one decree. *De Officio*, etc., II, vi.

done,[1] and shall turn instead to some of the greater names in France.

The greatest name was Bossuet's, and M. Lanson has affirmed (in his *Bossuet*, p. 198) that Bossuet made greater use of Hobbes in constructing his political theory than of Aristotle, French constitutional theory, Gallicanism, and the desire to refute Bellarmine.   In any case, Bossuet assembled the different parts of the Hobbian machine. Thus, in attacking Jurieu's liberal or semi-republican interpretation of the contract and of the people's ultimate donation of sovereignty, Bossuet maintained that in the primitive natural state of war there was no *people*, but only a herd or multitude, and that the miserable scattered herd " renounced the *right* that put everything in confusion."[2] Again, Bossuet held that without government " the earth and all goods are as much common property as air and light " (*Pol.*, I, iii, 4).   True, he rejected one form of the contract theory by insisting that contractual relations were political, and so that a pre-political multitude, collectively or severally, could not contract (5[e] *Av.*), and it may also be true, as M. Lanson suggests (p. 213) that, as a Christian, Bossuet was able, in the end, to throw gentler and lovelier beams upon man's wolfish nature than Hobbes was commonly supposed to have done.   In saying so, however, M. Lanson seems to have forgotten that *political* man, according to Hobbes, was " as a God " to his fellows, and that Hobbes might have been able to give *some* reasons for preferring the hard light of reason to the diffused illumination of the Church.   Hobbes might even have refused to admit that ecclesiastical faggots, or even candles, always made a *gentle* glow.

In various ways (as many Frenchmen had done before[3])

---

[1] According to Gierke (*Althusius*, 177 n.), Grasswinckel, Horn, and Felwinger were among the more notable exponents of absolutism, largely on Hobbes's lines.

[2] 5e *Avertissement* on Jurieu's *Letters*.

[3] See H. Sée, *Les idées politiques en France au XVII siècle* (*passim*).

Jurieu, Fénelon, Boulainvilliers and others tried to defend the liberal as opposed to the absolutist version of the contract theory. Hobbes, therefore, remained a force whether as demon or good genius, and he has been called " the chief master of Helvétius in the fields of morals " (Mondolfo's *Helvétius*, p. 15). In politics Helvétius followed Hobbes very closely indeed, although he attempted to deflect Hobbes's arguments into a perfectionist channel, and regarded justice, not as the result of political union, but as an equilibrium of forces, implied in any stable government, and persisting as such a government proceeded, at least half inevitably, to better things. The most important part of this historical narrative, however, concerns the relations between Hobbes and Rousseau.

(d) *Hobbes and Rousseau*

Rousseau had made some study of Hobbes. In his article upon Political Economy, for example, he developed the theme that a political body was a sort of living entity which was the measure of just and unjust and had a single will (q. Gadave,[1] 158 *sq.* n.). He meant by " Hobbism," however, the most arbitrary despotism (Letter to Mirabeau, ed. Hachette, No. 880).

Some of his references to Hobbes are rather difficult to follow. Thus he said (in *Emile*, Bk. V) that it was absurd to laud Grotius and execrate Hobbes, since both of them used the same methods, although Grotius relied on the poets and Hobbes on sophisms. (Their common error, it would seem, was too much rationalistic argument.) Again, in his *Discourse on Inequality*, Rousseau said, surprisingly, that Hobbes regarded men as intrepid in the state of nature, while Cumberland and Pufendorf made out that man was timid (p. 61 of ed. 1782). In this work, however,

---

[1] = *Th. Hobbes et ses théories du contrat social et de la souveraineté.* Toulouse, 1907.

Rousseau's criticisms of Hobbes were rather commonplace (97 *sqq.*). The noble savage was self-reliant, and not at all likely to interfere with others, since it was greed and civilisation that made men depraved and predatory. Even when the natural man was weak, as in his savage childhood, he did not in fact bite his mother or strangle his brothers ; and, as Mandeville had said, " even the wildest men are capable of pity."

Let us turn, however, to the *Contrat Social*.

The only part of that work in which Rousseau professed himself altogether Hobbian was the concluding section upon religion. Christianity, Rousseau there said, introduced a dual obligation into human society, with obvious consequences when a pretended other-worldliness became a this-worldly despotism. Hobbes was the only modern author who perceived both the evil and its remedy. Therefore he was hated. Yet even Hobbes did not see that the priestly spirit itself must always be too strong for good citizenship. Anything that weakened social unity was an offence. True religion must be a religion of humanity locked creedlessly in each man's breast. It should have no relations to any organised political body ; and, for political purposes, private worshippers ought to be a good deal more virile than orthodox Christians professed to be.

In maintaining (I, ii) that Hobbes, like Grotius and Caligula, regarded kings as divine and subjects as mere beasts, Rousseau may have been fair to Caligula, but certainly misinterpreted Hobbes. He echoed Hobbes, however, in his account of man's natural liberty towards *anything* he attempted (I, viii), in his insistence that the law of self-preservation was ultimate (I, ii), and in his statement that a malefactor was, in principle, an outlaw (II, v). On the other hand, he criticised Hobbian ideas shrewdly when he pointed out (I, iv) that a state of war was a political not a personal condition, that the majority principle itself was a convention (I, v), and that, strictly speaking, the general will could be represented by itself only (II, i, cf. III, xv). In general, his account of the contract contemplated Locke more than Hobbes, but Hobbes a good deal.

Rousseau's chief contribution to political theory was his conception of the " general will " and its relations on the one hand to individual citizens and their interests, on the other hand to the prince and his government.

Much of this theory, intentionally or unintentionally, was Hobbian. Rousseau held that political society arose by convention (I, i), its founders being free, self-directing, and equal by nature (IV, ii). The essential question, therefore, was by what act a people came into being (I, v), and the answer was that they had to invent a device according to which a man, on becoming part of the political body, continued nevertheless to obey himself only (I, vi). This would occur if men surrendered themselves *wholly* (*i.e.* unconditionally, III, xvi) to the general will. The general will or true sovereign must be absolute (III, xvi), indivisible (I, v), inalienable (II, i), and not itself subject to law or even to the social pact (I, vii ; II, iv, v ; III, xviii).

There is warrant, therefore, for Lord Morley's observation that the title-page of the *Leviathan* would have suited the *Contrat Social* had the crowned figure with the Stuart features been headless ; but if Hobbes, with some reason, was afraid of the criticism that his science of politics never got beyond the abstractions of Platonic ideas, Rousseau's speculations seemed very much more obviously to reach only the disembodied soul of sovereignty and to have little relation to possible practice. Such, at least, is the comment provoked by Rousseau's occasional excursions into actuality. His statement that the general will implied the equality of the citizens was a mere *non sequitur*. His attempts to show that the majority principle, or a cancelling out of votes, exhibited the general will (II, iii) were clearly futile, and dubiously consistent with his celebrated remark (III, xv) that the English were slaves except during a General Election. (Indeed, Rousseau suggested (II, x) that freedom might be irrecoverable once the yoke of the laws had been felt.) Again, his statement that the general will ceased to be general if it had any specific object (II, iv) disembodied his theory by its mere statement. And what could be made of his assertion that the general will was always what it ought to be (I, vii), and in its essence union for the common interest (II, iv), *although* it might be mischievous (II, vi) through the fallibility of its judgments, and *although* it was entitled to hurt itself if it wanted to do so (II, xii) ?

Regarding the government, prince, or executive, Rousseau maintained that it was the minister or instrument of the general will in relation to the individual citizens (III, i), and deduced an opposition in principle between the general will and any possible executive (*ibid.*). If the government " usurped the sovereignty," he said (meaninglessly, since he identified the sovereign with the general will) the contract was broken and the citizens became mere individuals (III, x). When the general will existed (in an assembly) there was no government (III, xiii). Hence deputies were shams, just like hirelings in the militia (III, xv).

These were not Hobbes's views, for Hobbes was concerned with the action of a permanent executive, that is to say, with government. If there is no bridge from the people's will to its government there can be no health in any political theory.

Diderot, in his article " Hobbisme " in the *Encyclopédie*, compared the two thinkers. For the one, he said, man was bad ; for the other, good. According to Hobbes, the state of nature was a state of war ; for Rousseau it was a state of peace. For Hobbes, law and government implied improvement ; for Rousseau degradation. The reason, Diderot suggested, was that Hobbes spent his days in

tumult and faction, Rousseau among the savants. "Change
the time, change the circumstances, and you change a
philosophy. M. Rousseau is eloquent and sentimental,
Hobbes is dry, austere, and rigorous. The latter saw the
throne in ruins, the citizens in arms against one another,
the country drenched in blood through the fury of Presbyterian fanatics. So he hated deity, ministers, and altars.
The former saw men knowledgeable in the sciences, torn
in twain, self-hating, delivering themselves up to their
passions, hungry for renown, riches and dignities, conduct-
ing themselves in a manner very inappropriate to the
illumination they had received. Therefore he hated science
and the scientists."

(e) Later Continental Influence

Although the contract theory in its various forms continued to be influential after Rousseau, it is usual to regard
that author's work as the close of an epoch ; and I shall
offer only a few desultory observations upon Hobbes's
later continental influence before I conclude by examining
his relations to later politics and jurisprudence in England.

It is difficult to agree with the enthusiastic Dr. Tönnies
that Kant's *Rechtslehre* was composed thoroughly in the
spirit of Hobbes (*Thomas Hobbes*, p. 275). Although Kant
postulated the social contract as a regulative idea, Kant's
ethic-ridden jurisprudence, his radical objection to the
ideals of utilitarianism, and his very un-Hobbian views of
punishment separated him from Hobbes, even regarding
the regulation of external actions, and in the only mention
of Hobbes's name I have noticed in his writings (apart
from a trivial reference in the *Correspondence*) Kant simply
remarked that Hobbes, in his empirical (and therefore
false) system of ethics had made positive law the tutor
of conscience, just as Montaigne relied on education and
environment (*Lectures on Ethics*, Eng. trans., p. 12).

Again, while it is tempting to compare Hegel's Great (Prussian) God of the state with Hobbes's *Leviathan*, it is more sober to admit frankly that any partial identity was due to the meeting of extremes, and that Hegel would have said about Hobbes precisely what he said about Rousseau, viz. (*The Philosophy of Right*, § 258) that Rousseau grasped the essence of the state in his principle of the general will, but ruined the authority and majesty of the state by regarding wills as individual and their union as a contract. Hegel's " public conscience " might have met with Hobbes's approval, but Absolute Spirit and the Concrete Universal would not have been readily understood in the neighbourhood of Malmesbury ; and Hobbes did not mean by " reason " what Hegel meant.

In other quarters, however, Hobbes was studied for his own sake. Thus Feuerbach, in his *Anti-Hobbes* (Erfurt, 1798), maintained that those who, like himself, were opposed to absolutism should not, like Jacobi, be content with producing an *Anti-Machiavel* (since Machiavelli dealt only with the practice of government), but should deal instead with Hobbes, the acutest and most consistent defender of despotism (Pref. and p. 276) ; and Feuerbach, attacking Hobbes and those who, like Grasswinckel, Wandalin, and· Masius, substantially agreed with him, produced a work that claimed to be a sort of commentary on Rousseau (Pref. xviii) and to answer the modish question (86) : " How far is this anti-Hobbes also anti-Kant ? " In a later age, as M. Gadave has pointed out (*op. cit.*, 183), Jellinek could think of no better way to explain the indivisibility of sovereignty than to quote Hobbes himself.

In France in the nineteenth century defenders of absolutism, such as De Maistre and Bonald, were ready to go back to Hobbes ; for both of them quoted Hobbes appreciatively (*e.g.* Bonald, I, 55) to prove that sovereignty was absolute of its own nature, and that the monarch who constituted the political body could not be limited by the subjects. Again, Comte proclaimed himself Hobbes's enthusiastic admirer. Hobbes and Bossuet, he said (*Cours de phil. pos.*, ed. 1864, vi, 257 and 260), had propounded a thoroughly healthy doctrine, and " the celebrated doctrine of Hobbes concerning the spontaneous domination of force constitutes at bottom the only capital advance that the positive theory of government has made between Aristotle's days and my own "[1] (*Système*, ed. 1852, ii, 299 *sqq.*). Similarly, C. de Rémusat declared (*Hist. de la phil. en Angl.*, I, 344) that Hobbes " had discovered the entire philosophy of positivism." Duguit (*L'État*, II, 252 and 257 *sq.*) repeated Hobbes's arguments concerning the distinction between temporary and genuine sovereignty, and tried to show on Hobbian lines that " mixed " government was an absurdity. A similar purport may perhaps be found in Hauriou's statement that " a little sociology estranges us from legal right, but a great deal of it brings us back again " (*Les facultés*, etc., p. 4).

(f) The Revival of Hobbism in England

In England the followers of the very unhistorical Bentham rediscovered Hobbes.

In his *Fragment on Government* (first published anony-

---

[1] In the *Philosophie Positive* (Leçon 55), Comte said that " the illustrious Hobbes " was " the true father of the revolutionary philosophy," that " the most important critical conceptions were due to him," and that Destutt de Tracy, " with the customary sagacity of his anti-theological instinct," had noted the fact. This " revolutionary philosophy," in the context, appears to mean a combination of secularism, " physique sociale," and phenomenalism or positivism. Here Comte believed himself to agree generally with the English philosophical radicals ; and he approved of their revived interest in Hobbes (ed. 1841, V, pp. 711 *sqq.*).

A recent and very competent writer (L. Strauss, in *Recherches philosophiques*, II, 610) has said that Hobbes was the true founder of liberalism (in the continental sense), that his absolutism was liberalism in the making, and that both the critics and the opponents of any thoroughgoing liberalism should go back to Hobbes.

mously in 1776) Bentham made a ruthless onslaught upon the insular complacency of Sir William Blackstone's *Commentaries*. Neglecting one of Blackstone's observations, viz. that it was "the *sense* of their weakness and imperfection that kept mankind together," Bentham was relentless but just to Blackstone's equivocations between the pre-political and the political meanings of the term "society," and attacked the whole theory of the original contract upon principles expressly borrowed from Hume. His thesis was that all such questions (IV, xvi) should be shorn of "metaphysico-legal" verbiage and reduced to simple utility.

Even so, however, it was important to consider what type of government, and what amount of government, utility did decree. It was not enough to wave "utility" to and fro like a brazier of incense ; and Bentham, even when circumstances made the Tory in him lie down with the philosophical radicals, remained a convinced authoritarian. He was concerned, all his long and active life, with the simplification and improvement of legal and governmental procedure, but when he had to deal with the nature of authority itself he slipped his competent hand into an iron glove. Thus, in the *Constitutional Code*, he said (I, ix) : "Into the composition of power, enter three elements ; intensity, extent, duration. . . . In the highest rank, to the intensity of power, it will be seen, no limits can easily, if at all, be assigned, without taking away, along with the power to do evil, the power to do good, and thus leaving evil unopposed ; to the extent still less ; to the duration with the utmost ease, as well as perfect safety." To say, with M. Halévy (*op. cit.*, III, 227 *sq.*), that Bentham developed Hobbes's thesis in a way that contradicted Hobbes by holding that the majority was the proper fountain of political authority because it was the best judge of the greatest happiness of the greatest number, is, so far as I can see, an unnecessary comment.

An authoritarian, paternal democracy had never been inconsistent with Hobbism ; and Hobbes had never thought so.

Bentham's little band of followers also became authoritarians, and rejoiced to find support in Hobbes. MacCulloch quoted Hobbes in the *Edinburgh Review* (July 1836) to the effect that anyone who tried to limit the sovereign power thereby invoked a higher sovereign. James Mill, in his Hobbian essay on " Government," declared for a first magistrate and for the union of legislative with executive power, but had no sympathy for the " doctrine of checks." As his son said (*Autobiog.*, 177 *sq.*) : " He thought that there was more practical good government, and (which is true enough) infinitely more care for the education and mental improvement of all ranks of the people under the Prussian monarchy than under the English representative government ; and he held with the French *Économistes*, that the real security for good government is ' un peuple éclairé,' which is not always the fruit of popular institutions, and which, if it could be had without them, would do their work better than they." Hobbes (whom James Mill admired in his politics as well as in his phenomenalism) had anticipated the French Economistes in this particular.

The most notable Benthamite writer on these questions, however, was John Austin, the jurist, who took his cue in the main from Bentham's *Fragment* (especially V, vi n.). According to Austin, law, properly speaking, was a command involving a superiority that *signified* might or coercive power. Moral laws were the compulsion of a consensus of equals ; but legal laws were the commands of determinate superiors, and from the nature of the case bound the subjects, not the law-givers, so that political subjection meant the habit of submission. The power of the sovereign was incapable of *legal* limitation, and entirely free from *legal* restraints.

This doctrine differed in some respects from Hobbes's. Its account of morality was different ; its developed Benthamite utilitarianism was relatively new, and its admirable critical examination of the contract theory (in the sixth *Lecture on Jurisprudence*) bore the stamp of a later age. Yet the correspondence between the Austinian and the Hobbian theories of sovereignty was so close that, according to Sir Henry Maine (*Early Institutions*, p. 354) Austin added little to Hobbes. And Austin himself admired Hobbes very much.

He made some criticisms, it is true. Hobbes, he said, exaggerated the extent to which an " independent " political body is self-sufficient (*Jurisprud.*, 2nd ed., I, 187). He was too much afraid of insurrection, and he should have derived his theory, not from the contract, but " from a perception by the bulk of the governed of its great and obvious expediency " (249 *sq.*). Otherwise Austin " knew of no other writer (excepting our great co-temporary Jeremy Bentham) who has uttered so many truths, at once new and important, concerning the necessary structure of supreme political government, and the larger of the necessary distinctions implied by positive law " (251). Hobbes's statement in his " masterly treatises " that " no law could be unjust " when properly interpreted, meant only that " no positive law can be legally unjust " (232 n.). Hobbes was no atheist (252) ; and his chapter on the duties of the sovereign showed that he appreciated the supreme desideratum in all these matters, an enlightened people (252).

Austin was a great analytical jurist, and Maine, in comparing Hobbes's method with Austin's, said that Hobbes, in at least one respect, was superior since he admitted the relevancy of historical questions, although his own historical notions were infantile. Some such comment was to be expected on the part of a writer who had shown so ably that status (in a rather untechnical sense) had preceded contract. It is doubtful, however, how far Hobbes was in earnest regarding the historical actuality of his mushroom men, and also doubtful how far it *was* unhistorical to hold that a government *by institution* arose by election in some assembly.

However that may be, Maine held that *after* the sovereignty of modern political states had arisen, the analytical jurists (among whom Hobbes and Austin were as good as any) did explain the abstract structure of such political communities. They forgot, indeed, that they were dealing with structural abstractions ; but they enunciated " self-evident propositions " regarding the nature of legally sovereign power (*Early Institutions*, p. 362). Beginners (*ibid.*) were " apt to stumble " because they did not understand what Austin and Hobbes were about.

Hobbes himself, I think, would not have solicited a higher testimonial. What he *meant* by a science was the explication of definitions. If, then, his definitions accurately showed what the instituted governments of civilised countries were, and must always be, unless political government were supplanted by some different form of community life, he would have asked for nothing more. He might have turned to historical and anthropological studies for amusement—and shut his Bible without a sigh—but he would never have employed history for scientific purposes.

If, on the other hand, he were told, as many later writers have told him, that what he really did was to present a mass of legal fictions in the similitude of self-evident propositions, he would have displayed his customary impatience of contradiction, and would have composed a reply (or, rather, many replies), usually savage, nearly always witty, sometimes amazingly effective, and frequently (I am afraid) quite unscrupulous. How he would treat the suggestions I have made sporadically in this book, I could not, with any modesty, pretend to guess. I know he would overwhelm me, and can only hope that my discomfiture would not always be earned. I suspect he would also discountenance most of my readers, if, as I hope they will, they discover questions and difficulties not explicitly manifest either in his writings or in my account of them. But it is time for me to stop. I have written the book with the object of stimulating the study of Hobbes in his own England. And Hobbes himself was so delightful and so important an author that even the dull surface of a patient commentary may, in a borrowed way, become attractive.

SHORT BIBLIOGRAPHY

I.—BIOGRAPHICAL

The rhyming *Vita* and the prose *Vita*, together with the supplement (Auctarium) to the latter (L. I). Hobbes-Analekten, published by Tönnies in *Archiv f. Gesch. d. Phil.*, XVII and XIX ; and also Seventeen Letters from Sorbière, republished by Tönnies, *ibid.*, III. For an account of this work see Croom Robertson in *Mind*, O.S. xv (reprinted in his *Philosophical Remains*).

Aubrey's *Brief Lives*, ed. A. Clark, Oxford, 1898.

II.—WRITINGS

See Section 2, Chapter I.

III.—WORKS ON HOBBES

(*a*) IN ENGLISH

G. Croom Robertson, *Hobbes*, in Blackwood's Philosophical Classics.

Sir Leslie Stephen, *Hobbes*, in English Men of Letters.

A. E. Taylor, *Thomas Hobbes*, in Philosophies Ancient and Modern.

G. E. C. Catlin, *Thomas Hobbes : An Introduction*, Oxford, Blackwell, 1922.

F. Brandt, *Thomas Hobbes' Mechanical Conception of Nature*, Eng. trans., Hachette, London, 1928.

(*b*) IN OTHER LANGUAGES

F. Tönnies, *Thomas Hobbes : Leben und Lehre*, in Frommann's Klassiker d. Philosophie.

W. Dilthey, *Gesammelte Schriften*, Vol. II, Teubner, 1923.

H. Moser, *Thomas Hobbes : Seine logische Problematik und ihre erkenntnistheoretischen Voraussetzungen*, Berlin, 1923.

R. Hönigswald, *Hobbes und die Staatsphilosophie*, Reinhart, München, 1924.

Baron C. von Brockdorff, *Hobbes als Philosoph, Pädagoge und Soziologe*, 2 ed., Bd. I, Kiel, 1929.

Z. Lubienski, *Die Grundlagen des ethisch-politischen Systems von Hobbes*, Reinhart, München, 1932. [Contains Bibliography.]

G. Lyon, *La philosophie de Hobbes*, Paris, Alcan, 1893.

R. Gadave, *Th. Hobbes et ses théories du contrat social et de la souveraineté*, Toulouse, Marques, 1907.

B. Landry, *Hobbes*, in " Les Grands Philosophes," Paris, Alcan, 1907.

R. Mondolfo, *La Morale di T. Hobbes*, Verona-Padova, 1905

G. Tarantino, *Saggio sulle idee morali e politiche di Tommaso Hobbes*, Napoli, 1905.

Beonio - Brocchieri, *Studi sulla filosofia politica di T. Hobbes*, Torino, 1927.

A. Levi, *La Filosofia di Tommaso Hobbes*, Società Editrice Dante Alighieri, 1929.

(c) OTHER DISCUSSIONS

B. Donati, in " Annali della Facoltà di Giurisprudenza," Vol. XXXI.

G. Jaeger, in *Archiv f. Gesch. d. Phil.*, XIV.

G. Sortais, *La philosophie moderne depuis Bacon jusqu'à Leibniz*, Vol. II, Bk. II.

A. G. Balz, J. Dewey, and H. G. Lord, in *Studies in the History of Ideas*, Vol. I, New York, 1918.

W. J. H. Campion, *Outlines of Lectures on Political Science*, Oxford, 1902.

L. Gumplowicz, *Geschichte der Staatstheorien*, Innsbruck, 1905.

G. Jellinek, *Allgemeine Staatslehre*, 3rd ed., Berlin, 1922.

Z. Lubienski, in *Journal of Philosophical Studies*, 1930.

F. Tönnies, in *Vierteljahrschrift für wissenschaftl. Phil.*, III, IV, V ; in *Phil. Monatshefte*, XXIII ; in *Zeitschr. für Philos. und philos. Kritik*, CVI (Literatur über Hobbes) : in *Zeitschr. für Volkerrecht*, XII.

INDEX

This index contains no reference (a) to Hobbes; (b) to his writings; (c) to matters sufficiently indicated in the Table of Contents ; and the compiler has exercised a certain discretion regarding the omission or inclusion of proper names t¹ ˙ seemed to him to be of minor importance.